Getting Published
in the Humanities

T0048855

ALSO BY JEFFREY KAHAN

*Caped Crusaders 101: Composition Through
Comic Books,* 2d ed. (McFarland, 2010)

Getting Published in the Humanities

What to Know, Where to Aim, How to Succeed

JEFFREY KAHAN

McFarland & Company, Inc., Publishers
Jefferson, North Carolina, and London

LIBRARY OF CONGRESS CATALOGUING-IN-PUBLICATION DATA

Kahan, Jeffrey, 1964–
    Getting published in the humanities : what to know,
where to aim, how to succeed / Jeffrey Kahan.
      p.   cm.
    Includes bibliographical references and index.

    ISBN 978-0-7864-5923-0
    softcover : 50# alkaline paper ∞

    1. Authorship.   2. Humanities literature — Authorship.
3. Academic writing.   4. Scholarly publishing — United States.
5. College teachers — Tenure — United States.   I. Title.
PN146.K34 2012
808.02 — dc23   2011038934

BRITISH LIBRARY CATALOGUING DATA ARE AVAILABLE

Front cover image © 2012 Shutterstock

Manufactured in the United States of America

*McFarland & Company, Inc., Publishers
  Box 611, Jefferson, North Carolina 28640
  www.mcfarlandpub.com*

To the Untenured.

Table of Contents

Introduction

or Five Reasons Why God Never Received Tenure at the University

For most Ph.D. students, the greatest day of their academic lives is their last: graduation. The campus is manicured and festive, tables overflow with cookies, chocolate-covered strawberries invite, everyone is well dressed and smiling, all thoughts of student loans are suspended. Once-aloof professors amiably shake hands and pose for pictures with your mother; the dean calls your name and you, magisterially decked in velvet robes, rise to the podium to accept the imitation sheepskin degree. Yet there is another graduation going on, one that is silent and unmarked by pomp and circumstance; here no family and friends are in attendance to acknowledge the occasion. It is the graduation of a faculty member to the ranks of the tenured.

Let's return to the newly-minted Ph.D. Once the confetti is cleaned up and the robes are packed away, a new challenge awaits: The search for an academic job. The newbie Ph.D. has crossed the ceremonial stage to get her degree. The new task at hand is to join the faculty, who sit silent in their wisdom and self-satisfaction. Yet, how does this newbie get to that ultimate graduation, where they can now look upon newly-minted Ph.D.s and say, "Yes, though no one here acknowledges it, I, too, graduated this year. I graduated into the ranks of the tenured, the untouchable, the ivory-towered. I cannot, unless under extraordinary circumstances, be fired; I no longer have to worry about job security or fret about paying my mortgage; I can (at last!) put aside the stress and finally fulfill my destiny. For what is education but the finding of the

1

self and the emergence of the self greater than the self?" *My time*, you can at last tell yourself, *has finally come.*

Sadly, only one in every two tenure-track candidates will get to this moment; the rest will fail (Louis Menand, *The Marketplace of Ideas*, 143). That is a shocking number considering the fact that every tenure-track candidate knows nothing but success. Every Ph.D. grad is, by definition, an overachiever. Consider: The total American workforce is about 155 million, of which only 1 percent have Ph.D.s. And yet these rarest of the rare, these brightest of the bright, are, about 50 percent of the time, unable to achieve tenure. That must be quite a shock for the tenure-track candidate: High school diploma, pass; college degree, pass; bachelor's degree, pass; GRE exams, pass; master's degree, pass; doctoral degree, pass; job interview, pass; five years to get together a portfolio worthy of tenure, fail.

Perhaps what is most amazing, a candidate gets basically one shot at tenure. Think about that. If an employee of Walmart leaves or is fired, we don't assume that the person cannot, or never will, work in retail again. Yet if someone fails in a tenure-track job, that professor is pretty much done in academia. This is not because there is some national blacklist; rather, your chances of winning a second tenure-track job are long because of the youthful and desperate competitors who stand ready to take your place. You know this group. You were, in all likelihood, once among their number: the many thousands of unemployed Ph.D.s who troll online job boards, who huddle with a strong air of desperation at national and regional conferences, who face tens of thousands of dollars in student loans, and who now teach as adjuncts for a pittance. A fall from tenured grace means a new job opening for someone else. Applications will be completed, letters of reference penned, and, with winged speed, some other part-timer will be plucked from purgatory.

Compare academic tenure to any other job that requires great intellectual skill and we may well wonder why we are doing what we are doing. A neighbor of mine works for Legalzoom.com. I asked him what it takes to be a successful lawyer. He replied, "Get a law degree, pass the bar exam, have a shitty attitude, and you'll be fine." By comparison, the formula for academia seems to be: Obtain at least five years more education than a lawyer and accrue at least $100,000 in debt, work part time for a number of years and, if you are very, very lucky, get a tenure-track job, only to be let go in five to seven years. Tenure isn't just a game; it's a lottery.

We can improve our odds at tenure considerably by writing and, more importantly, publishing. Yet, despite the obvious importance of publishing academic material, the activity remains a mystery to most young academics. Where to begin? What are publishers looking for? Are there guidelines for submission? Are there tricks to the trade? In this book, I will be showing you some of my strategies, gained by process of trial and, sometimes, catastrophic error. The chapters that follow will provide useful tips and examples to help guide the novice academic writer. In the course of this book, I will explain the following: why publication is now the virtual end-all and be-all of tenure; my own techniques for different kinds of publications; what I did wrong; how I corrected course; and how anyone with tenacity and common sense can succeed in this business. This does not mean that I can guarantee you that having publications will lead inexorably to tenure. Even with a significant publishing record, your department might still find a reason to let you go. Nor can I guarantee you a variety of publications. That will be up to you and the editors to whom you submit. But I can promise you that this book will remove much of the mystery concerning the process and outline a step-by-step approach to publishing — an approach that I have developed and which has served me well. In concrete terms, this book will explore:

1. Why not all publications are equal and why your university or college may weigh commercial publications differently than academic publications;
2. why e-publications do not yet carry the same academic weight as paper publications and why academic editions are *not* considered to be books ("academic editions" are works with limited scholarly contributions; for example, an edition of *Hamlet* with only a new introduction and notes);
3. how to set up a workable schedule that ensures you will have a sizeable body of publications *before* you submit for tenure;
4. how to spot a publishable idea;
5. how to approach the *right* publisher; and
6. why one publication leads almost inevitably to another and another.

In order to aid the reader, I have included samples of notes, books reviews, some of my own accepted book proposals, even replies to readers' reports. My aim is to create a variety of templates which might be useful to the tenure-track professor who is anxious to place work quickly and efficiently in a variety of academic contexts. You may decide to read this book from beginning to end; others may read just a chapter or two, though I would encourage the reader to skim through the entire book, which offers specific examples and advice for publishing projects. Many of the strategies involved are based on a foundational approach. What you learn in writing a publishable review will be of use in virtually all your larger projects, though some of the specifics of the larger projects may not be applicable to the smaller writing assignments.

The Changing Nature of Tenure

I'd like to begin, however, not by discussing academic writing, but the reason *why* publication has become so important in your tenuring process. At first blush, publication seems to carry too much weight. After all, publication is only a part of what we as university educators are expected to do. But gaining skills for publication is unlike any other aspect of academic work. Teaching is certainly important, but the skills necessary for good teaching are simple to seize upon. The tenure-track candidate has had years to watch good teaching and to copy it; the candidate has been tutored in the latest technologies to communicate with students. Committee work is important, but even professors who lack any sense of communicative charisma can be taught to be polite, cooperative, and useful. While teaching and committee work play a role, publication often remains the decisive factor in faculty retention. At a major research university, tenure may depend upon the publication of a book. More teaching-orientated institutions may require no more than an article and a few reviews. In all cases, however, publication carries additional stresses because, unlike other components of tenure, the factors in acceptance are:

1. Not clear. An assistant professor usually knows how well she is doing with students a week or two into the teaching term. Likewise, job effectiveness on a committee is usually apparent. However, the acceptance or rejection of an article or book may take up to, and sometimes over, a year. If the submission is rejected, all too often the reply is merely a form letter or a report that is unclear or contradictory.

2. The gulf between submitting a manuscript for consideration and its acceptance or rejection can be huge. It is not unusual for a book-length manuscript to be in play for over a year before a

decision is made. If it's accepted, it may take another year for a book to be published. If the manuscript is rejected, then the process needs to be started yet again. It took years to master the graduate essay, but there is no such luxury for academic publications. From the day candidates sign their first tenure-track contract, the clock is ticking. Yet no one teaches us how to do what is expected, and that's very frustrating, especially since rejection letters rarely tell us what we're doing wrong. Even acceptance letters don't tell us what we're doing right. So most of us muddle through, trying this or that, perfecting what works, winnowing away the rest. But it's often pure guesswork and many of us will likely run out of time without ever figuring out what is expected.

In addition to creating some context for the academic, our inquiry into the once sunny and now altogether gloomy history of tenure may be of use to the young academic's family and friends, who may not understand the extraordinary pressure of it all. Considering the job perks, a good salary, flexible teaching hours, and funds for travel, the tenured professor's life seems like heaven. Some may even feel a certain amount of anger towards academics, seeing them as venial eggheads who seem to have risen above the mundane concerns of job security. Yes, it's hard to feel any sympathy for the tenured professor, who teaches only a few hours a week, has her summers off, has health care, and flies on her employer's dime to conferences across the country, where she sips wine and gives the occasional paper written in jargon even her fellow professionals may not fully understand. Envy for academics is abundant; sympathy for the professor is virtually nonexistent.

And yet the general public does not understand the enormous pressures which come to bear on this elite lot. That may be of no more interest to the general public than, say, whether a banking executive worries about his cholesterol. But the new paradigm shift undertaken by even small liberal arts schools and colleges from a teaching to a research-driven agenda has profound implications for all of us. And while this book will in the main attempt to teach the tenure-track professor how to beat the university at its own game — to, in essence, give the university what it wants — we should be aware of the pitfalls of academic employment. Not only is academia a cutthroat business, it is almost certainly the shape of things to come for everyone. Thus, even nonacademics, perhaps especially nonacademics, have a stake in the university system, not only because institutions of higher learning train (or will train) our children but also because what is happening within most institutions of higher learning — growing job insecurity, layoffs, the hiring of part-time and underpaid workers, downsizing, stagnant or falling wages and early retirement packages — is happening in the general sector as well. In short, academics are workers, and like all workers, they are feeling the brunt of changing labor conditions. If the best and brightest can mount only a meek defense to the corporate beasts that now roam the halls of academia, then the rest of us are lunch meat.

We may note that it wasn't always this way: Everyone knows the phrase "publish or perish." But few today recall that a mere forty years ago the slogan was not "publish or perish" but "up or out," and its meaning was quite different. Whereas "publish or perish" enjoined the young assistant or associate to be a productive researcher, "up or out" merely demanded that the professor be competitive, polite, and, indeed, virtually anonymous. In fact, it was only a generation or two ago that universities were hiring anyone and everyone and often setting the bar for tenure so low that it was almost impossible to lose a job. In those days, there existed three kinds of tenure — automatic, non evaluative, and evaluative.

Automatic tenure was literally automatic. At Oklahoma State University and the University of Delaware, for example, assistant professors were hired on a three-year term and then rehired for three more years, upon the completion of which they were automatically granted tenure. At the University of South Carolina, tenure was even granted to assistant professors who had been employed by the university for 4 or more years. A decision of tenure, however, was made at the completion of the candidate's third year, so that, in essence, the fourth year was a matter of form. Iowa State University granted tenure as soon as the candidate achieved the rank of associate professor. The University of Arkansas automatically granted tenure after four years of employment or upon gaining the associate rank, whichever came first. The University of Wisconsin noted that automatic tenure could be sped up, if necessary: tenure was not "required solely because of the number of years of service." The number of years, four or five, to make a decision on the candidate was arbitrary. In theory, then, someone might be hired with tenure at any rank. The candidate did not have to submit a portfolio for tenure, nor did the candidate have to prove that she was a good teacher, that she was a recognized scholar, or that she added to the richness or diversity of the academic climate of an institution (B.N. Shaw, *Academic Tenure*, 17–28). Not bad for a job that was guaranteed until the professor in question voluntarily left the institution, retired, or died.

The second form of tenure was nonevaluative. In this system, the professor in question had merely to be "adjudged competent" after the full "probationary period" (B.N. Shaw, *Academic Tenure*, 24). The University of Idaho, for example, bluntly stated that "tenure is not automatic"; but here, too, no file submission was necessary. Rather, tenure was adjudicated by the board of governors after a review of letters of reference written by the candidate's chairperson, dean, and university president (B.N. Shaw, *Academic Tenure*, 27). The University of Washington and the University of Florida conducted open votes within their respective departments; if the majority approved, the candidate was granted tenure. Auburn University opted for a "secret poll of all tenured members of the department" and a letter of recommendation, yea or nay, written on behalf of the entire department, which was then forwarded to the dean. If the vote was against tenure, the department had also to write a letter justifying its decision (B.N. Shaw, *Academic Tenure*, 53). And if, for whatever reason, tenure was denied, the candidate in question had the right to appeal and the right to look over all aforementioned documents and reports on her performance. This happened so infrequently, however, that, of the 80 state universities and colleges surveyed in a 1971 study, only 34 gave concrete rules for the appeals process. The rest reported no set guidelines at all, presumably because there was no need for an appeals process. After all, how could one appeal a nonevaluative decision? Being hired for a tenure-track job was a de facto granting of tenure unless the candidate was a professional disaster, a total psychopath, or a career criminal. Reasons for denying or breaking tenure agreements included immorality or misconduct, incompetence, neglect of duty, incapacity (such as incurable madness), conviction of a felony, or — get this — treason.

The third form of tenure was the rarest: fully evaluative. For those comparatively few colleges or universities (34 of the 80 institutions sampled) that had bothered to set up the formal process of actual evaluation, the most often cited requirements were as follows:

1. Outstanding teaching ability, cited by 34 out of 34 colleges and universities;
2. outstanding research ability, cited by 33 out of 34 colleges and universities;

3. outstanding professional degrees and achievement, cited by 25 out of 34 colleges and universities;
4. outstanding scholarly publications, cited by just 17 out of 34 colleges and universities;
5. outstanding cooperation and general service, cited by just 17 out of 34 colleges and universities;
6. outstanding character and personality, cited by just 9 out of 34 colleges and universities. (The above information is from B.N. Shaw, *Academic Tenure*, 50.)

We may note that publication was equally weighted with "general service." However, "general service" is a rather nebulous term which might include teaching, committee work, or merely being collegial. We may note that "general service" and "character and personality" can be combined as "social skills." If we cite teaching as a "social skill"—which, in large measure, it is—then publication becomes a distinct afterthought in the overall tenuring process at most universities.

There were noted exceptions. Seven of the original pool of 80 institutions (less than 10 percent) placed a premium on publication. We may here further note that some of these institutions were not Ivy League. The University of California, for example, was, and remains, a state school; further, not all of its campuses enjoy the same level of prestige (UC Riverside, while a fine school, does not carry the same clout as, say, UCLA or UC Berkeley). Yet all tenured faculty at Riverside, even in the 1970s, had to put together a file which included a letter of recommendation written by the department chair, an up-to-date biography and bibliography, and copies of research publications or other scholarly or creative work—this according to professors I have interviewed who were tenured in that decade. Riverside's old guidelines also carried a few warnings: "In decisions about tenure, teaching and research carry more weight than does service." However, teaching carried less weight than publication: "Speaking very generally, it would appear reasonable at a research university to devote a significant amount of time [to] one's scholarly and research activities, [and] equal or somewhat less time to teaching after the courses are well-established" (*UC Riverside Advance and Promotion Manual*, 11).

A brief comparison of the old, three-tier system of tenure (automatic, nonevaluative, and evaluative) to the present reality of solely evaluative tenure can be jarring. It used to be that a book assured one of becoming a professor. Now, a book is often needed just to get a job or even an interview. Still more outrageously, you are now likely to be interviewed by senior colleagues who have less education than you do! In 1969, for example, a third of professors were not Ph.D.s, and, as we have already seen, the pressure to publish was, in that era, nearly non-existent (Louis Menand, *The Marketplace of Ideas*, 121). So, in effect, the people interviewing prospective new faculty often have fewer degrees and less publications than those they are rejecting.

Let's put aside the outrage. After all, someone hired circa 1969 may have, in the course of a robust career, served the institution well. Further, while we might not be thrilled with the level of competition for academic jobs, most of us accept that the bar for a lifetime appointment should be higher than the ability to stay out of jail. An applicant should be evaluated, and, of course, the evaluation should be to a high standard. But the present reality is that the bar is higher than it has ever been before and that there are fewer and fewer tenure-track jobs. Why this is so isn't really all that clear.

America's Economic Boom and Tenure

Since 1970, the average income of Americans has risen from $17,000 to $27,000; the average house size has grown by about 50 percent; the stock market, even with the recent downturn, is up elevenfold (the Dow in 1970 was around 1,000; in 2011, it was around 11,000); the number of cars in the country has increased by 120 million; and the percentage of people with personal computers has risen from zero to 70. And what did universities do during this unprecedented boom period? They did two things: They hired more administrators and, whenever possible, rid themselves of tenured faculty. At UC Berkeley, a prestigious but still public school, the management staff between 1993 and 2007 grew 259 percent; the full-time faculty grew by just 1 percent (Chris Hedges, *Empire of Illusion*, 94). Numbers of faculty hires across America tell much the same story. In 1975, 57 percent of all university and college faculty were tenured or on a tenure track; by 2007, the number was down to just 31 percent. The numbers for 2009 and 2010 are expected to show further erosion (Robin Wilson, "Tenure, RIP: What the Vanishing Status Means for the Future of Education," in *Chronicle of Higher Education* Online, July 4, 2010). Most experts now estimate that no more than 27 percent of university academics are tenured or on a tenure track. Young academics are the most affected by this trend: Ph.D. placement between 1989 and 1996 dropped, depending on the discipline, anywhere from 11 percent to 37 percent (Louis Menand, *The Marketplace of Ideas*, 147). In 2008 and 2009, job openings in English dropped by 21 percent (Chris Hedges, *Empire of Illusion*, 108). In the classics, the job market is virtually non-existent (Hanson and Heath, *Who Killed Homer?*, xix).

Since at least 1970, universities by and large have shifted away from the traditional educational values of a liberal arts education (i.e., discussion and contemplation) in favor of corporate principles (i.e., cost cutting and efficiency) (Frank Donoghue, *The Last Professors*, 81, 83). Administrators at most universities, even while hiring more of their own at higher and higher wages, have staunchly held the line on faculty wages and, in some cases, have further driven down costs to absurd levels. Sometimes, graduate students earn more than Ph.D.s who do the same work. In 1997, Cary Nelson reported that at the University of Illinois, a graduate teaching assistant earned about $2,800 per course; but, upon receiving her Ph.D., she was rehired for $1,200 per course (Cary Nelson, "Between Crisis and Opportunity," *Will Teach for Food*, 5). And there are still worse and lower wages out there. Studies published in 2001 and 2004 found that some university adjuncts work for as little as $1,000 a class, which, when divided by contact hours necessary for students, grading, and course preparation, comes out to about a quarter of the legal minimum wage, or, at the time, $2.12 an hour (Frank Donoghue, *The Last Professors*, 56; 148, fn. 3–4). Remember, these people are not high school dropouts applying to a big box store. They are the intellectual (un)privileged of the country, and they make less than the secretaries and janitors they see on campus each day.

But the newly-minted Ph.D., mired in student loans, is a victim of supply and demand. In 1978, the National Research Council's Board on Human Resource Data and Analyses reported that the number of Ph.D.s awarded in the United States essentially had doubled in each decade over the past century: "Quarter-century landmarks show that in 1900 the annual output was about 300; in 1925, about 1,200; in 1950, about 6,000; and in 1974, about 33,000" (NRC 1978). After a brief period of contraction in the late 1970s and early 1980s, Ph.D. output reverted to its normal pattern of growth. In 1995, a total of 41,000 doctorates were issued (NRC 1996); in 2006, that number jumped to 60,616; in 2009, the number grew to 63,000. Projections by the National Center for Education Statistics and the Institute for Education Science for the next ten years suggest that the number will rise still more, topping out at 106,700 by 2017 (http://nces.ed.gov/programs/digest/d08/tables/dt08_268.asp?referrer=report).

The numbers can depersonalize the sense of panic often experienced by Ph.D.s in search of academic work. If one adjunct won't accept pay that is far less than that given to high school dropouts, another desperate former graduate student will. The swell of recent grads has created a highly-trained, overly-specialized cadre of the underemployed and the woefully underpaid who occupy adjunct or nontenure-track jobs. Despite their elite education, these people are in fact the equivalent of migrant workers, or, as they are sometimes labeled, "freeway fliers" — a term which suggests both the difficulties of their multiple commutes and their numbers, comparable to flocks of birds, migrating from one campus to another. They work for astonishingly low wages, usually without union representation, and generally receive no health or retirement benefits; one upside: they do qualify for food stamps.

The Profitable University

We may here note that higher education is now structurally and financially dependent upon a ready supply of cheap labor as a way of balancing its own ballooning costs. Let's do the math. The average salary for a tenured professor is about $80,000, plus retirement and medical, so let's call it $100,000 a year. Add to that the professor's conference and research fund expenditures, and possible teaching assistants, and your full professor is probably costing the university closer to $160,000 a year. Subdivide that by the norm, a load of four classes a year. Each class costs the university about $40,000. Some universities have substantially higher teaching loads, but we're dealing with averages here. Adjuncts make anywhere from $1,000 to $6,000 per course and, on average, don't receive any retirement 401K funds, don't qualify for medical benefits, and have no job security. Thus, even at the high end of the salary scale, the adjunct will cost the university about $24,000 for four classes, as opposed to $160,000 for the tenured professor's four classes. That means that the university could hire four adjuncts to teach *all of the tenured professor's classes*, for about one eighth of the cost. On October 22, 2010, the *Wall Street Journal* reported that the Texas University system had created a

265-page spreadsheet which "amounted to a profit-and-loss statement for each faculty member, weighing annual salary against students taught, tuition generated, and research grants obtained." The chancellor is now using the data in his deliberations as to whether tenured faculty members who cost the university money should be pink-slipped. If the chancellor has his way, we can expect "a radical reshaping of academia, with far more emphasis on filling students with practical information and less on intellectual pursuits, especially in the liberal arts," not just in Texas but throughout the nation (Stephanie Simon and Stephanie Banchero, "Putting a Price on Professors").

It may seem that academia is merely following the corporate lead. All workers, academic or otherwise, are worse off today than back in 1970. In 1970, about a third of all American workers were unionized; by 1983, that figure had dropped to about 20 percent (see Bureau of Labor Statistics, http://www.bls.gov/news.release/union2.nr0.htm). In 2009, only 7.8 percent of workers in the private sector were unionized — about the same percentage as in the early 1900s (Chris Hedges, *Empire of Illusion*, 168; Bureau of Labor Statistics set the number at 12.3 percent). Yes, we can say that academics share many of the burdens experienced by all American workers. But the differences between American academics and nonacademic laborers outweigh their similarities. The economy might regulate the number of jobs available in the nonacademic world, but within the so-called ivory towers of higher education, tenure has nothing to do with prosperity. As we have seen, even in the good years, universities generally cut back on tenure-track hiring.

That the requirements for tenure have changed over time will strike many as surprising in that the common myth about universities is that they are untouchable ivory towers. In fact, the changes for tenure, especially the rise of publication as the defining factor for tenure and promotion, reflect the ongoing conversion of the university from a place of teaching and thinking to a commercial enterprise devoted to customers and profits. The corporate takeover of the university seems to be nearing completion. I speak here not just of millionaires who commonly sit on university boards but also of businesses themselves that have created rival institutions of learning. The University of Phoenix may be the best example, but we should not overlook the fact that major corporations now either partner with universities or, as in the case of Microsoft, have created their own universities, complete with degrees.

No, that's not quite right. It's worse than that. Confronted with a volatile economy, changing demographic trends, weakening public opinion, lagging state and federal support, restructuring administrative operations, debt management, capital renewal pressures, and endowment management, the university is not following a corporate model. Rather, corporations are now following the university model. After all, corporations have to pay at least the minimum wage; yet, as we have seen, universities pay far, far less to many of their part-time professors. As Hanson Heath and others have recently noted, universities are now more comfortable talking about money than in the past, far more so than they are interested in discussing education. Administrators are no longer former academics but "officers" who justify their enormous salaries by rubbing shoulders with and outdoing the practices of business tycoons. The salaries of their employees are recorded as merely another cost, no different than calculating the heating and cooling of classrooms or the cost of maintaining other facilities owned by the university-corporation. Education is the product on offer, and keeping customers happy, if not always challenged, is now the priority. It is perhaps only a slight exaggeration to say that customer satisfaction is now only rarely about giving students an actual education. L.G. Bolman and T.E. Deal said as much when they reported on one "jaundiced college president [who] lamented that his main job seemed to be providing employment and parking for faculty, football for the alumni, and sex for the students" (L.G. Bolman and T.E. Deal, *Reframing Organizations*, 196). The remark may be read facetiously, but there is a grain of truth in it: Administrators administrate budgets, and the last item on their agendas is often academics.

The New Paradigm and Academic Publishing

Let's set aside for the moment whether these changes are good or bad. The fact is, they are here. How has the shift in education affected publication? Has it made the academic's job harder or easier? The answer is surprisingly complicated but, to begin with, we may note that the university is also using changes in job requirements to get more labor out of its faculty at no extra cost. A survey conducted in 1993 of all universities, public and private, revealed that faculty members spend on average 59 percent of their time teaching or in teaching-related activities. The growth in student-centered learning and the rise of internet-based activities — Blackboard, instant messaging, and email — I have certainly raised the number of contact hours still higher. Moreover, this 59 percent does not take into account "non-instructional activities," which include course preparation, grading, or office contact hours (Daniel T. Layzell, "Higher Education's Changing Environment," in *Faculty Productivity*, 3–37; 20).

Thus, while official classroom teaching hours have remained stable, the number of contact hours has ballooned. We can understand that, from a customer service point of view, making professors more available may increase consumer satisfaction, but contact hours also cut into research and publication time. Further, having a professor wired to a group of students does not necessarily tell us much about the quality of instruction. We assume that more contact hours will make students feel that their needs are being addressed, but these needs may be emotional rather than intellectual. Having someone to guide a student to the library is hardly the same as teaching the student about the books in it.

From the vantage point of a faculty member interested in publication, the new realities of academia are, frankly, a nuisance. Emails, tweets, and the like cut into valuable research time. Yet from an administrator's point of view, they are a godsend. Administrators, after all, like to know what their workers are doing, and emails, tweets, office hours, etc., create a paper trail, a detailed record. But thinking can't be measured, and most administrators are ill-equipped to evaluate a faculty member's intellectual activity. Thus, the administrator has but one way of evaluating the brain power of its faculty: academic publication. In an op-ed piece published by the *Los Angeles Times*, Naomi Schaefer Riley, author of *The Faculty Loungers: And Other Reasons Why You Won't Get the College Education You Paid For*, noted that professors are paid more the less time they spend in the classroom and the more time they spend researching because, in her view, "it is easier to measure the quality of research and scholarly writing [i.e., whether it is published in a peer reviewed journal or not] than the quality of teaching" (Naomi Schaefer Riley, "Cal State Mission Drift," *Los Angeles Times*. June 15, 2011).

Taking the business model still further, academic productivity is no longer a measure of just the amount produced but also *the efficiency with which the product is produced*. Corporations are evaluated by balanced books and growth projections; a faculty member, similarly, is expected not merely to do what she has done in the past, but to grow correspondingly as a teacher and a researcher. More, not less, is expected with each passing year. Continual increases in productivity may be unfair or even unwarranted, but the expectation is there. This explains why universities do not take into account changes in technology and accompanying shifts in customer expectations when addressing faculty workloads or contact hours. The university expects its faculty to do more and more on the same pay — a seeming model of robotic efficiency. Barry Munitz — whose résumé includes posts as a senior administrator at the University of Illinois and the University of Houston, a business executive at Maxxam, Inc., chancellor of the California State University system, and, as late as 2006, the chief executive officer of the world's wealthiest art institution, the J. Paul Getty Trust — is unapologetic about what he expects from faculty. And what he expects is more, more, more, more: "If faculty do as they have always done, society will get no more than it has always had." Munitz finds the possibility that faculty members might do the same or less than they have in the past to be "very destructive" ("Managing Transformation in an Age of Social Triage," 21–48, 37).

Changing Research Models

The nature of what faculty do in the classroom is also a factor in what they write about, and that, too, is under siege. To begin with, the traditional academic relies on a high degree of autonomy. Traditional faculty members, especially in the humanities, were expected to work independently. Today, the professor is encouraged to work collaboratively with students. In 1994, Roland W. Schmitt summarized a ULCA symposium on the future of the university system by stating that research in the classroom has been too long confined to the graduate level. He recommended that all students at all levels participate in collaborative research because "academe needs to recognize and build on the value of industrial collaboration in the education of its students" ("A Symposium Summary," *Reinventing the Research University: Proceedings of a Symposium Held at UCLA on June 22–23, 1994*, 237–244; 243). Since his summary findings, published in 1994, his views have moved to the mainstream. In 1996, Jan Sinnott of Towson State University and Lynn Johnson of the National Research Council jointly advised that universities shift to a "problem-focused" approach because a "problem-focused university" will be positioned "to establish and maintain good working relationships with the industrial sector" (Jan Sinnott and Lynn Johnson, *Reinventing the University*, 155). In that same year, the Carnegie Foundation concluded that students require "active learning."

In 2004, the transformation was so widespread and entrenched that Roger C.H. Downer could declare the triumph of "student-centered learning" in all disciplines. Arguing that a content-based lecture system was thoroughly out of fashion, students, he proclaimed, should be "responsible for at least some of the content before they enter the classroom" because "the interaction between the student and the teacher will [then] be more productive, with the student transformed from the role of receiver to that of developer of knowledge" (Roger C.H. Downer, "Innovation in Undergraduate Teaching: Student-centered and Research-led learning," 65). Daniel T. Layzell ("Higher Education's Changing Environment," 24) offers a useful chart of the changes he sees in academic teaching:

Old Educational Model	Versus	Present Corporate Reality
Modular learning		Synergistic learning
Independent research		Teamwork and cooperation
Leadership		Consensus building
Prerequisite-based learning		Flexible "need to know" learning
Eccentricity, creativity, and style		Conservative codes and behavior
Cling to traditional practices		Ability to change
Standardized testing		Flexible performance reviews

Education is no longer about thinking but about doing; student learning is not a matter of personal growth; rather it is about free research labor. Education, in short, has become "projectified." (This nifty term is the creation of Bino Catasús and Bengt Kristensson Uggla, "Reinventing the University as the Driving Force of Intellectual Capital," 74).

We can, I think, agree that the rise of collaborative or group projects is designed to prepare the student for the realities of the workplace. That is all well and good. But we must likewise acknowledge that the university is abandoning its higher calling: to educate people not just for a career but also about their culture, their country, and their relationship to the community, nation, and planet; to see themselves not just as competitors but, in the case of the humanities, as custodians of western philosophy. The traditional system of inquiry and debate, originally designed to get students to question and to think, has been scrapped. What we have instead is a system that trains people to work together within set discourses of knowledge. Kim Cameron, professor of management at the University of Michigan, writes matter-of-factly that a good manager is an uncreative manager who wants equally uncreative workers: "For the most part, [business] organizations are designed to foster stability, steadiness, and predictability" (Kim Cameron, *Positive Leadership: Strategies for Extraordinary Performance*, 8). While this new educational model is practical in that it trains workers for the needs of industry, it never asks its students to question why they are taught what they are taught, or why they are taught to do what they do. Education is now, more than ever, geared toward career development, job placement, and lifelong learning opportunities; it is about providing a highly-skilled workforce and maintaining a competitive edge; it is about the latest technology and professional responsibilities. It is not, at least in the main, about informed debate or personal and intellectual growth.

It seems increasingly clear that the changes in teaching methods seem to strike at the very heart of what a university used to stand for. But a more urgent task for the tenure-track professor is to understand how *team-based learning makes it that much more difficult to publish research*. What I am about to say is not a hard and fast rule for everyone. Team-based research is, in rare circumstances, a positive for a stressed academic, who, faced with emails, Facebook updates, Twitter postings, office hours, interactive lectures, and grading, may see group work as an opportune time-saver. After all, topflight students can often help with research. Yet, if students are collaborators with their professors on research projects, it stands to reason that outstanding schools will have outstanding students, aiding in the production of outstanding work. This means that if you are an assistant professor at Duke University, you have a considerably smoother path to publication, since your students are doing work that for the most part does not need to be re-contextualized for high-brow academic publication. The Duke professor is likely teaching to and collaborating with graduate students who are themselves careerists, and the resulting work is likely not only of high caliber but is also very likely already cast in the jargon of academia. Even in the humanities, these students may do summaries of research materials, double-check quotations, proof manuscripts, etc., etc. These students, if used correctly, should speed up the writing process and may even offer new ideas that aid the professor's thesis.

But what of the tenure-track professor who does not teach at Duke or an Ivy League school, what of the assistant professor in a class filled with students who are generally unsophisticated or who come from "somewhat restrictive backgrounds" or who, for religious or personal reasons, object to the subject matter of the research? In such cases, professors may be limited to teaching on a basic level, to stressing fundamentals, and to following conventional teaching patterns. In such instances, collaborative learning may be possible, but the results of that learning many not be complex enough to warrant publication. In essence, this unlucky assistant professor has to engage in time-consuming collaborative work and then engage in personal research, written without the aid of a room full of bright, sophisticated graduate students to speed and spur production.

Controversy Kills

A key to getting an academic job is to publish. As Emily Toth notes in her book *Ms. Mentor's Impeccable Advice for Women in Academia*, "You cannot wait to be brilliant.... You must aim to publish early and often. That is the only way you'll distinguish yourself from the hordes of people who apply for every tenure-track job" (18). Good advice. But the tenure-track academic has to be careful not to be too controversial. We all know the story of Galileo, who, despite scientific evidence, was forced to yield to theological and civil norms by renouncing his support of Copernicus. We might here note that today serious academic inquiry is being shunned in the name of "politically correct" image-making. Many readers might believe that academics retain the privilege to say and to write whatever they like, but they would be wrong. Gary A. Olson has recently clarified the limits of academic freedom and concluded that it is a very narrow space: "Academic freedom involves the concept that faculty members may engage in research on controversial subjects (and, by extension, discuss those subjects in their classrooms) without fear of reprisal. This refers specifically to academic subjects and is not a blanket protection for any and all speech in any venue" (http://chronicle.com/article/The-Limits-of-Academic-Freedom/49354/).

In practical terms, this means that anything that is now embarrassing or even politically incorrect may be grounds for dismissal of tenured faculty. This makes some sense. While every press is likely to publish something it later regrets, every book bearing the university's colophon is a reflection of the institution's interests, perhaps even its core values. Pulitzer Prize-winning journalist Chris Hedges has noted that since 9/11 universities have become still more sensitive to the kinds of messages and discourse practiced by their faculty, many of whom, tenured or not, are now "too scared" to speak their minds, even within their own disciplines, "for fear of being fired" (*Empire of Illusion*, 91). In 2004, Dr. Richard M. Sternberg, who holds two Ph.D.s — one in molecular evolution from Florida International University, the second in systems science from Binghamton University — "was pressured to resign" from his post as editor of the scientific journal *Proceedings of the Biological Society of Washington* over his decision to publish a paper in support of intelligent design. Similarly, Guillermo Gonzalez, an astronomy professor who had discovered several planets, was denied tenure at Iowa State University because of his views on intelligent design (see documentary film *Expelled: No Intelligence Allowed*, 2008, directed by Nathan Frankowski). Norman Gary Finkelstein, a political scientist, obviously offended his De Paul University tenuring committee, who denied him tenure despite praising Finkelstein "as a prolific scholar and outstanding teacher." Finkelstein's primary fields of research are the Israeli-Palestinian conflict and the politics of the Holocaust (see "Joint statement of Norman Finkelstein and DePaul University on their tenure controversy and its resolution," DePaul University, September 5, 2007. http://newsroom.depaul.edu/NewsReleases/showNews.aspx? NID= 1655). John Lewis, an associate professor of history at Ohio's Ashland University, was denied tenure because he wrote and lectured on objectivism — the philosophy of third-rate novelist Ayn Rand. Ashland University eventually granted him tenure on the condition that he agree to be placed on paid leave and then resign from the university the following term.

We can understand that a corporate-minded university, operating in a competitive academic landscape, has no desire to see itself on the six o'clock news as subsidizing the writings of anti–Holocaust literature or preaching the quackadoodles of creationism. The commonsense approach has a dangerous downside, however. The university's ties to corporate sponsors and the need to avoid any and all offense to its potential customers means that the university can no longer afford to push the status quo. The mystique of the high-minded, economically insulated paradise of ideas has obscured both the realities of the job market and the corporate mentality that now governs higher institutions. The university must be universal, which in a commercial sense means it must be all things to all people, or, put another way, offensive to none of its customers. Thus, when a faculty member writes or says something that is too controversial, despite the institution's lip service to academic freedom, that same academic is in danger of damaging the ability of the university to reach out to customers who are not necessarily interested in having their views challenged.

Institutions of higher learning must now play a careful game. The university needs star academics — defined by publication — in order to bolster and to propagate its intellectual image in the marketplace. Yet the academic publication market is geared toward highly-specialized subject matter, which must challenge existing doctrines to be worthy of publication. In essence, what the university needs to promote and what it promises to publish are at odds with each other. The academic press deals in the marketplace of ideas; the university, while requiring academic publications of its faculty, deals in the marketplace of customer relations. No wonder so many young academics feel that they are in a no-win scenario. In terms of teaching and contact hours, an assistant professor must do more than any colleague hired in any other era and must still find the time to produce more publications than has ever been required of older colleagues in the very same department. The work must be interesting enough to warrant publication but not confrontational enough to warrant attention by the general public.

Yes, it all looks pretty grim — dire even. But let's take a deep breath and step back for a moment. There is no doubt that the new system in place has its problems, but that doesn't mean you can't be part of the problem. After all, few of us lead a life of utter conviction. Who is for more pollution? No one. Yet, how many of us drive a Prius? Very few. How many of us think junk food is good for us? Very few. How many of us eat junk food? Very many. My point is that, unless we're willing to change careers, we need to keep our feet on the ground here and deal with the harsh reality of securing publications for tenure. After all, challenging authority is rarely a way to win over the boss or to advance a career.

For many, leaving academia may be the only way to keep principles intact. For William Deresiewicz, a former associate professor of English at Yale University, that was clearly the case. He left his plum job because he refused to bow to the new corporate mentality of the university (see his "The Disadvantages of an Elite Education"). To Deresiewicz and others who refuse to bend to the new dictates of commercial academia, who like to dance in the rain, who won't wear power suits to work, who are unwilling to surrender who they are for the small rewards of a steady paycheck, I say, "I respect you." I really do. But for the rest of us, we've come too far, invested too much, worked too long to chuck it all away. No, we know the odds are long, but we've come this far. Why not fight for what we want and what, we feel sure, we deserve?

Unsympathetic University Presses

The above-cited difficulties might be collectively moot if the only obstacle to publication were actually finding the time to write. After all, even an exhausted community college professor could forgo sleep and burn the midnight oil in a heroic attempt to turn out a manuscript of sufficient academic promise. Many do. But the odds are stacked against them. And here is perhaps the worst news of all: Given the momentous changes in academia, one would think that university presses would also be changing with the times by accommodating to the kinds of writings that are increasingly the bent of academic practitioners. But no. The difficulties of tenure-track professors are not at all troubling to most university presses, which can happily continue to accept traditional-approach books written with aplomb by those Ivy League professors. As a result, the struggling assistant professor at a middling school may well have little to show in terms of publication when it comes to submitting a tenure file. In fact, university presses have followed academic institutions in establishing what seems to be a permanent cycle of fiscal restraint by publishing fewer and fewer books. Yes, that's right; just as you are expected to publish more and more, there are fewer and fewer places to do so. Perhaps what is even more egregious, some university presses are now demanding that academic writers (who are likely desperate for publication) share the production costs. That's right: many academics now need to pay for the privilege of having their work published. This is easy enough for the tenured professor with a research budget, but it is a further humiliation for recent graduates, who are underemployed or unemployed. Worse, considering that publication is a key component of tenure, it's likely that these same presses will be raising the amount they charge to these utterly desperate academic authors. There are far fewer jobs, far more candidates for those jobs, a rising premium on publication, fewer places to publish, and now the costs of publication are being pushed onto the scholars. The task at hand is of biblical proportions.

Ten Things You Need to Know

1. Universities are moving toward abolishing tenure — your time is running out,
2. given the competition, you have one chance to get this right.

3. A key to tenure is publication.
4. Expectations of publication are unreasonably high.
5. The university's corporate mentality blocks your ability to meet its lofty expectations because it expects you to have more student contact hours, thus limiting your ability to research and write.
6. The university's new-found interest in group work impedes the research efforts and interests of a typical humanities-based academic.
7. University presses only want studies which challenge the status quo.
8. You can be fired for publishing something that challenges the status quo.
9. Fifty percent of tenure-track appointees will fail to achieve tenure.
10. Oh, and here is the answer to the question of why God never got tenure at the University:
    a. He took too long to get his ideas onto paper;
    b. He was writing for general readers, not scholars;
    c. He refused to collaborate with students;
    d. His published views were too controversial; and
    e. His book was not published by a university press.

CHAPTER 1

The System

In 2006, I could finally rest easy. After reviewing my dossier, my university had bestowed tenure upon me. As part of the tenuring process, I had assembled all my teaching assessments, recorded my activities on various university committees, documented my service to the community at large, assembled letters from my chair, dean, and a variety of friendly scholars willing to lend their support. I included a list of my publications along with a plastic tub housing the hardcopies, which consisted of two books, seven editions, two essay collections, three articles, ten notes, and 15 reviews in various journals, all written between 2001—the year of my tenure-track hiring—and 2006—the year I was at last granted tenure. In the four years since I was granted tenure, I have added three more books (one of them coauthored), published two more critical editions, edited and contributed to two essay collections, and published nine articles, two encyclopedia entries, two notes, and three book reviews.

How have I amassed this impressive research portfolio? Was I (or am I) a genius of some sort? I wish! A compulsive writer, maybe, but not a genius. My GPA had never been exceptionally high. I had never been an honor student. After graduating from a very good school, I was short-listed for exactly zero jobs and slogged it out for eight years as a part-timer until I finally published a book, which then secured a tenure-track job at a tier-three private university. In short, given my track record and eventual place of employment, no one expected me to publish much. How, then, have I exceeded all expectations? This book will attempt to clarify my system, which depends upon a rhythm of writing and submission.

Before you can come up with a strategy to ensure your tenure, you need to know the rules. The value of publication may vary widely from institution to institution and, while this book will be citing examples from specific institutions, we must acknowledge that my own situation may not exactly fit the reality of your home institution. I treated tenure like a military expedition. Whether that is right or wrong for you is a personal decision. But as Shakespeare says, "In matters of defense, 'tis best to weigh the enemy more mighty than he seems." As far as I was concerned, my university was not yet my home institution. It was the enemy. For reasons that will become clear in the next chapter, nearly my entire experience as a Ph.D. student had been adversarial; my time as an adjunct had been marked by uncertainty and the feeling that I was being exploited, no doubt because I *was* being exploited. There was nothing in my professional experience to suggest that tenure would be any different. The university had a prize that I longed for—tenure—and my mission was to capture it. I was wrong to think that way. In reality, my university, I now see, was on my side. My department had chosen me over equally qualified candidates; in searching for and selecting me, the university had already spent much treasure and had no wish to do so again. I was given a faculty mentor and attended a variety of new faculty orientations, each designed to introduce and to welcome me to the university and its culture. If I were on a tenure track at this point in my life, my attitude toward the process would be healthier and less adversarial.

Ground Rules

My first day as a new hire at the University of La Verne was a busy one. I wasted no time. I went down to the personnel department and asked for information concerning tenure. Just what was expected of me? I was given some general information and told to consult the dean, who then informed me that the rules for tenure were set by individual departments. (This is probably the case at your institution as well, but it is best to do the leg work. Have everything in writing.) I then met with my department chair, who explained to me that the department was reasonably flexible in its standards but that it expected (a) excellence in the classroom, (b) scholarly activity, (c) community service, and (d) collegiality.

I took some notes, studied them for a day or two, and then met with my chair again: "OK, fine, so there are these assessment standards, but, err, umm, how much is enough?" My chair didn't understand the question. I continued, "Well, you say here I need to teach to a high standard. You quantify standards numerically on teaching evaluations, so what number should I have in mind? You state that community service is necessary. What kind and how much? Likewise, you write that collegiality is important. That's difficult to measure. Could you please define activities in which I can thereafter report that I have been 'collegial'? Lastly, you say that publishing is important, but how much and of what kind? Just what has everyone else done in terms of publishing?"

More discussion ensued. In terms of teaching assessments, we agreed that all fully tenured faculty of the Department of English should consistently maintain a points average that met or exceeded the university's standard, as defined by its own student surveys. In terms of public service, we agreed that each member of the department seeking promotion should present one community-oriented paper every two years and be a member of at least one professional organization. Collegiality, a nebulous term, was thrashed about. We defined it as being demonstrated in dozens of ways, some great and some small: by faithful attendance at department meetings, programs, and other functions; by accepting and fully cooperating with academic policy once it has been agreed upon by a majority of the department; by taking seriously one's responsibility to colleagues on a committee; by helping a colleague with scholarship; by taking an absent colleague's class; and by being willing to accept teaching assignments occurring at unpopular times.

But in the matter of publication, he was silent. He explained that some members were extremely active, some were not. I assume, in retrospect, that he didn't want to set hard and fast requirements in case I would fail to meet them. However, I saw his silence as further proof that I could be canned at any point. After all, if the department refused to state its moving target, then it might thereafter argue that I had failed to hit it. I explained my worry and, to his credit, he agreed to work with me on creating a reasonable set of publishing goals. Here is what we came up with:

PUBLICATION: HOW MUCH IS ENOUGH? (OUR POINTS SYSTEM)
The Department of English suggests the following for any promotion in rank: 25 points over any 5-year period. The indications of valuable scholarship include, but are not limited to, the following:
1. Authoring books of literary criticism (25 POINTS)
2. Editing a book, collection, or journal (15 POINTS)
3. Publishing articles in professional journals (14 pages or more) (10 POINTS)

4. Publication of notes (13 pages or less) (3 POINTS)
5. Publishing reviews (2 POINTS)
6. Presenting conference papers (1 POINT)
7. Conference proceedings (.5 POINT)
8. Participating in scholarly organizations. Membership in and attendance at the meetings of professional organizations may be indications of scholarly activity (.5 POINT)
9. Research grants (Internal: .5 POINT; External: 1 POINT)

I urge the reader to do the same. Sit down, today if you can, with your chair and agree in writing upon a reasonable point system based upon what you need as a minimum for tenure submission. Find that minimum and then pad it, just in case. Why? Because you can never be certain that anything you write will be published—or, if published, that it will be published within the term of your tenuring requirements. No, it was clear that if I were to get 25 points, I really needed to aim for about 50 points. That is to say, I needed to have all the articles, reviews, and conference stuff accepted *just in case the book I was working on was rejected*. Remember, what you have done before your tenure appointment is zeroed out. The day you begin your new job, you have, so far as your tenuring committee is concerned, ZERO publications.

Let's be clear. It is not enough to accumulate points; you need to vary your points as well. You can, for example, join 50 scholarly organizations and attend their conferences. Yet the 25 points gained in doing so will be fairly worthless to your tenuring committee. Obviously, what your committee wants to see is that you have been productive, not just attentive. Likewise, presenting papers at 25 conferences over a five-year period may impress some, but what about an actual publication? Let's also keep in mind that there are publications and there are publications. In my own field, *Shakespeare Quarterly,* Oxford University Press, and Cambridge University Press are the summa cum laude of Shakespeareana, *Shakespeare Survey* is the magna cum laude, and Ashgate and Routledge are probably the cum laude. There are, as well, a variety of presses, particularly vanity presses, that have far lower reputations. So publication, in and of itself, is not enough. Of course, everyone wants to publish with Oxford or Cambridge. We will be dealing with the suitability of projects and presses in the coming pages, but the point here is that you should discuss all this with your chair and come up with a reasonable and actionable strategy. The remainder of the chapter considers different aspects that might be included in such a strategy.

Earning Points

*Participating in scholarly organizations;
conference proceedings*

My earliest experience at a conference led me to believe that I was wasting my time. I had just graduated; I was unemployed. There was a local conference; the entry fee was low, so I applied and was accepted. I was given a very early morning slot. As a consequence, the room was more than half empty; those who were there seemed more interested in queuing for sweet rolls and coffee than in listening to a presentation. Most chatted among themselves — old friends who had already been through the tenure wars. No one seemed very interested in what I had to say. Their indifference made me, perhaps, more nervous. I sweated profusely the very first time I laid down my notes on an oaken lectern. I was told I would have twenty minutes to speak and that I should leave time for questions. I spoke for precisely seventeen minutes. An uncomfortable silence ensued. Somewhere from the back of the room I heard the tearing of sugar packets. The moderator offered a polite question, one which might have been answered by anyone with access to Wikipedia. A follow-up question by someone who had returned late from the sweet table did not address the subject of my paper. Still, I responded as if I were an expert on that subject, too. More silence followed, and then I sat down, relieved it was over.

I suppose that, had I already been on a tenure-track appointment, I would have felt that I had done well. But I was not on any such appointment. Unlike the rest of the people in the room, I had come on my own dollar, and the muted response to my paper infuriated me and filled me with a sense that there was no need to go to any more conferences. After all, when it came to my own slim field of specialization, there were few on earth, I felt confidently (or overconfidently), who knew as much as I did on the subject. Ergo, any discussion of my work was one-sided. I was fielding polite interest but not really learning anything. I had not yet figured out what conferences are for. I thought conferences were designed as promotional vehicles, i.e., "I have a new book out; let me read you a passage and then, in discussion, effortlessly volley your soft-lob questions." Indeed, conferences have two facets that encourage this view: (1) each conference usually has a keynote speaker who discusses or reads excerpts from a new book; and (2) many conferences, almost all large conferences, have a room for book vendors wherein they display their newest publications. So, yes, I felt that these conferences might be fun — or, more likely, stressful — events, but they were not really useful for exchanging information.

That was a major error. The fault was entirely my own. In order to get more material published, I should have used — and now do use — conferences not as a platform to discuss what I know but to learn about what others know. It's not like I just go up there and say, "Hi, here's what I am thinking about today." I have a paper written out, but I am not yet married to its ideas. Conferences are my first chance to try out a topic, to see if it creates any meaningful discussion, and to take notes on any books that are similar. In essence, I turn the tables on the audience. They become my resource and — surprise, surprise — it works! Why? Because conference attendees like to feel useful and to enjoy showing off their own knowledge. There are 100 brains in the room, all with Ph.D.s. Isn't it likely that someone knows something that can benefit me?

To really get something out of this process, you will have to put your ego to one side. Of course, it's great to hear that your work is fascinating, but you don't learn anything that way. Instead, simply begin by saying that this is a work in process, that it is formative. And then just go for it. The questioner is likely to begin politely. Be honest. When you don't know, say so. Too often in my early conference discussions I simply shifted to safe ground.

WRONG WAY TO ENGAGE IN CONFERENCE DISCUSSION
QUESTION: "Is there a link between forgery and identity and Fredric Jameson's idea of cultural capital?"
SHIFTING ANSWER: "There is no doubt that when dealing with forgers, identity is always a key issue. In forging the names of others, a forger is shifting his own identity away from his family and those who gave him, well, his 'given name.' After all, every newborn has no say in his or her name, blah, blah, blah."

I have avoided the real question, which is designed to get me to acknowledge Fredric Jameson's work. What I should have said was this: "Interesting. I really don't know his work enough to formulate an intelligent reply. Can you give me a brief rundown, perhaps suggest some titles for me to check out?" Yes, you might look a bit flatfooted if you adopt this strategy. But that's all right. You have learned something, and, after all, isn't it better to learn what is wrong with your idea now, after investing only a few hundred hours on the paper, rather than later, after you have invested tens of thousands of hours on it? Consider the conferences as a dry run for journal or press submission. The people in the room are there to help you, if you will just let them.

There is another great reason to go to conferences: Schmoozing. As a Ph.D. student, I had always held schmoozing in low regard. Polite conversation, fine; intellectual discussion, even better; but schmoozing, at least in my mind, inferred groveling, laughing at unfunny phrases, and generally "sucking up." And no one was a bigger suck-up than Nigel Athens. Who? Nigel Athens (not his real name) was a fellow Ph.D. student at the University of Bexhill-on-Sea (not my real alma mater — the use of pseudonyms is explained in the next chapter), and he was the master of schmoozing. He knew how to tell an inoffensive joke and how to keep a conversation going; he had an endless amount of interesting observations and anecdotes. Nigel became, almost overnight, something of a pet to the professors; he was offered scholarships, he won prizes. He deserved it; he worked hard and was brilliant. And he was professional. When going to class, I had worn a Black Sabbath T-shirt and faded jeans; Nigel wore a starched dress shirt as white as confectioner's sugar. Yet even Nigel hadn't figured schmoozing out fully and made some laughable errors. His dream was to become a director at the local, highly distinguished theater. So he got a job bartending right across the street from the theater and began schmoozing with actors and directors. I always wondered how he thought that turning point would come. In my mind's eye, I guess he thought that the chief director would walk in, order a wine cooler, exchange some casual banter with the barkeep, and then say, "I like you, boy. How about you direct Chekov for me?" Yes, schmoozing, I felt, was beneath me. I was a fighter, not a fawner, and while I might die in despair, I would not drown in my own hypocrisy.

Well, I've mellowed with age. I now recognize that it's only hypocrisy if you don't mean it. To begin with, there is nothing wrong in acknowledging the good work of others. After all, it's kind of cool to meet famous scholars, people you have been reading for years, and to discuss their ideas with them. For the most part, scholars are generous with their time, especially when the topic is how interesting they are! More important, important scholars are, well, important! I'm not suggesting you go the Nigel Athens route in the hope that someone will offer you a dream job on the merit of color-matching your shirt and tie. What I am suggesting is that important scholars are often asked to edit collections of essays, and they generally ask people they know and respect to write for these collections. You might not be asked the first time or even the twentieth, but sooner or later you are bound to be in the running for this sort of assignment — if you attend conferences and mix politely and intelligently with the right sort of people. Also, these same bigwigs often sit on the boards of journals, and journals — unlike publishing houses — are often strapped for submissions. If one of the board members knows you, she may be more willing to work with you and even offer you tips on a paper before formal submission.

That's why I suggest you join at least two professional organizations, and that one of these organizations be a very conservative one, likely filled with academics nearing retirement. In my own case, I joined the Shakespeare Association of America and the Association for Literary Scholars. The Shakespeare Association was a given. It is the leading organization in my field, and its conferences, seminars, and symposia feature the cutting-edge ideas of the profession. But I also joined the Association of Literary Scholars (ALSC) for wholly different reasons, and many young academics in English literature probably think it was a dumb move. The organization consists mostly of greybeards and was, from its inception, comically dubbed the Anti-Modern Language Association (Anti-MLA). The ALSC makes no bones about its differences with the MLA, which is often more interested in the political and theoretical implications of literature than in the creative process of writing and the aesthetic pleasures of reading.

As someone whose own writing gravitates to the biographical and quirky, I had little or no sympathy with approaches that downplayed or obscured the author or the gratifications of the text. But I didn't join the ALSC just because I found the organization to be aesthetically pleasing. *I did it because it was filled with greybeards.* To many, that makes no sense. The energy and new ideas are coming from the new generation, not the old — but, as a member of the new generation, those people are my rivals. The greybeards are not. Moreover, the most distinguished of these greybeards are people who have toiled in academia for years, people who have published lots of books, people who know all the editors, people who sit on the boards of a variety of journals, people who edit collections of essays. As a young academic looking for publishing outlets, can you really afford to ignore this lot of successful people, people happy to mentor *your* success?

The first year I joined the ALSC, I was put on a panel with Richard

Knowles, one of the foremost critics of *King Lear* in the world. Oh, and the organization also had a young scholars' travel grant. I applied for and won that as well. (I note that the Shakespeare Association is now offering young scholars not only travel awards but also research awards. Find like organizations in your own field and apply for everything!) I soon struck up a friendship with Stanley Stewart, one of the founders of the organization. He invited me to dinner. Joining us was Thomas Hester, editor of the *John Donne Journal*. As I will explain in my final chapter, all these people would come to play a vital role in my publishing career. The point to keep in mind here is that you don't want to jump from one organization to another. Conferences are not cheap vacations. They are networking opportunities. That means you want to join one or two organizations and become friendly with its members by seeing them year after year. Make a point of being sociable. Collect cards; send out pleasant emails emphasizing how much you enjoyed chatting at the conference. State that you look forward to seeing them again. Don't be pushy. Be cordial, sincere, and then leave it at that. Sooner or later, you will connect with people who can help you.

You should also get involved in a local conference. Despite my early negative experience, a local conference — something you can drive to — is really worth investigating. In California, for example, the Cal State Universities have an annual Shakespeare conference. The cost is a mere fifteen dollars, and a box lunch is included. I try to make this conference whenever it is in the Los Angeles basin. The attendees are a smart and friendly lot, and I use the conference to try out new ideas or projects. If the conversation goes nowhere, it's no big loss. I'm only out $15.

Before we leave the subject of conferences, I should note that there is a kind of conference that merges both vacation and publication: The French conference! Our Franco friends have conferences all over their splendid country — conferences set in chateaus, castles, and monasteries. Their dinners are 4-star and often accompanied by classical quartets that play for your pleasure. Best yet, the French usually publish the proceedings of the conference. (Best to check ahead of time to see if, in fact, the conference in question is publishing the proceedings.) These papers are not vetted beyond the synopsis that you submit to the conference organizers. As a consequence, their qualities are uneven, but it is still a publication. Keep in mind, however, that these conference proceedings often take years to produce and are of varying quality. Two of my own proceedings papers took five years to come to market — this despite the fact that I handed in my paper the day after the conference ended. I would not recommend too many of these sorts of publications, which often look like cheap phone books.

Ideally, you want to publish in conference proceedings and then publish a revised and expanded version as an article in a peer-reviewed periodical. Some readers are likely surprised by this. Some may even think it the academic equivalent of double-dipping. But that is because you have yet to see the conference as a dry run for publication. The conference is evidence that you have been producing material; at the conference, you are supposed to present your ideas and to discuss them with colleagues. Then, as the result of revisions springing from this process, you will be better able to place your work in a peer-reviewed journal.

Lastly, if there is a faculty research lecture series on your home campus, you want to get on that circuit, too. Anything that will raise your profile as a researcher at your own university is a good thing. There is no point in raising the profile of your institution at a conference while keeping a low profile of your activities on your own campus. Every time you address an audience, whether it be your students, an international or small local conference, or an on-campus departmental lecture series, you are representing your university and selling yourself. You have every right to discuss your work — not in a brash or egotistical manner, but in a simple and straightforward way. Research is one of your responsibilities, but it does you no good if you don't engage others in your interests.

COUNTING TALLY: You need 25 points. By presenting at five conferences in five years, you have earned five points. Congrats! You have just earned one-fifth of the points you will need for tenure.

Book reviews

Reviews are both critical and superfluous to the fortunes of a book. They are critical in that a good review can create some academic buzz, which, in turn, leads to more attention for the writer, the writer's academic home, and the publisher. They are superfluous, however, to sales. Since the book is so expensive, a good review is hardly likely to get scholars to shell out 100 bucks for it. It is more likely academics will simply check the book out of the library. Still, reviews can make or break the public perception of a book—all-important when the public, in this case, is your peer group. Yet, despite the importance of reviews, no one likes doing them very much, and often the people most capable of writing useful reviews simply don't have the time to write them. (That's the thing about busy people. They are busy for a reason. The better they are at something, the more people ask them to do stuff.)

That leaves an all-important opening for the young academic, who, even as an unknown, can often snag a major book for scholarly review. A newly-minted Ph.D. likely has no pending commitments and thus has more time to undertake reviews. But why should a journal seek you out as a reviewer? Short answer: they shouldn't and they don't. But you can be proactive. Simply go over to your university library and look at the new acquisitions on offer. Find something that is in your field, read the book, ask yourself if you could write an adequate review of this work — "adequate" will be explained — and set to. Be timely, as it is likely that the journal already has the book on a shelf and the book editor is looking for a reviewer. Reviews are usually between 1,200 and 2,000 words in length. It should take you about four days to read the book and three or four more days to write the review. So in a week, you should be able to submit a review. Now all we need to do is select the journal. Easy! Simply pick a journal in the field that does reviews and check to see whether the book has already been reviewed. Then simply pop the review in the mail to the book editor along with a letter stating that your dissertation was in that particular field, that you feel you have a good grasp on the subject, and that you would appreciate it if the press would consider publishing your review.

I'm not going to lie: in my early days, I'd sometimes get back a letter thanking me for my work but, alas, the book was already promised to some established star in the firmament. About 80% of the time, however, I'd get my review published. It wasn't because my reviews were brilliant. Now that I sit on the board of two journals, I know why my reviews were accepted: They were filler. Let me explain. The journal must publish a set number of issues per year, yet academics often fall behind in their publishing commitments. So, rather than having three articles and two book reviews, a journal might only have two articles and two reviews set for press. This leaves the editor or editors in the unenviable position of having to find meaningful filler for the issue, and you have provided it.

While the review in and of itself is unlikely to make a deep impression on academia, a review is still a publication—one that appears in a peer-reviewed journal. Not only does the review carry some academic weight, it also serves as good practice to keep up your writing chops and allows you to stay current in your field. Moreover, the readers of the journal have no idea that you were not specially assigned this very important book; for all they know, you were commissioned to write the review because of your expertise.

We also need to discuss the tone of your review. There are, in general, two kinds of reviews: positive and negative. But have you ever noticed that, in most instances, the positive reviews are written by the really important people and the negative reviews are written by people you have never heard of? In my field, I call this the "MacJackson Effect," named after the highly-distinguished MacDonald P. Jackson, emeritus professor of English at the University of Auckland and the author and editor of an enviable body of works published by Oxford, Cambridge, and other top-tier publishers. "MacJackson," as I call him, is one of the greats. His reputation is unassailable. So when MacJackson reads a book, he can say things like "I really learned a lot reading this book," "this book brought a perspective that had me rethink my own ideas on the topic," etc. He can afford to be generous or to admit his own ignorance. Of course he can! He is MacJackson!

But you are not, and you cannot write, "Hey, I really learned a lot reading your book," because academics reading your review will simply ask themselves, "Well, if you knew so little about the topic, why are you reviewing this book?!" No, for a newbie Ph.D., the tone most be polite but disappointed. If MacJackson's underlying message is, "Wow, great book," yours must be, "Good book, interesting book, flawed book, here's why." And now you catalogue the book's failings. Every book has one— some far more than one. You don't want to get a reputation as a hatchet man here, but you also have to show your competence in the field. If you find an error, point it out. However, don't go on for the full 1,000 words in a negative tone. Be fair, and be right. And know that what you are doing will hurt. Nicholas Royle sums up the publishing game nicely: "Nearly twenty years ago, I began what is so inanely called an 'academic publishing career' with a short review of a book by Christopher Norris…. The review was taken up by Geoffrey Bennington who … savaged Terry Engleton's review of my review" (Nicholas Royle, *The Uncanny*, 120).

This may sound like I am advancing only the worst tendencies of the profession, that I am advocating that your review be mean because the profession is a hard and cruel one. I am sure that there are other ways of going about getting reviews; I am sure that there are other avenues available to the unknown and untenured assistant professor. I can only tell you what worked for me. Moreover, I can also tell you that no one in my 20 years of academic publishing has ever called me out for being too hard on an author. I also note that many academics, even very famous ones who don't need to bother about tenure, continue to write rather biting reviews. Still, you really should take some care who you review. As a newbie, you don't want to review (especially negatively) books by important, established authors. For one, the journal has likely already farmed out that book for review and sent it to a very distinguished person in the field; moreover, because of the author's and reviewer's reputations, the journal is more than likely willing to wait on the review. In addition, it makes no sense to be negative about someone who is important and who may, in the adjudication of your article or book manuscript, recall that you were the peon who wrote a hostile review. No, what you want to do is to pick a new author — someone whose reputation is not yet established.

Even here you might want to be careful. Remember, just as you are struggling to gain that tenured job, so, likely, is the author you are reviewing. Recall that your tenuring committee can only judge your publications on what you submit. So the author does not need to include reviews done on her book, hostile or otherwise. Still, you might want to go easier on an assistant professor, just as a matter of professional courtesy. After all, what goes around comes around. Negative reviews might be fun to write, but they are also nasty to read.

It should be pointed out that many publishers collect these reviews and send them on to the author. Opening up a letter from your publisher only to discover a negative review can be very painful. (The first time I received a negative review I wanted the earth to swallow me whole.) But negative reviews are common and are part of the job. You can take some solace in the fact that your reviewer is often an untenured, junior faculty member who is merely doing what is necessary to survive in the profession. That survival depends on publications. The downside, however, is that the author you have attacked won't forget your name. You will have made an enemy, one who may one day sit on a journal or editorial board; one who may doom your latest publishing project; one who may want to write an equally nasty review of one of *your books*. It has never happened to me. But I may have been lucky, and I'm not advocating that you rely on luck.

In my initial iteration of this book, I included a negative review I had written some time ago but had decided not to place because, despite the fact that I felt that I had scored some good points, the tone was too hostile. In fact, I can further state that the tone was too hostile *because* I was looking to score points. A review shouldn't be about proving that you, the reviewer, are smarter, more knowledgeable, or better positioned than the author you are evaluating. The point is not to audition yourself. A book review is not a job interview, and no one I know, even the most brilliant of reviewers, has ever included a review as a writing sample for a hiring committee. As I said, I was going to include an old, unpublished review, mostly because I hate throwing away anything I have worked on; I always believe you can revise and redraft something into a workable and publishable project. But, just as the proofs to this book arrived, I received an email from someone I have never met, Celeste Woo, who teaches at Empire State College/SUNY.

Empire is a small, predominantly liberal arts school with a ridiculously low in-state undergraduate tuition of only $5,270 per year. More than 60 percent of the students study part time. Its most popular major is business, which accounts for almost 40 percent of its students. The school has a hard time saying "no" to anyone, accepting 83 percent of its applicants. Compare Empire to New York's Columbia, which has a tuition of $45,000 a year and accepts about 9 percent of its applicants.

Celeste is not at a famous school and likely struggles with heavy teaching loads and flimsy research resources, but she is both smart and productive. She has already published a handful of peer-reviewed articles and a book on Romantic theater. We have never met, but she contacted me out of the blue to share an advance copy of her review of my book *Bettymania and the Birth of Celebrity Culture*. As part of her review, Celeste added a bibliography of other related studies, an ungainly but not uncommon practice. For the purposes of this book, I have cut that laundry list. Other than that, I herein reprint Celeste Woo's report in full, along with my own running comments. The review is partially positive, partially negative:

Bettymania and the Birth of Celebrity Culture. Bethlehem, PA: Lehigh UP, 2010.

    Jeffrey Kahan clearly has a penchant for analyzing quirkiness within theater and performance history. A scholar of British Romanticism as well as of Shakespeare, Kahan has authored monographs on Edmund Kean, the *enfant terrible* of Shakespeare acting history, and on William Henry Ireland, the notorious Shakespeare forger. He has edited several of Ireland's works, and a multi-volume set of "Shakespeare Imitations, Parodies, and Forgeries, 1710–1820." Extending his innovative analysis, he has also issued a textbook discussing the writing principles operant within graphic novels, further showcasing his talent at bringing texts from the margin into the mainstream of academic discourse. The readers of *Shakespeare Newsletter* may recognize his name from the several recent editions of Shakespeare plays that Kahan has edited for the New Kittredge series.

[So far, this is a wonderfully positive report, and I now feel sure that I know how Caesar felt just before Brutus stabbed him in the groin.] In *Bettymania and the Birth of Celebrity Culture,* Kahan presents the first book-length analysis of a colorful character named William Henry West Betty, whom one might dub the "Shirley Temple" of the British Romantic era. [I had wanted to make that very connection but didn't. Still, I am impressed. She understands my iterative processes.] Master Betty, as he was known, was all the rage, taking Scotland, Ireland and eventually London by storm as a theatrical wunderkind. A "tween" in contemporary parlance, Betty was marketed as the "Young Roscius," a deliberate reference to David Garrick. He made headlines for successfully playing many Shakespearean parts, including Hamlet, Macbeth, and other roles surprising for a child actor.

Kahan's study is excellent, going well beyond mere biography and presenting a cohesive, accessible analysis of the Betty phenomenon from a cultural studies vantage point. Kahan argues that "Bettymania" reflected political attitudes as well as the rise of consumerism and of a celebrity culture that is quite recognizable in today's terms: a culture of wild fan behavior and sophisticated PR. The back cover blurb highlights one of Kahan's most brilliant points: that "the disintegration of Betty's popularity was not a sign of celebrity culture's failure but of its appropriate function. One idol must be replaced with another." [This point is actually stated in the conclusion as well but, yes, so far so good.]

Kahan's analysis joins a growing body of Romanticist scholarship on celebrity, such as Luckhurst and Moody's *Theatre and Celebrity in Britain: 1660–2000* (2005), Ghislaine McDayter's *Byromania and the Birth of Celebrity Culture* (2009), and Tom Mole's *Byron's Romantic Celebrity: Industrial Culture and the Hermeneutic of Intimacy* (2007). Mole has also edited a collection, *Romanticism and Celebrity Culture, 1750–1850* (2009). Richard Dyer's seminal work, *Stars* (1980), inaugurated much of the current fruitful work on stars, fandom, and celebrity. [I quoted most, if not all, of these studies, but that information is in the notes, so she has read the book, it seems, with some care.]

In *Bettymania,* Kahan provides an important contribution to Shakespeare scholarship, Romanticist discourse, theatre history, and cultural studies. His work on Master Betty differs from classic actor studies such as Kalman Burnim's *David Garrick: Director* (1961), which presents meticulous archival research and simple biographical narrative, with little overarching argument. Kahan's approach is more akin to that of scholars who have analyzed Shakespeare's afterlife and continuing cultural meaning, such as Barbara Hodgdon, Péter Dávidházi, Graham Holderness, Richard Burt, and myself. Kahan's work strikes me as most reminiscent of Marc Baer's book-length analysis of the Old Price Riots in the early 1800s; like Baer, Kahan trains his focus upon a relatively short and outrageous theatrical phenomenon, and analyzes its significance with verve and insight. [That is heady company, but with every compliment, I feel sure that the dagger will soon come out. She now moves into a chapter-by-chapter review, stressing aspects of the book that might be of use to scholars.]

The wit and humor that Kahan displays throughout his study attest to his enjoyment of his subject matter, and make his book a pleasurable and accessible read. Copiously researched, *Bettymania* shows Kahan's flair for nosing out amusing anecdotes, which he shares with relish as well as incisive commentary. For instance, his chapter on "Kemble's Revenge," which relates how the haughty and resentful John Philip Kemble cleverly and subtly retaliated against this upstart Betty, is rife with lively tales that support Kahan's convincing and compassionate analysis of the adult actors' psyches.

Kahan begins his study by observing the techniques that Garrick employed to promote himself, arguing that his self-marketing efforts, successful as they were, paled in comparison to the "businesslike media machine" that Betty ran, "which sought public endorsements, paid critics for positive notices, issued daily health bulletins, leaked private correspondence for press release, repackaged the boy actor for regional markets, and profited directly from official or souvenir merchandise" (17). Besides this very contemporary-sounding PR apparatus, Betty's stardom owes a debt to Words-worthian notions of childhood and innocence, as Kahan points out [24–25].

His first chapter chronicles the intriguing reasons and ways that Master Betty was branded differently in Scotland, Ireland, and then England. His narrative is highly spirited and entertaining. Drawing analogies to "Garrick Fever," when a young sprightly Garrick heralded the professional demise of his predecessor, James Quin, Kahan argues that Bettymania was a "decidedly nostalgic and thus conservative enterprise" [59]. He follows with an instance of his witty and perceptive analysis, characterizing the fad as reliant upon a "Romantic adherence of innocence and ignorance" which resulted in "a kind of pretzel logic, twisted and half-baked" [59]. His parsing of the convoluted and overdetermined meanings superimposed upon the star serves to illumine various strands of the era's sociocultural discourse (again resembling Baer's analysis of Kemble and the Old Price Riots). Additionally, Kahan's detailed discussion of actors' contracts and salaries, the workings of benefit performances, and the spate of child performers that arose in Betty's wake is immensely useful: careful and clear in presentation.

His positioning of Betty as an influential and hitherto unrecognized figure within the development of Romantic discourse, and of Shakespeare's impact within it, is his most provocative assertion. Analyzing the gendered resonances of the sensibility ascribed to Betty, Kahan argues that Betty's Hamlet was deeply admired because of the contrast with Kemble's approach to the Dane, Kemble being famed for his stoic, dignified, and sublime characterizations. Betty occasionally used his youth to excellent effect, playing Hamlet with a feminine delicacy and tenderness that an older man perhaps could not have carried off, and highlighting his filial relationship with Gertrude.

Kahan makes note of moments when Betty's choices as an actor made a virtue of necessity: unable to intimidate the full-grown woman playing Ophelia to his Hamlet, Betty chose to showcase Hamlet's delicacy and sensitivity (109). Kahan argues that Betty's Hamlet likely influenced subsequent Hamlet actors, including Sarah Bernhardt. Here, Kahan's point is extremely thought-provoking, and rather underdeveloped: it would be worthwhile indeed to speculate further upon the interaction between Betty's Shakespearean interpretations and the Romantic obsession with Shakespeare, and with Hamlet in particular. Even the folks who abhorred Betty, including Coleridge, Kemble, and Siddons, may owe some portion of their views on Shakespeare to their negative reaction against the Betty craze. Throughout, Kahan presents his reader with nuanced and thoughtful analyses of the Betty fad, delineating the myriad reasons for Master Betty's meteoric rise to fame as well as his downfall, and using Bettymania as a case study for a greater understanding of today's celebrity obsession. The voyeurism, mystification, and idealization that were projected onto the child star resemble what today's superstars encounter, not to mention the fickle and transitory loyalty of their once-adoring public.

[But now Celeste does what she is supposed to do — point out the book's flaws, clinically and mercilessly.] Kahan does miss several opportunities to draw fruitful connections with other discussions within Romantic scholarship, such as the proliferation of studies on Sarah Siddons and the maternal sensitivity she was known for evincing. A discussion of sensibility on stage, in relation to the evolving understanding of "Romanticism," would productively tie his study with the several fields he already engages with: Romanticism, theatre history, and Shakespeare studies. [She's right.] Moreover, he could have positioned his monograph in relation to other studies that argue for more serious critical attention to be accorded to actors, such as the *Players of Shakespeare* series released by Cambridge UP in the 1990s, and more recently, Jonathan Holmes's study of the RSC, Tony Howard's *Women as Hamlet,* and my own monograph on Romantic-era Shakespeare performers. [Again, she's right, but it does sound a bit odd that I am told that the book would have been better had I cited her!]By the same token, Kahan's fascinating discussion of Betty's perceived transvestitism, the obsession of some of his fans with his biological gender and physical body, and the Chevalier d'Eon is quite brief. [Yes. Again, she's right.] He reads Betty as "liberated to traverse the boundaries of class and clothing" [115] without contextualizing his interpretation within the copious scholarship on cross-dressing. [A point scored. I do confess it.]

Overall, Kahan's study would have benefited from more references to other critical strands, such as discussions of Garrick, since Betty was billed as a new Garrick, and the two were mystified in similar fashion. His discussion of the parallel between Bettymania and Byromania would certainly have been enhanced by connections to McDayter's and Mole's books on Byromania, but these latter were probably not yet released while Kahan was authoring his book. Also, Kahan's use of actor memoirs led me to think that his points would have been strengthened with more theorizing of the nature of these "memoirs," such as has been done by the many scholars studying eighteenth-century actresses. In particular, I will draw attention in my bibliography [excised for the purposes of this book] to two recent studies by Felicity Nussbaum and Laura Engel — too recent for Kahan to have mentioned them in his book, but they constitute evidence that Kahan's exploration is timely and part of a dynamic scholarly conversation on celebrity culture and theatrical "marketing." [Hmm, this is a bit rough. I am blamed for not having read books that had yet to be published. But it does suggest that my work fits into a growing body of research. That is a good thing, as I am likely to be cited by a variety of studies both central and peripheral to Romantic theater. She then closes with a summation, which is positive.] Kahan's *Bettymania* is a marvelous and memorable analysis of a phenomenon not likely to be taken too seriously until now. He closes with a potentially powerful rumination on the interplay between social civility and celebrity, eloquently concluding, "Though Bettymania only lasted a season or two, modern celebrity culture, nourished by the evanescent thoughts and dreams of millions, has proven to be the center that continues to hold" [156].

To tell you the truth, because I am a veteran of the academic wars, when I saw the initially positive statements, I began skimming. What I really wanted to read was the negative stuff. Does that make me a masochist or a realist? I'm not sure myself. Not that her opinion matters much. The only reviewers who really count are the press. I had convinced them it was a good book. The press' board had thought so as well. I was pleased with and proud of the book, but, to tell the truth, I knew it had flaws. Almost all books do. And I knew that a smart reviewer would find those flaws.

After reading the review, I did not consider Celeste Woo an enemy, nor did I write to the journal to which she stated she was going to submit to demand that the review be retracted or revised. I did not put her on a hit list. Instead, I did the mature, professional, and right thing: I replied via email that I appreciated both her compliments and her criticism, that my book would have been far stronger had she been one of the readers. I then asked whether I might use her review as a template for young academics. My consolatory reply caught her off-guard. She was bowled over that I would want to reprint a review that was not entirely glowing: "I am impressed at your integrity — most authors I think would simply be peeved that anyone dared to criticize something in their book" (email dated: 27 September 2011). That is considerate of her to say, but the truth is that I expect to be bashed a bit in every review and every report. That is part of expectation of publication. I further invited her to join me for coffee at an upcoming conference to exchange information.

I suppose that she had her own reasons for sending me the review. Perhaps she was feeling out how I would react to a partially negative review; but that would suggest that she thinks I'm important, and I am not. So she has either made a mistake about my influence, or, more likely, she is trying to develop me as a low-level (i.e., fairly unimportant) ally. If the latter was her intent, she succeeded brilliantly. In the future, I might send her an early version of my next book and ask her for some pointers. I further hope that she will trust me enough to do the same when her next book is ready for press submission. The point is that just because she wrote a review that did not proclaim me the second-com-ing-of-Steve-Jobs or a brilliant game-changer does not mean that she considers my work worthless or that I should consider her to be my enemy. If, as her reply email suggests, my reaction was less hostile than is the norm in academia, then so much the better for me. The way I see it, a polite and thoughtful email, followed by a cup of coffee or a beer, is a cheap price to pay for an ally who is smart and who may, at some point in the future, be of aid. Young academics are all in the same drifting boat, but sooner or later one of them is going to become a captain. So why not be civil and respectful to everyone, not just because it's the right thing to do morally but also because it's the smart thing to do politically? Despite the fact that I am older and more experienced than Celeste, we are colleagues with like interests. She knows things I do not, and, hope-fully, vice versa. She has published with presses that I have yet to approach and vice versa. She, therefore, knows editors I do not, and vice versa. Nor can I know whether Celeste will be at Empire State forever. Who knows? One day she may be at Columbia, with a slush fund of thousands to bring in guest speakers from all across the country. She would have to win a lottery to get that sort of job, but then again, *she has already won a lottery* in getting her job at Empire State. Anyone who has a job in academia is lucky, and, for some out there, that luck will hold. Why shouldn't I seek her counsel and her friendship? If I can do her a good turn, I will, not because I am thrilled with having my shortcomings pointed out in print, but because I now have yet another friend with whom I can vet ideas, another colleague to have a drink with at conferences, another contact who may offer me advice on how to approach publishers. Further, as in the case of every negative review I have ever read concerning my own work, I agreed with most of the criticism.

To reiterate: We need to keep in mind that not all reviews you will write will find a publication outlet. Some journals may reject your review or may be awaiting a review on the same book by a famous scholar or specialist. That being said, book reviews are worth doing, especially since you are likely reading new books for your other publishing projects anyway! Why not turn your research notes on the newer books you are already consulting into a publishable review? Further, despite the limited narrative options available to the unknown academic, a few book reviews, especially those placed in topflight journals, always look good. Why shouldn't they? While it is possible that many of these same journals will be unknown to some members on your tenuring committee, they will certainly be known to your chair, who will, likely, be asked her opinion of your scholarship. A few reviews *on their own* are not going to impress your chair or anyone else, but a few reviews, *coupled with other kinds of publications*, demonstrate that you are a working scholar, and that you are keeping up with the general trends in the field. At worst, you are gathering a list of publishers who may be interested in a book on a similar topic. That in itself is valuable! And, of course, you need not tell anyone that your published reviews were unsolicited. If your chair or members of your tenuring committee assume that you have been solicited for opinions on newly-published, cutting edge-work, so much the better.

A few last things to keep in mind: Don't offer your review to more than one journal at a time. You don't want to get two or more acceptances and then have to withdraw. It looks bad. Besides, journal review editors are generally helpful and prompt. And they usually need the copy. If one journal says no, then move on to the next and so on. Try e-journals if all else fails. (On the relative value of electronic versus traditional print, see a later section of this chapter.)

POINTS TALLY: Assuming you write two or three reviews a year and place one per year, you will, in five years' time, have five published reviews, worth 10 points.

Notes (13 pages or less) (4 POINTS)

There are, at last count by the MLA, some 25,000 journals out there, so finding the one that will publish your article may seem like only a matter of submitting to enough of them. But there is that time factor again.... A far less time-consuming way to publish is to target your journal first. Again, because I am an English major, I'll draw from my own field, though the lessons to be learned are applicable to any of the core humanities fields. Most people think that you come up with an idea, write it up, and look for a journal. And most people do it this way. But, if you think about it, that's really inefficient. The smarter way is to first target the journal you want to write for and then see if there is something you can offer them that you think will be of interest.

Be aware, however, that you have to balance the journal's interests with the demands of your tenuring committee. Some journals are peer-reviewed; some are not. Since we're dealing with academic journals in both instances, some may wonder, well, what's the difference? In the main, a peer-reviewed journal will take your name off your submission and send it out to an expert (sometimes two or three experts) in the field for what is called a "blind review." A non-peer-reviewed journal will not remove your name and will not send it out. Usually, the reading is done by the editor, who may or may not also consult a colleague in the field. For obvious reasons, peer-reviewed journals enjoy a higher standard than most non-peer-reviewed journals. Whether a journal is peer-reviewed or not should be noted in the submission information, listed (usually) on the inside flap or prefatory pages of the journal. (More on the importance of this prefatory information will be found in our discussion of articles below.)

OK, so you have found a journal you think is a good one. Your research interests dovetail nicely with some of the stuff the journal has recently published. What next? Well, this may sound unnecessarily stupid, but it needs to be said: Does your targeted journal actually publish notes? Believe me; I am on the board of two journals. You would be surprised how many people make this simple mistake and, in so doing, lose valuable time. A "note" is anything less than 13 typeset pages, or about 20 pages of double-spaced Times Roman 12 font.

A note is not just about the number of words. A note seeks to do things that are, in many instances, different from, say, an article. Because of its relative size, a note ideally does not seek to change or to overturn an important ideal or foundational concept. A note is a small space for minor claims, something which may warrant further investigation; a note may also build upon or refine an existing claim. Let's play a game. Out of the following, identify which subjects are best suited for notes and which for articles:

Test Case Number 1:

No one has fully investigated the way Shakespeare's plays have been appropriated by the Bank of England. In this note/article, I will discuss the ways in which the BoE used Shakespeare to forward its own agenda. My data is drawn from public advertisements and hitherto unpublished sources.

Note or article? Although this sounds intriguing, its claim of creating a new field of investigation is far too grandiose for the limited space of a note.

Test Case Number 2:

A Fair Warning has been classified as impossible to date. This is not entirely accurate. The source of the play is a murder that took place in 1573. The play, therefore, was composed some time after that date. The play's most recent editor, Cannon, argued that since the play makes mention of "pipe smoking," it was probably written in or after 1586 — the year Ralph Lane, first governor of Virginia, introduced that pastime to Sir Walter Raleigh. The compositional end date is derived from the title page, which states the year 1599. Further scholarship has been unable to pinpoint the play any more exactly. But *A Fair Warning* has enough intertextual borrowings to cut down this rather spacious fourteen year *terminus ad quo* and *terminus ad quem* to a two year *immo*. More specifically, I will argue that the play borrows heavily from a key passage of the 1597 version of *The Spanish Tragedy*. If I am correct, it is logical to conclude that at least parts of *A Fair Warning* were written between 1597 and 1599.

A good topic for a note — a minor claim that seeks merely to refine what is already accepted by academia. You are here building upon established scholarship, not seeking to overturn it. Your claim is merely that we can at least establish some parameters.

Test Case Number 3:

In Act 3, Scene 13 of Kyd's original *Spanish Tragedy*, a character named Bazulto appeals to Hieronimo for justice. They understand each other's grief. Each has a son that has been murdered. In 1601, Jonson was paid by Henslowe to add some lines to the play. Of Jonson's additions to *The Spanish Tragedy*, the most famous is the painter scene. The scene is placed just before the entry of Buzalto and his appeal for justice. According to the poorly set text, the painter is named Buzardo. Like Buzalto in Kyd's original, this Buzardo also has a murdered son. Buzardo and Buzalto: the two names are nearly identical; their histories are suspiciously identical and they appear in back to back scenes. Could the compositor have misread the name in Jonson's addition? Could Buzardo be a misreading of Buzalto ? There is internal evidence concerning Q2's compositor and external evidence concerning Jonson's hand, as well as the aesthetic and commercial concerns of both Jonson and Henslowe, which suggest, albeit do not prove, that Buzardo is a misspelling of Kyd's original character Buzalto.

Yes, a note. You are not claiming that all the editions have been wrong, merely that you have an idea that may warrant further investigation. All you are claiming is that the compositor may have misread Jonson's handwriting, and this may explain why these two extremely minor characters are in many ways similar.

> Test Case Number 4:
> In March of 1929, Robert E. Howard, best known as the creator of Conan the Barbarian, wrote a Shakespeare parody entitled "Bastards All!" The title comes from Posthumus' diatribe on women:
>> Is there no way for men to be, but women
>> Must be half-workers? We are all bastards; all ...
>> [*Cymbeline*, 2.5.1–2]
> To Posthumus, the problem is one of self-identity. If women can't be trusted, then it's possible, even likely, that all mothers can't be trusted. Hence, each man, in Posthumus' mind, shares the anxiety that the man he calls father is not the man who sired him.
> Significantly, "Bastards All!" has at least two literary fathers. One is Shakespeare's *The Merry Wives of Windsor*, in which Master Ford hires Falstaff to test his wife's virtue. In this attempt he is thwarted by his wife, who, knowing of the plot, outwits them and, along the way, humiliates Falstaff. At the end of the play, Ford, now sure that his wife is faithful, apologizes to her, and, together, they plot a final humiliation of the knight. In "Bastards All!" Sir John Falstaff— renamed "Sir John Crappo"— intends to seduce Sir Onan's wife and then extort money from her husband to keep the incident quiet. Implicitly referring to the source tale, Sir John admits that, by this new plan, he hopes to "reverse the order and cozen a man by his wife, instead of being cozened by a man and a wife."
> The second potential source is not Shakespeare's, though it is Shakespearean....

Article. While the topic seems interesting (at least to me!), I'm already a page in and I don't know what the McGuffin of the so-called note is. Your project is more likely better suited to an article or, less likely, a book.

Remember, notes don't have to be twenty pages of word-processing. In the field of English, the journal *American Notes and Queries* and the older UK version, *Notes and Queries,* both publish notes as short as a page. Check out your targeted journal for the general length requirements. OK, because notes are so small, let's look at a full version, with commentary outlining the dos and don'ts of note writing (for the sake of simplicity, I have deleted all source citations):

"As Cold as Any Stone": A Connection to Ovid's *Metamorphosis*? [The question mark signals that this is a modest claim.]

The description of the death of Falstaff in Shakespeare's *Henry V* is surely one of the most poignant in the bard's canon. At "the turning o' th' tide" (2.3.13), Mistress Quickly notes that she felt a gradual change overcome Sir John's body: "I put hand into the bed and felt them, and they were as cold as any stone; then to his knees, and so upward and upward, and all was as cold as any stone" (2.3.23–25).

The tidal aspects of Falstaff's death are generally accepted as a significant symbol of the jolly knight's mutability. This mutability might be also an aspect of Falstaff's seeming metamorphosis from flesh and blood to stone. In his edition of the play, Gary Taylor notes that the reference to stones may have some echo of Plato's account of the death of Socrates, but he ultimately dismisses the notion, pointing out that no English translation was available to account for such a parallel. The Arden editor T.W. Craik believes that stones may be a reference to testicles, and he cites a short note by Gary Taylor in justification. Taylor, however, does not include this reading in his edition of the play. Instead, he merely refers to the Plato reading he evidently distrusts. Clearly, these lines remain in need of further gloss. [The survey of editions signals that you are engaged in an ongoing scholarly debate. Reinforce that you are *not* disagreeing with existing scholarship.]

I have a less ribald reading, but one that fits well with Falstaff's tidal associations: [You are not shaking the academic world but rather mildly suggesting that there may be some small addition to be made. You are building upon accepted scholarship but not stating that what came before is wrong. You are arguing that there may be some minor loose ends.] The image may well have come from one of Shakespeare's main sources, Ovid's *Metamorphosis*. In Book One of Ovid's *Metamorphosis*, Deucalion and Pyrrha survive a flood (an aquatic disaster associated with tides) and repopulate the earth by throwing stones over their shoulders, which magically grow into humans: "Of these we the crooked ymes, and stonie race in deede,/ Bewraying by our toyling lief, from whence we do proceed."[4] [Ground your speculation in textual fact.]

Both Jonathan Bate and Robert S. Miola believe that Ovid was Shakespeare's favorite author. This is reflected in Shakespeare's frequent use of Ovid in many of his works: Ovid's *Metamorphosis* is a direct source for a number of Shakespeare plays, including *Titus Andronicus* and *A Midsummer Night's Dream*. But the book was also a source for specific passages in many of Shakespeare's histories, including his second Henriad. Jonathan Bate has traced Ovid's influence in a number of passages, including *2 Henry IV*, 2.2.165–6 and 2.4.164–5; *Henry V*, 4.8.32. [Remind the editor of this speculative note's connection to accepted scholarship.]

More to the point of this particular passage, Ovid's *Metamorphosis* is a book that deals with both natural and unnatural transformations; Shakespeare's Falstaff has already been linked to the changing faces of the moon, the turning of the tide, and Saturnalian revels. [Closing paragraph reiterates that you are building upon a well-regarded critical opinion.] Referring to Falstaff as "cold as any stone" and dying at the turning of the tide may not simply signal the death of Falstaff but also his links to material resources from whence Shakespeare so often mined comic material. [Point out that your minor claim *may* extend our understanding of Shakespeare's use of resource materials, but that it does not radically alter our primary reading of the play itself.]

Because of the flexible length requirements, notes are easy to write. Better yet, journals that specialize in notes don't have a long turnaround process. I've never had to wait longer than a few weeks on the submission of a note. I also have the feeling that, because of the speculative nature of many notes, the threshold for publication is a little less stringent.

COUNTING POINTS: Assuming you publish one note in five years, you have earned another 3 points.

Articles

We're moving into the "Big Boy" stuff — the materials that will really impress your tenuring committee. Notes, reviews, and conference proceedings all indicate that you are active, but to what end? If this question mystifies, let me explain. So you have targeted a journal or a press, and you think you have an idea that will work. Then you find a conference that will allow you to air your idea. You solicit opinions, helpful comments, etc. You do some research into the topic and read up on the latest scholarship, for which you write a book review and place it in a journal. You have some stuff in an article that works well, but some just doesn't fit. Do you just jettison it? Heck no! Turn it into a publishable note! I think you're starting to see how *one project* can result in *multiple publications*. So far so good.

But let's get back to something I discussed on notes — targeting a journal. Targeting is all the more important when it comes to articles, since articles are more time-consuming and carry greater weight. So, let's repeat what bears repeating. Pick a peer-reviewed journal. You will notice on the prefatory materials of that journal the name of the editor and, under that, a list of the board members. One or more of those members is going to read your article and decide its fate.

Let's say, for example, that I am writing on *Frankenstein*. My thesis is that Victor has a fear of incest and has built the monster as a way of dealing with (by murder) the target of his fear, his cousin and fiancée,

Elizabeth. I have done a database search on *Frankenstein* and have decided to submit to the journal *Studies in Gothic Fiction*. I have checked as to whether they publish only theme issues. (For the sake of simplicity, let's assume there is no special theme; the journal is open to all aspects of the Gothic.) I now go to the library and look at an issue. I open the front cover, and this is what I see:

> Editor: Franz J. Potter, *National University*
> Associate Editor: Curt Herr, *Kutztown University*
> Editorial Board: Colin Marlaire, *National University*
> Melissa Bradshaw, *DePaul University*
> Katherine D. Miller, *San Jose State University*
> Dale Townshend, *University of Stirling*
> Jamieson Ridenhour, *University of Maryland*
> Roy Bearden-White, *Southern Illinois University*
> Margarita Georgieva, *Université de Nice Sophia Antipolis*

I read the fine print. Yes! It is a blind, peer-reviewed journal. When I submit, the readers will not see my name. But does that mean I won't know who is reading the paper?

While it is impossible to know for certain who will review my essay, this list of editors is an excellent place to start. Certainly, these readers will likely be the first academics to see the paper. (In some cases, an external reader may be brought in, but by and large, the editorial board will handle all submissions.) So, at this point, I need to do some research on the editorial board:

> Editor: Franz J. Potter — edited a collection *Monster Made by Man* (2004).
> Associate Editor: Curt Herr — edited Elizabeth Bonhote's *Bungay Castle* (2006).
> Editorial Board:
> Colin Marlaire — theory guy. He posted a biographical statement for a conference, which was then posted online. It reads: "He is ... concerned with the impact of economic changes on both Culture and the individual, the implications of imperialism and colonialism on the literature of both the colonizer and the colonized, and the role new technologies can play within the classroom."
> Melissa Bradshaw — cowrote a book on the American Gothic.
> Katherine D. Miller — has published three collections of fiction.
> Dale Townshend — published "The Haunted Nursery, 1764–1830," an essay on the Gothic in children's literature of the late eighteenth and early nineteenth centuries, which appeared in *The Gothic in Children's Literature: Haunting the Borders* and fits with our interest in incest (New York: Routledge, 2007).

Jamieson Ridenhour — recently edited Lefanu's vampire tale, *Carmilla*.
Roy Bearden-White — a graduate student. He probably handles book reviews.
Margarita Georgieva — specializes in translation but shows some interest in children's literature and the Gothic.

Can we eliminate any of these board members as potential readers? Yes, we can! Since your paper has nothing to do with vampires, the American Gothic, children's literature, or creative fiction, we can exclude Melissa Bradshaw, Katherine D. Miller, Jamieson Ridenhour, and Margarita Georgieva. Roy Bearden-White is unlikely to be trusted with much. Potter's work has an obvious *Frankenstein* theme — a man-made monster.

I order Potter's book and read what he has to say. Maybe I even cite it positively. I certainly don't want to be harsh. Remember that publication is a means to an end. Attacking the very editor who will decide whether my paper gets published is a bad move. This does not mean that my paper is nothing but a kowtowing exercise. In reading Potter's own work, is there something that I can find that I believe to be genuinely interesting, and can I build on it? In reading *Monster Made by Man*, I note that Potter writes in a jargon-free manner. He's historical. He likes to cite dates after the first mention of a book. I go through the introduction and the stories that follow. It's a collection of nine rare Gothic tales, which shows that *Frankenstein* is not just a story about a monster assembled from various body parts; it's also a novel assembled from earlier tales by various authors.

I note that of the remaining board members, Marlaire is theory-orientated and Townshend writes on childhood. Both might serve as readers. (Of course, if they farm out the paper, I will have no control over the choice of readers, but more on this anon. At this point, we are concentrating on our known list of potential readers.) If I write my paper with a mumbo jumbo of theory, it's likely that Potter will send the paper on to Townshend and Marlaire; if I write it in plain-speak, I have a better chance of getting Potter as a reader. And I want Potter. Why? Because he's the general editor, and if there is a split of opinion, his voice will carry more weight. I cut a long-winded section on theory from my paper. Marlaire is now out of the picture. I am now pretty sure that my paper will be read by Potter and Townshend.

OK, now how do I make my readers interested in my incest theme, since neither writer has tackled that subject directly? Well, I know that

Potter is interested in historical correspondences and Townsend is interested in children. So issues of lineage could be worked up. I also need to mention some theoretical aspect. Likely, I'd write up something like this as an opener:

In Horace Walpole's Gothic play *The Mysterious Mother* (1768), the widowed Countess of Narbonne slips into bed with her son — who thinks he is sleeping with yet another woman. Years later, he ends up marrying Adeliza, the child of his union with his mother. The author thought this plot was so horrid that he limited the print run to just 50 copies and distributed it only to close friends: "I thought it [the subject matter] would shock, rather than give satisfaction to an audience" (251). [Historical aspects to please Potter.] The reader, however, can quickly discern that Walpole does not see incest in and of itself as merely an aesthetic gross-out; the fact that he distributed the play among a close/incestuous circle suggests that incest can also be a stand-in for other activities — including, in the case of the play's distribution, friendship and support. Indeed, as Karl Zender (2002: 175) explains in his essay on Faulkner, incest can be linked not only to an Oedipal anxiety — a son's love of a mother — but also to any number of antiauthoritarian acts. [Theory to please Marlaine, just in case.] As a further example of Oedipal anxiety, we may turn to the Marquis de Sade's "Eugénie de Franval: A Tragic Tale" (1800), in which a father raises his daughter as his spiritual and sexual partner but demands that she refer to him as "brother" and "would not have his daughter call him by any other names" (François, 246). [Historical aspects to please Potter.] Monsieur de Franval's demand suggests that sibling incest is somehow less egregious than parent-sibling coupling. The opposite is true in Mary Shelley's *Frankenstein* (1818). Victor's creation of life without sexual union can be read as an attempt to avoid incestuous contact both with his betrothed, Elizabeth (his cousin in the 1818 edition; his adopted sister in the 1831 edition), and, symbolically, with his mother. Victor's mother dies from scarlet fever she contracted from Elizabeth. Before she dies, she holds both Victor and Elizabeth by the hand and makes them swear they will marry each other: "Elizabeth, my love, you must supply my place" (26). [Opening thesis statement.]

Are we working the system? Sure we are! But we are also making our readers' jobs easier. Let us say that Potter received an article that began just with the following thesis statement:

In Mary Shelley's *Frankenstein* (1818), Victor's creation of life without sexual union can be read as an attempt to avoid incestuous contact both with his betrothed, Elizabeth (his cousin in the 1818 edition; his adopted sister in the 1831 edition) and, symbolically, with his mother. Victor's mother dies from scarlet fever she contracted from Elizabeth.

Before she dies, she holds both Victor and Elizabeth by the hand and makes them swear they will marry each other: "Elizabeth, my love, you must supply my place" (26). [Opening thesis statement.]

Potter might decide that he'd be a good first reader, but he might have a heck of a time figuring out who should be the second reader. In such an instance, he may be tempted to look for an external reader. Why? Because the paper is not a natural fit for his own editorial staff. By adding material that fits the exact interests of the board members, I gain more control on who is likely to read it and demonstrate that my paper is a good fit for the journal.

True, this is a lot more work than just writing an article, but I am no longer just writing an article and hoping for the best. I am targeting a journal and crafting my ideas in a way that will fit the research agendas, interests, and sympathies of its readers. Giving the journal what it wants means giving the editors what they like. If that sounds commercial, so be it. But being useful to those who have the power to help your career is also a logical and straightforward path to success.

COUNTING POINTS: Let's assume, conservatively, that you write and place one article in five years. Add another 10 points.

Collaboration list

There are two very good reasons and a ton of bad reasons for engaging in collaboration. Before we get to the pros and cons of collaboration, we need to point out the obvious. There are different kinds of collaboration: collaboration with your students, collaboration with a colleague of your own age and standing, and collaboration with a senior academic. Each has a different dynamic. Collaboration with your students — and this may be a surprise, considering what I said about it in the introduction — can be positive if handled correctly. Obviously, the level of your students will have to be taken into account, but even if you teach solely to undergraduates, you can still use them in the proofing phase. I regularly give each student two or three pages from my bibliography and have them order the books. Then, once the books are collected, each one sits down with me and together we proof the quotations. If I feel both they and I can get something useful out of it, and I can save some time, I will then assign other rudimentary tasks. If you have access to graduate students, then you might assign an annotated bibliography project on your research topic. While you won't be quoting from these annotations, they might help you compile a short list of works that you need to look at in some depth.

The reasons you may seek out collaboration with another faculty member probably rest on two factors: time and friendship. You may have said to yourself, "Hey, if I only have five years, then working with someone on a joint project might bring me yet another publication I can put in my dossier." That may be fine if, in fact, your collaborative project is just one of your many publishing projects. Don't put all your hopes on just one major work, especially a collaborative work. That's just dumb and dangerous, especially if that collaboration is with a fellow assistant professor. Here's why. The tenuring process has a habit of turning friends into enemies. No matter how strong your friendship is with your fellow assistant professors, on some level they are rivals. In fact, I know of no tenured faculty in the same department who remained friends after going through the tenuring process together. Remember, only 50% of assistant professors survive the tenuring process. It's not hard to imagine a scenario in which the department decides to tenure just one of you. It may even come down to your collaboration. Who wrote most of the article? "I did," you say. "Look, my name comes first on the publication." "No," your former friend and partner says, "that's just alphabetical. I did most of the work." Proof, in such cases, is all but impossible to substantiate and credence of claims will come down to relationships with other members of the department (i.e., who has more friends and allies). If you have been the real scholar and your partner has been the coffee-socializing gadfly serving on four committees, then you lose. Your partner/rival has more friends than you. And friendships count. Accept it as a fact of life and move on. My advice is, when it comes to working with an assistant professor: Don't do it.

Under what conditions, then, would collaboration be helpful and useful? That one is easy. You want a senior fellow in your department or from another college or university, someone who has published a few books or maybe edits a journal, someone who has a lifetime of respect and contacts built up among publishers. Why? Again, it's simple: The difference between you and your senior colleagues is that they have a reputation and proven track record; you don't. That makes a huge difference when some overworked editor slogging through a hundred proposals a day comes across your joint submission: "Hey, I know that person" is something the editor is likely to say when coming across your collaborator's name! And that recognition factor is often all that is needed.

The right condition for collaboration might be easy to see, but let's be clear. If you think that collaboration is a time-saver, you are probably wrong. There will probably be more talking about writing than actual writing, and that might not be a bad thing. Part of the pleasure of working with a senior fellow is having a mentor who can help you in academia, and much of that work can be coping with the stress of the job. But collaboration must also be efficient and productive. That means that you need extremely clear roles in the collaboration. Who is doing the research and on what? Is there grant money involved for research-related travel? Who is filling out the forms? Which one of you gets to hang out at the biblioteca in Madrid for a week and who gets the "thrill" of checking proofs?

And which one of you is doing *all the writing*, because one of you will. Why? To begin with, you and your collaborator probably have different writing rhythms. Maybe one of you reads, makes notes, and contemplates for months on end and the other rattles off copy at a daily rate. Getting together at the end of the month, one of you may have 20 pages of workable text, the other virtually nothing. Hey, people work in different ways. That doesn't matter. The issue is whether you can tolerate and adjust to differing modes of production.

I recently did an interview with Roy Thomas, a comic-book writer of some note. All comic book writers work with artists, so they are all experts on the grief of collaboration. Thomas' most famous partner was the artist Barry Windsor-Smith, with whom he produced the award-winning series *Conan the Barbarian*. Here is what Thomas had to say about collaboration: "The only thing you ever have to know about partnership, of course, is that each of the partners did ninety percent of the work." It is safe to say that academics will experience still more problems; comic book writers are trained to produce in teams, while academics are trained to work alone.

There is also the matter of style. It takes a thick skin not to be upset when you submit to your partner what you believe to be perfectly acceptable prose and it is either rejected outright or revised to reflect your partner's voice. My advice: Live with it. Humanities-based academics generally work alone, but you decided to collaborate. You picked a senior fellow in order to ride the coattails of reputation. That is what you wanted, and that has nothing to do with style points or ego. Keep in mind that you have no reputation to speak of; your partner does. If the book fails, the senior partner is taking the hit because no one expected you to do anything. Why should they? No one has ever heard of you! Your partner is the more senior and distinguished writer. Be honored by the collaboration.

COUNTING POINTS: Let's assign half-points for all collaborations and further assume that you were able to write an article with a senior fellow and place it in a peer-reviewed journal. Assign yourself another 5 points.

Editions

OK, here is the good news. Unless you are editing something like a Shakespeare text, where you have multiple versions and manuscripts that require collation as well as a massive amount of commentary, most editions can be undertaken quickly. Better yet, the finished result is something that looks like it carries the full value of a book, although it does not.

There is another good reason for wanting to edit a text: connections. The text you edit will likely appear in a series of some sort managed by a general editor with whom you will work closely. The general editor of a series is usually someone with a great deal of prestige, and your relationship with this same editor may lead to further projects. I'll be discussing this later in the book. I have also noted that general editors often have informal meetings for everyone working on the series. These meetings usually take place at national conferences. In my own field, general editors of various Shakespeare series have invited me to wine receptions or meals to meet other editors. This affords an excellent opportunity to market yourself and to make connections with other academics across the country and, sometimes, around the world.

Now the bad news: editing is extremely tedious. Even if the text is available in some electronic form, everything will have to be checked word by word, comma by comma, against a printed copy. This can be backbreaking work. There is also a skill in good note-making. Some people pick it up right away; for others, what to include is a mystery. In the main, you want to be as factual as possible. Because of its tedious and mechanical nature, not many people are interested in doing editions and this is, of course, to your advantage. As with notes and articles, your first step is to canvas the market. It's likely that some readers feel that no one in their field of, say, psychology is interested in editions, but Oxford and other presses bring out editions of the writings of Freud. No matter what your field, there are likely texts that publishers might want to see back in print. Once you have located publishers who handle editions for your field of the humanities, look over their lists. Get a feel for what interests them. Then check their catalogues for forthcoming editions. This is vital, as you don't want to work (even preliminarily) on an edition that the press has already published or commissioned.

Next, find a text that fits what you think would interest each press. Write up a letter of inquiry, stating your interest and qualifications, and add a sample page of the proposed edition, along with a statement that outlines the importance of your edition. And then do absolutely NOTH-ING on this project until you hear from the press. For one, as we have seen, writing an article can spawn a number of other publications along the way: book reviews, conference papers, notes. Editions are unlikely to produce any publications other than the edition itself. It is, therefore, obvious that it is more efficient to write an article than edit a text, and you need to be as efficient as possible. Editions should NOT be undertaken on speculation. To do so is to waste months, perhaps even a year. Just hold tight. What should follow is a contract from the publisher or a polite rejection. DO NOT, repeat DO NOT, edit a text on the hope you will be able to place it. Almost certainly you will not.

A sample of an edition proposal is included in the appendix — just the overview; the text sample has been suppressed. But we also need to ask ourselves why, given the tedious and time-consuming nature of editing, do editions get less respect than books? The answer is pretty clear. The prefatory materials and notes combined usually come out to about 40 or 50 pages. In this sense, editions are glorified journal articles — maybe not even that, since articles have theses and undertake original research, while editions usually do not. (Oh, yes, occasionally you will come across an edition based on a newly-discovered manuscript or approach. But for the most part when we pick up an edition we know what we're getting: an introduction and set of notes to a novel or play that has already been available for some time.) Lastly, you want to inquire among your colleagues in your own department, as well as among the members of your tenuring committee, how they feel about editions. Some people — people who have clearly never edited a text — don't value them at all. Others — again, mostly people who have never edited a text — look at editions as if they were full monographs, I assume on the supposition that anything that has its own cover is a book! It bears repeating: Don't do work that no one will value and don't do just one kind of

work. Make sure your submitted dossier demonstrates a range of publications.

Here is a good trick once you have a contract or an edition in hand:
Do another project alongside your edition. Here is what I do. I'll get a
photocopy of a first edition, retype maybe 50 lines of a text a day, then
highlight any words or passages that need annotation and write up the
notes for those 50 lines. All told, that process takes me about three hours.
Then I rotate into a more creative project, a book or an article I am writing. For the most part, edition work can be done mechanically, roboti-
cally. Editing is, in large measure, factory work and should be seen as a
break from the more demanding intellectual labors required for articles
and books.

COUNTING POINTS: Let's assume you edit ONE text over five
years. Add 15 points to your tally.

So far, we have covered the kinds of publications that offer the most
opportunity and access. There are other forms of publication, some of
which are quite prestigious but are often more difficult to come by. In
this section, we'll go through some of these rarer work opportunities,
cognizant that these are publishing tasks that probably won't come our
way.

Essay Collections, Journal Work, Editorial Boards, Encyclopedia Entries

Essay collections are becoming rarer, but they are still out there. In
the main, these are not open to general submission. Usually, what happens is that someone, almost always an established scholar of some sort,
gets a group to agree to write on a specific theme. A proposal is then
generated and submitted to a publisher, who, on the strength of the
theme and the names attached, agrees to the collection. Because of the
trust involved in this process, it is essential that most of the contributors
are bigwigs in the field. This is another reason to go to conferences, as
your seminar leader may be planning an essay collection. But even in
this case, there is no guarantee that there will be room for your essay.

If you are not invited to join a contracted collection but still want
to be in one, you might want to look at the calls for essays at
cfp.english.upenn.edu. However, you should be aware that almost none
of these collections have a publisher attached. Usually, the project cited
involves an editor who is trying to put a collection together on the off-

chance of securing a publisher. That means you can spend a year writing and revising an article and then come to find that the entire collection collapses because the editor has failed to find a home for it. If you are going to go this route, make sure your general editor for the collection is an established scholar, i.e., someone with three or more books to their credit. In many cases, these collection proposals are put together by assistant professors with no more experience or pull than you have, and, in almost all cases, their collections fail to find a home.

A still rarer circumstance would be that you start or join a journal in some editorial capacity. I have noted that general editors are almost always extremely well-established in the field; however, book editors for a journal are not. Sometimes, they are graduate students. The position, we may therefore infer, involves thankless and menial tasks, and, as such, you might offer your services. Your job will be to search for the appropriate reviewer for a given book and to read reviews that come in unsolicited by scholars (like you). (See the section in this book on writing reviews).

Being on an editorial board is a sweet deal. You usually read a paper or two a year and write a report on it; maybe you are even involved in the proofing of the copy. In exchange, you get your name listed in every issue of the journal. Being a reader for a university press is somewhat more demanding in that you will have to read and comment on an entire manuscript. Usually the latter comes with some slight stipend—maybe a hundred and fifty bucks or so. The value, in terms of merit points for tenure, is, again, open to interpretation. Colleagues on your tenuring committee with little publishing background may think that you are doing quite a bit of work, but active scholars may know better. On the other hand, an invitation to review a text is usually extended to established experts in the field, and, as such, the publisher's request for your opinion is an important career marker. You have established yourself and your opinion matters. In terms of points, let's give it an extra 2 points based simply on prestige.

As for encyclopedia entries, again, these are difficult to come by. I have published a few, but they came more by way of luck than of effort. I'll be discussing why one publication leads to another in my final chapter, but for now we might note that these entries usually go, or should go, to an expert in the field—in short, not you. These works are not peer-reviewed.

COUNTING POINTS: The value of an essay in a published collection is open to interpretation. On the one hand, it's in a book; on the other hand, the book isn't peer-reviewed. Value in terms of points? It's hard to say. If the collection is with Oxford or Cambridge, it might be worth quite a bit. To be safe, let's value the essay as worth slightly less than that of an article in a peer-reviewed journal (5 points). Editing a collection for a major press is probably worth the same as writing an article or doing an edition (5 to 7 points). Editing a journal will depend on the quality and prestige of the journal and your activities. Editing a peer-reviewed journal can be time-consuming, but it does bring the university quite a bit of prestige; being a book review editor can be time-consuming and probably brings almost no prestige. Let's call it 1 point. As for encyclopedia entries, let's value them as similar to book reviews (2 points).

E-Publishing

Today, all publishing includes some form of e-publishing. Even if your book is only coming out in paper format, Google, for example, will likely have an excerpt of your work on the web; Amazon.com, if sales of your work warrant — and they rarely do — will do the same for its Kindle. Your journal work will, similarly, be transformed into a PDF for database consumption. So the question isn't whether you can choose between e-publishing and traditional publishing. E-publishing as a component of paper publishing is now the norm.

A more difficult question is how your tenuring committee will value a *pure* e-publication—that is, a publication that exists only in cyberspace. To some, e-scholarship does not yet have the same credibility as traditional publication, though the gap does seem to be narrowing. Further, depending on your project, e-publishing has certain advantages over traditional publication. To begin with, it is a far better forum for work that needs constant updating. Let us say, for example, that you are writing a book on performances of a certain Shakespeare play. Updating a book will be possible only after the initial run is sold off and only if the publisher sees the need for a second edition. Online, however, you can add endlessly to your project. Then, too, there is the issue of typos and corrections. Of course, in an ideal world you and your proofer have caught all the manuscript's errors. But you don't live in an ideal world, and in our own reading of other people's books we come across typos or factual errors virtually on a daily basis. That is both irritating and embarrassing for a writer. But e-publishing now allows for instant correction.

One thing most readers will agree upon is that e-texts offer an ideal landscape for concordances, stylometrics, and other mathematically based analyses and functions. The value of these works will doubtless grow as our imaginations rush to meet the power of these new online tools. Just the other day, I was reading about Ian Lancashire's new work on Agatha Christie. Lancashire took 16 of Christie's novels, written over more than 50 years, and fed the text of each into a computer program. He noticed that as Christie aged, her word choices and usages remained fairly stable — until she was about 80 or so. Then something odd happened. Her use of words like "thing," "anything," "something," and "nothing" increased. At the same time, her use of unique words fell off by about 20%. "That is astounding," wrote Lancashire. "That is one-fifth of her vocabulary lost." Lancashire consulted with linguists, pathologists, and psychologists and then concluded that the author had developed Alzheimer's (see Jad Abumrad and Robert Krulwich, "Agatha Christie and Nuns Tell a Tale of Alzheimer's").

Whether Lancashire is right or not is not the point. Indeed, discussion of the matter will doubtless spur others to review the data, to dispute the processes, or to suggest that Christie was purposefully limiting her language in keeping with other more spare writers, that she was simplifying so that her translators would have an easier time of it, or that she grew less careful as a writer because she could no longer be bothered to write more than an off-hand draft. I am speculating here. But the point is that Lancashire has not just written a paper, he has created a new field of research and debate for Christie scholars.

Yes, the time for paper may be almost up, and the power of computers may offer us new insight or avenues for further debate, but e-publishing has its issues. To begin with, e-publishers need to do a better job labeling pages. When you open a Web page it is not entirely clear, unless you look carefully at the browser address, who is publishing that work. That needs to change. The colophon of Oxford on a book denotes instant academic credibility. But on the Web, any yahoo can put up information — information that has not been vetted. It would help, of course, if all Websites or pure e-publications were vetted and thereafter included in traditional library databases. But, as of this writing, most databases deal only with printed word copies and so avoid e-publishers altogether. That may change, but, the database indexing of e-publishing is virtually nonexistent.

There are other aspects of e-publishing that need to be worked on.

Looking at various online editions of texts, for example, there does not yet seem to be a universal format. That is a problem. Traditional print editions follow an editorial page format that dates to at least the middle ages. We recognize what editors ungraciously call "the tyranny of the textual apparatus"—the numbered lines, the dense footnotes, etc. We have been trained to read in an "up and down" process of text to note and back again. That is, we all recognize a poor system that breaks up the flow of our concentration.

E-publishers and programmers understand that the Web offers new ways to address this old problem, but no one has standardized a solution. Some e-editions opt for hyperlinks that take you to a new page. Others have pop-up boxes. Still others opt for permanent captions. Some dispense with footnotes altogether but have highlighted or blinking text to alert the reader to some significance. There is also the problem of authoring e-texts. Because of the varying formats, academics need to have some knowledge of a variety of cyber codes: HTML, SGML, XML, etc. This puts an undue burden on scholars who are having a hard enough time simply writing a publishable paper without having to worry about its e-coding. Until we have a clear and uniform format, e-editions will suffer due to their own idiosyncrasies.

The question is, can you afford the time to write for an e-publication, knowing that some of your tenuring committee might dismiss e-publishing out of hand? Of course you can't. You might begin by seeking written clarification on the value of e-publishing. Consult your chair, dean, and provost.

Get a list of the people on your tenuring committee and seek their counsel. If you find that you have to justify what you need to publish on the Web, then that in itself is your answer. You want to talk about your work, not explain the utility of the Web or the growing prestige of a startup publisher.

Another thing: You will be asked to copy all your publications for the committee to peruse. If you have an e-edition in which you have, say, five hundred hyperlinks, printing and presenting the work will be virtually impossible. If paper is still the dominant form, then my advice is to stick to paper. "Book" publishers that exist solely online might be an idea whose time is coming, but it is probably not coming quickly enough for your tenuring process.

COUNTING POINTS: For reasons stated above, ZERO POINTS. Stay away.

Internal and external grants

When you land a grant, you are doing more than just getting some money or getting a course release. Grant proposals are a form of research writing and their acceptance is a sign that the academic community values your work. External grants — grants outside of your own university's grant system — are particularly important and look good on your tenure sheet. Anything that brings outside revenue into the department is a big positive.

In terms of internal grants, you need to discuss this thoroughly with your chair. You might begin by asking whether the department or the college of arts and sciences offer classes off for research. If so, there is probably a committee that approves course releases. You might want to get on this committee or make friends with those who are on it. Probably some of you are thinking, "Oh, no. I don't want to apply for a course release. I don't want to come off as a prima donna. I want, rather, to be seen as a workhorse." That's a bad idea. Frankly, no one is paying much attention to what you do. By inquiring about release time, you are reminding people that you are busy with a robust research agenda. Also, you have, as a member of the faculty, a perfect right to know what resources are available to you and to take full advantage of them. Let your chair and dean know what you are doing. It will confirm their faith in you. After all, they selected you for the job you have at present. You want them to know that you are doing your best to be as productive as possible.

Next, you want to apply for as many internal grants as possible. Does your project involve transcription? Perhaps you can use funds to hire a student worker who can help you check the accuracy of your manuscript. Do you need to secure the rights to any images for a project? These can be quite costly (usually about $200 an image); there might well be a program in place at your university to help pay for those images. Next, you want to apply for as many external grants as possible to pay for your research-related travel or publication costs. If your university has an office of sponsored research, there is probably a grants officer who can point you in the right direction.

The following is by no means a complete list of places you might want to look at: The European Institutes for Advanced Study (EURIAS) offers an international researcher mobility program. It accepts proposals for 10-month residencies in any one of the 14 participating institutes, located in Berlin, Bologna, Brussels, Bucharest, Budapest, Cambridge, Helsinki, Jerusalem, Lyons, Nantes, Paris, Uppsala, Vienna, and Wassenaar. Keep in mind that a long grant of this nature is not what you want. For one, the competition is fierce. For another, it's not a good idea to take off a year from your university while you are still seeking tenure.

A better bet for a young assistant professor would be to apply for short-term summer grants. You might look at the Huntington Library, which offers a variety of short-term (as short as one month or a summer) grants to use their facilities. The pay is quite good—about $3,000 a month. A month or three months in sunny California, with the Huntington paying for your apartment, food, and fun money, is all good. It's also a fantastic opportunity to network with older established scholars. (See chapter 5.) The Newberry in Chicago, the Folger in Washington, D.C., and various libraries at Yale and Harvard offer similar research opportunities. The New England Regional Consortium offers $5,000 for you to work on your own project for eight weeks. Indiana University's Lilly Library, the Honolulu Academy of Arts, and the Ransom Library in Austin, Texas, all offer fellowships. That's right, you can get paid to do your own work, so long as you do it at their institutions and use their facilities. It sounds too good to be true, but, trust me — it is true! And this is in addition to your salary at your home institution.

There are also a variety of institutions that will fund your non-travel–related research. The Bibliographical Society will pay you to edit texts. The American government's NEH offers a variety of research opportunities, among them up to $38,000 in fun money to edit or translate an out-of-print text. Note that no contract in hand is required for the application of these funds, though obviously a signed contract will strengthen your application. The American Philosophical Society offers some short- and long-term grants, depending on your project, as does the American Antiquarian Society. And there are private patrons of the Arts as well. Each summer, Norton Island hosts three sessions for thirty established artists, musicians, and writers to develop and to share their work in an extraordinarily beautiful and remote wilderness setting. You get your own log cabin and cooked meals served in a communal setting with the other artists in residence. (All applications should be lined up well in advance. As we will see in the next chapter, when submitting a proposal you should list all the grant money which might, in some way, offset the publisher's printing costs.)

As with article writing, you need to target the right sort of grant agencies. Don't write to anyone and everyone hoping for the best. Target your best potential sponsors and write something that will impress them. Have a colleague who has had some success look over your applications. If you know no one who can help in this regard, then reach out to the agency itself and speak to someone there. It never hurts to make contact. Stress that you are anxious to do a good job, but that you are inexperienced. In my experience, someone is usually very willing to offer advice. If applying to a library for a fellowship, pick up the phone and speak to the special collections curator in your field. Does the curator know of any other materials, apart from those listed online, which might be of interest? Having a few items on your application which show your familiarity with the collection will go a long way toward securing your funding. You want to be able to pinpoint why you need to be at *that* library.

Keep in mind that a library is *paying* you to do research. It is an honor and a privilege to receive a grant, and aside from putting in some long hours doing your own work, you should spend some time befriending fellow academics and thanking the library staff. This is work, not play. You want to be invited back to the library or invited by fellow academics to visit their institution, write for their journal, contribute to their contracted essay collection, etc., etc. So buy someone a cup of coffee and ask what they do, have fun, make friends—but, again just as important, build a network of allies.

COUNTING POINTS: Let's assume that you successfully land one internal and one external grant over a five-year period. Both of those accomplishments go in your vitae and should be added to your tenuring dossier submission. Give yourself 1 point for an internal grant and another 2 points for an external grant. That's another 3 points.

Overall Points Tally

So, how many points have we earned so far? As stated, editions are difficult and not worth your time, collections are primarily by invitation, and traveling to Europe for a conference with published proceedings may be beyond you, but most of the other activities are very manageable. At the conclusion of five years, you should have at least the following:

One peer-reviewed article	10 POINTS
Presenting conference papers (5 in 5 years)	5 POINTS
Publishing reviews (2 in 5 years)	4 POINTS

Publication of notes (1 published)	3 POINTS
Research grants (internal and external)	3 POINTS
Participating in scholarly organizations (2 of them)	1 POINT
TOTAL:	26 POINTS

Again, you need to check with your chair to see what will meet the minimum requirement. For all but the tier-one institutions, this will probably suffice, but why do the minimum? In fact, doing the minimum is dangerous. One rejection of an article or note and you are below the line. Better to do far more than is required. And, of course, what would really help seal the deal is a book contract, which will be discussed in the following chapter.

Ten Things You Need to Know

1. You need a plan, and should develop one as soon as possible with your chair.
2. Know thine enemy—find out who is on your tenuring committee and make friends with them.
3. Explore all course release and funding programs at your place of employment.
4. Join academic organizations.
5. Go to and participate in conferences and check your ego at the door.
6. Write unsolicited book reviews.
7. Be efficient—turn failed chapters into workable and publishable notes.
8. Explore collaborations and editions.
9. Apply for external grants.
10. Most importantly, target your publisher.

CHAPTER 2

Revising the Dissertation

This book, I am guessing, will have multiple types of readers. Some of you may already have a tenure-track job; some of you may be among that vast pool of underemployed part-timers. Both are common on virtually every university campus in North America. No matter your background — whether you are publishing with the hope of securing tenure or publishing with the hope of gaining a tenure-track job — when it comes to submitting your first book, most of you will turn to your doctoral dissertation. Certainly it was that way for me, and it remains the same for virtually every newly-minted Ph.D. I have ever met.

Because you have been dealing with your dissertation for a number of years, I'm betting you think it's a monumental achievement. And it is! Congrats! But that doesn't mean that your dissertation is, de facto, publishable. Nor was it meant to be. The dissertation served its purpose — to get you your degree. It was never meant to be published. The differences between a dissertation and a publishable academic book may not be clear in your mind. Their respective content often looks much alike. Both will have formal introductions, chapters, footnotes, appendices, and bibliographies. But there are differences. A book expands the field and shapes those who read it. It must be seen as a benefit to the academic community. It is something that came from nothing — mental energy turned into paper and ink. On the other hand, a dissertation is designed for you to prove other things. For example, you could:

(1) Do research — i.e., collect, evaluate, and summarize a great deal of information;
(2) come to some conclusion about your chosen topic; or
(3) add to the existing body of evidence in some way.

Of course, you can do 1 and 2 without tackling 3, but you can't do 3 without tackling 1 and 2. Further, the emphasis will be on 1 and 2, but not 3.

Whether your dissertation is publishable or not, it will hang around your neck for years. After all, when you were interviewed for your tenure-track job, they asked you about the subject, what you had discovered, and what your future interests revolved around. In short, your interview team probed whether you had plans to publish your dissertation or convert it into a series of articles and judged from your replies your likelihood of success.

Beginning the process of converting your dissertation into a book is made more difficult because you are very likely emotionally tied to the project. Even 17 years after completing my Ph.D., my attachment to the project is highly personal, far more so than the other books I have gone on to write. The conversion of the dissertation into book form usually happens during a perilous time for the young academic: right after graduation. As such, it is not surprising that this chapter on converting a dissertation into a publishable book is also the story of my struggle to find tenure. While this chapter will, to quote Pushkin, mingle the "intellect's cold observation" with the "heart's reflections," I am not sharing my experience because I am writing a *Chicken Soup for the Soul* story of overcoming long odds. I am sharing my experience because it shaped the immediate post-doctoral years in which I slowly learned what publishers want.

That learning process took me seven years. That is to say, if I had landed in a tenure-track job right out of graduate school, I would not have been able to generate sufficient publications for a standard five-year review. But I was lucky. I didn't have five or six years to learn how to publish. It took me eight years just to get a tenure-track job, and then I had to wait another five years before I was eligible for tenure. The result was that when I finally came up for tenure, I was prepared. I knew how to get published. But it took me thirteen years to learn what I am sharing with you now. I am hoping that whoever is reading this book does not need to struggle as much as I did, that tenure comes faster for you. The downside of that hope is that you don't have the "luxury" of time to learn the tricks of the trade. You need to start publishing from day one. Right now.

What follows is a story. If a reader doesn't feel compelled to learn from my mistakes, then I encourage you to skip the next 3,000 plus words of this chapter and start reading again where I discuss how I cut down my dissertation and slowly learned the art of the query letter and proposal, maybe at the header "Cutting the Dissertation Down to a Manageable Size." For the rest of you willing to follow along, I have certain caveats I want to get out of the way. We are talking about my experience in the early 1990s. We are dealing with people who have all since moved on, retired, or died. Many people have been compressed into a single person or deleted; names have been changed, and characters fully fictionalized. This may seem lame in the digital age, where so much information is openly available via the Internet. Still, I have no desire to impugn the reputations of these extremely qualified people or, by citing my actual institution, impugn those who have taken their respective places. Moreover, what I write might not have been experienced by my fellow students or, I stress, may not in full or in part mirror reality. This is a narrative and, like all narratives, borrows freely from the genres of tragedy and comedy. This is not a "tell all," and besides, names and places really aren't important here, anyway. What counts is why my topic made a mediocre Ph.D. dissertation but, conversely, contained the makings of a publishable book.

Why a Mediocre Dissertation Might Make a Good Book: A Story

In terms of the selection of my dissertation topic, I was lucky. I had been left on my own. That doesn't sound like luck, but it was. I had not been co-opted into a larger project of dissertation supervisors at the University of Bexhill-on-Sea, England. I distinctly recall walking into my university's formidable library and thinking, *Now what would I like to write about?* I knew there would be stuff on databases which would add to my research, but I wanted to have a tactile sense of the major works. On Shakespeare's meter, there were about 50 books, mostly from the 19th century. On "performance," there was a vast array of stuff, ranging from books on specific theaters to actor biographies. There were books on Shakespeare's comedies, histories, and tragedies in daunting stacks. But then I saw it: a very small pile of books on Shakespeare forgery and a still smaller lot — a handful of pamphlets, a confession, and one 20th century study — on the Ireland forgeries of 1795–96.

For those of you who don't know the story, I'll fill you in. In 1795, a seventeen-year-old boy said that he had discovered a trunk of papers, many bearing the signature of William Shakespeare. Among the papers were letters, legal documents, original drafts of *Hamlet* and *King Lear,* and two unknown plays, *Vortigern* and *Henry II.* The papers were inspected by a variety of experts who were divided; most believed them to be genuine, while some dismissed them as forgeries. After the first of the "new" Shakespeare plays, *Vortigern,* was met with disastrous hostility, all but a handful of supporters admitted their error of judgment. Still, no one suspected that the discoverer, William-Henry Ireland, had actually penned the forgeries. He spent much of his remaining life trying to prove he was the author of his own fraud. The original plays and many of the original papers were thought to have been destroyed in a fire. There was, therefore, not much to go on in terms of original archival materials.

The topic was screwy, but I was intrigued. I proposed it in my meeting with my dissertation supervisor, Francis Fame — not his real name, of course — a small and thin-boned man who somehow made a room heavy with his responsibilities. Fame had a habit of avoiding eye contact. He seemed to be always peering over my shoulder, as if someone more interesting was vying for his attention. For my first Ph.D. conference with my supervisor, I was invited to tea. I entered Francis Fame's office, crammed with the spookiness of Dickens' *Old Curiosity Shop.* Somewhere in the distance, an old wall clock decided to strike. The hissing of steam was followed by a rattle and then the banging of a cracked pot with a stick. I sat opposite Fame:

FAME: Well, my boy, what would you like to write on?

ME: Well, I was thinking about Shakespeare, perhaps the Ireland forgeries.

FAME: Have you read Schoenbaum's chapter?

ME: No.

FAME: It's in his *Shakespeare's Lives.*

[I made a note.]

FAME: It's rather comprehensive.

ME TO MYSELF: How can it be comprehensive if it's just a chapter?

FAME: (continuing) I wonder whether a study of the Ireland forgeries is enough for a dissertation....

ME: I know, but maybe I could also edit the play?

FAME: Isn't it already in print?

ME: There is a printed version, published in 1799; we have it in the library.

FAME: Well, that might be sufficient.

And with that brief exchange, I began a project which completed my doctorate in 3 years and landed me not one but eventually two books.

I state all this not to revisit that fateful afternoon at idyllic University of Bexhill-on-Sea but because I had unknowingly hit upon a subject which, while not a great Ph.D. topic, was suitable for publication. Note that my supervisor was not keen on the project initially because he felt that there wasn't enough material to demonstrate my ability to do thorough investigative research and synthesis (points 1 and 2). And he doubted that there was material enough for point 3. The lukewarm reply — "Well, that might be sufficient" — suggests that he would not have been surprised if, in a few months, I returned chagrined and started the process all over again with another topic.

And he would have been right. After all, although I liked the topic, I had in part picked it because there were so few documents on the subject. I therefore felt that I could master the material fairly quickly. What then? Would I have enough to write 350 pages or would I run out of materials before I reached my page goal? What I had stumbled upon, however, was a very publishable project: a topic which had not been thoroughly investigated in over 150 years, a topic that had been treated as a one-off crime. Once I realized that forgery is not merely a crime but a response to the aesthetic needs of the culture, I was off to the races. In addition, all previous studies had followed a newspaper clipping which stated that the manuscripts to *Vortigern* had been destroyed in a fire. All that was left from Ireland's original 1795 forgery was a quarto published in 1799. Yet one day of research at the British Museum proved that all that scholarship had been mistaken. The British Library had not one *Vortigern* manuscript but six, and I found yet another one at the Folger Library in Washington, D.C. I also rediscovered the sheet music used for the play's two songs.

On my return to my university, I contacted the chair of the music department, showed him the scores, and asked if they were markedly Elizabethan or whether they conformed to the late 18th century. The answer was essential to understanding whether Drury Lane offered *Vortigern* as a museum piece or as a workable, modern — and by modern I mean 1796!! — play. He told me it was a rather average score, not at all different from traditional theatrical fair. I then asked him for the name of his best classical music majors. He gave me the details. A few days later, we were all in one of Bexhill-on-Sea's music rooms, recording the score. I added that to my doctorate as well. Now it consisted not only of the original materials but also of information on how the materials had been lost and how shoddy scholarship had overlooked for a century what I had found in a week. Once I had the copies of the manuscripts of the play, I then compared them to the printed 1799 version. I found massive differences and, what was more exciting, many authorial hands. I could now collate those differences, spend some time identifying the various hands involved, and piece together who wrote what.

The more I thought about it, the dissertation would practically write itself. I could start by creating a theory about the cultural factors of forgery — aesthetics in the 18th century, the threat of Napoleonic invasion, etc. I could compare the Ireland forgery to other recent forgeries, such as the Ossian forgeries of Macpherson and the Chatterton frauds, and then argue that there was a reason why these three frauds occurred within 30 years of each other. I had stumbled upon what I was later to call "the golden age of forgery." In collating the manuscripts, I had already matched some of the hands. The vast majority of the early manuscripts were in W.H. Ireland's hand, but the revisions were in that of his mother, some were by his sister, and some were in the hand of R.B. Sheridan, manager of Drury Lane. I could now prove that Ireland's forgery was a criminal enterprise (a conspiracy?!). In short, I had an average dissertation — average in that it did no more and no less than any other acceptable dissertation. But unlike most dissertation, it also had the makings of a publishable book.

This was going to be fun! And it was! I really enjoyed every day of the writing. It was a puzzle that needed to be put together. It was slow and laborious work, but it was ultimately exhilarating when I completed the project. Along the way, I really bonded with my subject. I came to see that I was not merely writing a research thesis; I was writing a self-portrait. What I was putting on the page was not only a way of looking at the topic; it was also a means of exploring some deep-seated issues about my own identity. (I have found that invariably to be the case. Looking back on your own dissertation, unless the topic was foisted upon you by a dissertation supervisor, I'm betting that what you picked was highly personal — so personal that its full implications were hidden even from you when you picked it. You discovered only in the doing why it was that you chose that specific topic.)

After nearly 3 years of work, I submitted my dissertation. It would take, I was told, a few weeks for a decision to be rendered. In the meantime, I bought a backpack, took a boat to France and a bus to Portugal and then camped on the beach, ate barbequed sardines and drank cheap wine. I checked in with the school every week and, after three weeks of working on my tan, I returned there fit and relaxed. I entered an office, where I found Francis Fame and my external reader, Perry Daniels — not his real name, but an author of several books on Shakespeare — deep in conversation. Perry Daniels rose silently from his chair. He was about my height. He cocked his head and strode toward me as I walked toward him. I put out my hand and stepped on his foot. "Beg pardon," was all I could muster. At that moment I had a sinking feeling that I would be flunked because I had stepped on his foot. To his credit, he sought to calm me. He shook my hand. "Congratulations. This dissertation will make a great book." That was a moment of great relief. It was short-lived, as I will explain.

The Importance of an Academic Affiliation

Why am I falling into a bit of personal memoir here, dear reader? Not just to excise dread furies from my memory. Rather, I am writing all this because of the huge disadvantage you might face if you write to a publisher on anything other than an academic letterhead. It's unfair, but let's face it — if you were an editor with a huge pile of manuscripts to go through and received something from Stanford and something from Tuscaloosa Community College, your first thought would be that the Stanford applicant has a better project. After all, the Stanford-based academic probably has more resources to draw on: a state-of-the-art library, research grants, conference travel funds, and the like. In addition, the Stanford academic is probably surrounded by topflight minds who have offered their own insights. The language of the manuscript is likely jargon-filled, perfectly in keeping with the linguistic sludge so commonly published by many academic presses. So, yes, an applicant from a name university has a huge advantage over a no-name applicant from a no-name school. It therefore follows that someone with no academic affiliation has still worse odds for overcoming the university press editor's snap judgment.

But we are jumping ahead of the story. I had just been told by my external supervisor that my dissertation would make a great book. How did my internal supervisors react? Fame nearly jumped out of his armchair, as an animal does in the joy of attack: "But we have some reservations." And then for the next two hours he grilled me on what seemed minute word choices. I answered all his questions. Then Perry Daniels asked me what I thought of the play itself. I said that I thought it moved really well and was exciting and fun, especially for Shakespeareans who could identify lines and situations that Ireland had borrowed from other plays. Then I stumbled by saying that not every Shakespeare play was a masterpiece and that *Vortigern*, while in some respects a bad play, was no worse than *The Two Gentlemen of Verona*. To this statement, Francis Fame replied irritably that *Vortigern* was "infinitely worse than *The Two Gentlemen of Verona*." It doesn't sound like much, but from someone who had exchanged only a handful of words with me, someone who was my dissertation supervisor, someone who had grilled me for two hours, this last statement put things in their proper light. In the blink of an eye, I saw him as a fell opposite. We were enemies, Fame and I. In Francis Fame's mind, I had denigrated Shakespeare — I suppose because I was arguing that a good Shakespeare forgery is just as dramatically legitimate as a mediocre authentic Shakespeare, or, worse, that every writer, including Shakespeare, borrows from other writers. Imitation is supposed to be a form of flattery, but I was exposing Shakespeare as unoriginal, a writer no different from other writers and, in a sense, no better than other writers.

In the end, Fame pointed out some minor revisions, which I completed in two days. But Fame's ire had not been placated. Indeed, I had no idea how irritated Fame was with me until I saw his letter of reference. It was a few sentences, maybe five or six. It outlined the years I had attended, the work I had done. My work was labeled as "interesting." Yet the letter was mechanical and disinterested, and it was ridiculously short. It was, even to my untrained eye, unsuitable.

Still, I sent it off with my vitae. I was shortlisted for exactly zero jobs. The following year, I sent Fame an email requesting a new letter. He did not reply. I thought to myself that this was like Samuel Johnson's relationship with his tutor, who was "a very able man ... but to me very severe; but I cannot blame him much. I was then a big boy; he saw that I did not reverence him; and that he should get no honour by me. I had brought enough with me to carry me through; and all I should get at his school would be ascribed to my own labour."

It is possible that I am being too hard on my dissertation supervisor. The reality is that Fame was (and still is) a busy man. It's very possible that, confronted with a multitude of tasks, he dashed off a quick letter and then moved on to another project. In any case, with only a tepid letter from my Ph.D. supervisor, I didn't get any job interviews. Besides, even if I had received a glowing testimonial, the job market in the 1990s sucked — doesn't it always? Who is to say how different my life would have turned out with a better letter in hand? Perhaps quite a bit; perhaps not at all. After all, I did have an abrasive personality and appearance, so I might have (and probably *would* have) blown any number of face-to-face job interviews.

My new fear, however, was not that my school would do nothing to help me but that my former dissertation supervisor might actively block me. Without realizing it, I was sabotaging my own chances of success. My thought process at the time went something like this: Fine, so Francis Fame was unlikely to help me find a job or a publisher. What's in a name? It's a question I had asked myself when writing on forgery. Now that same question came back in another guise. Fame had enormous power because he'd published so much. He was a known commodity, like Shakespeare himself. But I was not Fame, had no reputation, and, given his hostility, there was no point in listing him as a reference for the project. I had read his letter for the job market. That hadn't worked out so well. So I had to get my book published without mentioning my home institution or my dissertation supervisor — huge disadvantages!

That thinking was, I now recognize, sheer paranoia. I had no reason to believe that Francis Fame or any of the faculty at the University of Bexhill-on-Sea cared about or thought about me one way or another after granting me my degree. Heck, they had hardly noticed me at all when I was a Ph.D. candidate. Still, your Ph.D. is an all-consuming affair. It's likely the only thing you've been thinking about for the last three to five years of your life. It is almost impossible to imagine that a project that was all-important to you is a rather piddling one to your supervisor. In my mind, I began to construct elaborate and highly destructive narratives in which academic publishers were keen to publish my work and immediately contacted my dissertation supervisors to ascertain the value of my project. Fame, in these nightmare scenarios, would then, for the overriding good of Shakespeareans around the world, ensure that I was blackballed. What a fantasy of self-importance I had created! The truth is that even with a favorable letter by Fame or someone like him, the project had little chance of success. (On the actual chances of successfully publishing your book, see Chapter 4.)

How did I survive my own self-destruction? Here I speak not of finances, which were pretty dire, but of my emotional state. For the most part, I dealt with (or tried to deal with) all of the aforementioned events constructively. OK, I was second-rate then, but that did not mean that, like Maugham, I could not be the first of the second-raters.

Cutting the Dissertation Down to a Manageable Size

So, dear reader, my point here is that I had little going for me after obtaining my Ph.D. I had no publications to my credit and no job prospects, and I wasn't listing my home institution in my query letters. And then there was the issue of the dissertation itself. Perry Daniels had said that my dissertation would make a "great book." Yet no one had told me what I still needed to do to transform it into a book. So I began a detailed study of the books publishers were bringing to market and then compared them to my dissertation. The most obvious issue was one of length. In all, I had about 650 pages. Doing a word count of an average university press page against my own pages, I understood that 650 pages in Times Roman double-spaced would come out to about 425 pages typeset. Most books run to about 200 pages. In point of fact, I had *two* books: one a study/biography and the other an edition of a play. Further, even if I divided my dissertation into two books, the main book, the study of the forgeries, covered too much ground. Was my target subject eighteenth-century theater, aesthetics, or a minor Romantic writer? Was I writing a case study of literary forgery or a book on Shakespeare's reputation in the eighteenth century?

As for the edition of the play *Vortigern*, that would be a still harder sell. A quick look at the shelves of my local Barnes and Noble revealed that, aside from Shakespeare, the pickings were slim, even for playwrights such as Jean Genet, George Bernard Shaw, and Oscar Wilde. There were a handful of anthologies of Jacobean drama and a series of rare Elizabethan and Jacobean plays, the Revels and Mermaid series. But my forger was not an Elizabethan or a Jacobean. He wrote in the early nineteenth century, an era that favored poets over playwrights. Even as a playwright, William-Henry Ireland's canon was slim. He never wrote another play that was staged, so his reputation among theatre historians was at best a footnote. There was also the availability of the play *Vortigern*. In 1970, a facsimile of the 1799 version had been issued and was widely available for scholarly citation. I was arguing that the 1799 version bore only slight resemblances to the actual play as performed in 1796, but I was doing so in a doctorate, not in a book. So I had to overcome scholarly bedrock to even have a reason to get the play published. Here was a play written by a forgotten playwright which had been staged for just one night. Worse yet, I understood that getting the play itself published was unlikely if I could not first interest a press in my study of the forgeries. In my heart of hearts, I was really hoping that my book on the Ireland forgeries would come out first, it would become a best seller, and then the same press would publish the play as a companion volume. Boy, was I dreaming!

Nuts and Bolts Issues

Separating the two projects (a study of the forgeries and the play itself) was not difficult. I simply lopped off the edition and its collations from the main study of Ireland and the forgeries. But even after cutting the overall size of the book in half, I still faced a variety of nuts and bolts issues. In looking over my favorite books of Shakespeare criticism, I noted that their introductions outlined the importance of the subject but did not give a chapter by chapter synopsis. My introduction did the opposite. I made no claims to importance, but in painstaking detail pointed out the various flaws of previous studies and described how my study would prove to be a corrective. Then, in paragraphs and pages, I outlined each chapter. Sometimes I used a quote in my synopsis of, say, Chapter 5 and then used the same quotation in the actual chapter. No book that I had read did that.

So, to begin with, I turned 20 or so pages of synopsis into one paragraph and pretty much junked the entire review of previous studies. I also cut down on the footnotes. A dissertation is in large part designed as a project that demonstrates your ability to do archival work and documents your findings. It encourages an exhaustive approach because it catalogues all you, as a researcher, have learned. A book is not designed to show off your learning but rather serves as a text to teach those who, by and large, already know something of the subject area. So my 300 or so footnotes per chapter, some of which were over a page long, were chopped down or eliminated. I still catalogued all quotations, but all sidebars, all notes that simply cited prior studies to demonstrate breadth, were cut, as were the full citations in the bibliography. Instead, I concentrated on writing a new section for the introduction — again, no more than a longish paragraph — on how my study, while offering a new approach and presenting new materials, fit within a growing discourse concerning authenticity and the value of the printed word. As a newly-minted Ph.D., I wanted desperately to be seen as an important new voice, central to the field. I did not want to be the lone crank at its periphery. My instincts, in this regard, served me well. In most cases, academic publishers sell only a few hundred copies of each book. It's important for them to understand how your book fits into a larger and ongoing academic discourse.

That process sounds easy, but it took me, on and off, three years. The finished project was far from perfect. Were I to write the book again, it would be a far different and far better book, but nearly two decades of writing academic books and essays has passed and I now have a fuller sense of my strengths and limitations. First books are just that — first books. Still, looking back on the project, I was doing a lot of things right. But I blew probably the most important aspect of the submission.

The Inquiry Letter

I had discovered *The Writer's Handbook*. It can be found in the reference section of most public libraries. The book is an invaluable resource that explains to writers what publishers are interested in. But the subject areas were not clear. One press would express an interest in "literature," another "theatre." But did that mean that one press would be interested in any and all aspects of literature, or that another would be interested in any and all aspects of theatre? And I was still wrestling with the nature of my book-length manuscript. Was it about Shakespeare forgery or a study of a Romantic forger? Should I send the proposal to presses that dealt with Romanticism, Shakespeare, theatre history, or all three? To be safe, I sent my proposal to all the applicable presses. What had I to lose except stamps and (still more) self-esteem? I sent off letters of inquiry, outlining my project, what I felt would be new to scholars, and why I felt the book would be successful. I herein reprint my inquiry letter for what in time became my first book, *Reforging Shakespeare*.

Let's compare notes. Take out a pen and write in the margins what you think I did wrong, then check your notes against my own comments:

Jeffrey Kahan
1 Wood Ave, apt. 306
Westmount, Qc
Canada, H3Z 3C5

April 3, 1996

Lehigh University Press
Linderman Library, 20 Library Drive
Bethlcham, PA 18015

Dear Sir,

I would be grateful if you would consider the following proposal:
Proposed book: *Reforging Shakespeare.*

Reforging Shakespeare charts the bizarre but true story of William-Henry Ireland, a 17 year old boy who fooled the academic and theatrical world with his Shakespeare forgeries. At first the forgeries were mundane: legal papers, promissory notes, mortgage deeds, but as each was unquestioningly validated, William-Henry grew more bold, and bizarre. He "found" Shakespeare's love poems, significantly different versions of *Hamlet* and *King Lear*, love letters to his wife, even a lock of Shakespeare's hair! But boldest of all was his "discovery" of a lost play: *Vortigern*. Theatre Royal Drury Lane offered a lucrative contract for its world premiere. The Duke of Clarence engaged a box, the poet laureate wrote the prologue. Supporters filled the house to ensure a positive reception. But as the curtain went up, no one could suspect the disaster that was to ensue.

A story that includes many of the most famous literary, political and theatrical figures of the day, *Reforging Shakespeare* is a tale of greed, selfishness, deception and a son's need to love an unloving father.

Reforging Shakespeare is written in a vivid and lively manner. It is written for a wide audience, though fully documented for more specialized readers. This book has the potential to be a best seller! It will appeal to academics and any one interested in a cracking good story. I think it fits into a Peter Ackroyd-style biography.

I look forward to your comments concerning *Reforging Shakespeare.*

Reprinted with my comments:

Jeffrey Kahan [I did not include "Ph.D."]
1 Wood Ave, apt. 306
Westmount, Qc
Canada, H3Z 3C5 [No academic affiliation in address looks bad.]

Lehigh University Press [I had not checked whether Lehigh published Shakespeare or had an interest in Romanticism.]
Linderman Library, 20 Library Drive
Bethlcham, [City is misspelled. It should be "Bethlehem."] PA 18015

Dear Sir, [I did not name the editor; looks like a form letter. What if the editor is a woman?]

I would be grateful if you would consider the following proposal: Proposed [Repetition.] book: *Reforging Shakespeare.*

Reforging Shakespeare charts the bizarre [Academic presses are not interested in a bizarre story but rather why the story is bizarre.] but true story of William-Henry Ireland, a 17 year old boy [Spell out numbers; add hyphens for adjectives.] who fooled the academic and theatrical world with his Shakespeare forgeries. At first the forgeries were mundane: legal papers, promissory notes, mortgage deeds but as each was unquestioningly validated, William-Henry [Should use the full name; this is too colloquial.] grew more bold, and bizarre. [Repetition of "bizarre."] He "found" Shakespeare's love poems, significantly different versions of *Hamlet* and *King Lear*, love letters to his wife, even a lock of Shakespeare's hair! [Using exclamation marks, especially ones that mark an inability to understand the subject's behavior, is not the way to go.] But boldest of all [Alliteration is a nice touch, but the tone is too colloquial.] was his "discovery" of a lost play: *Vortigern.* Theatre Royal Drury Lane offered a lucrative contract for its world premiere. The Duke of Clarence engaged a box, [Grammatical error.] the poet laureate wrote the prologue. Supporters filled the house to ensure a positive reception. But as the curtain went up, no one could suspect the disaster that was to ensue. [This is not the back cover of an Agatha Christie novel.]

A story that includes many of the most famous literary, political and theatrical figures of the day, *Reforging Shakespeare* is a tale of greed, selfishness, deception and a son's need to love an unloving father. [None of these are academic issues, yet I am addressing an academic press.]

Reforging Shakespeare is written in a vivid and lively manner. [As opposed to what? Written in a dull and lifeless style?] It is written for a wide audience, though fully-documented for more specialized readers. [In short, the book is not yet revised suitably for one kind of press or readership.] This book has the potential to be a best seller! [Academic presses are not set up for bestsellers; books that retail for $100 don't sell well.] It will appeal to academics and any one [Spelling error.] interested in a cracking good story. [Again, not an Agatha Christie novel.] I think it fits into a Peter Ackroyd-style biography. [Ackroyd does not publish in academic markets. If making the comparison, pitch the book to Ackroyd's publisher or his agent.]

I have enclosed a sample chapter and a short except from the play, *Vortigern.* I look forward to your comments concerning *Reforging Shakespeare.*

Please look over my notes. I had nowhere in the query letter stated my academic credentials, where I had earned my Ph.D., or what sorts of unpublished archival materials I had unearthed or where I had unearthed them. I had not enclosed a vitae. Perhaps just as vitally, I had not mentioned any grants for the project. Of course, I didn't have any grants; I didn't even know you could get them. But they are vital in your query letter and proposal for two reasons: (1) Grants obviously off-set publishing costs, a plus for any borderline business; (2) the odds of publishing are long, but external funding suggests that some scholars have already vetted the project and think it worth pursuing.

Dealing with Rejection

As soon as I had mailed off the proposals, I set to work writing another one. This one dealt with the edition of the play *Vortigern*. Yet, even while I was writing that proposal, the rejections for *Reforging Shakespeare* started coming in. Sometimes they came in one a day, sometimes 5 or 6 in a day. Sometimes a week would go by with no word, and then yet more rejections. I studied these rejections for clues as to what I was doing wrong, but most were simple form letters. One press, Lehigh, asked to see the entire manuscript. I sent it off, but aside from Lehigh, there seemed to be no interest in my project.

But then I got lucky. A dear friend from my Ph.D. days, a fellow student, Marie-Christine, had reached out to me. She knew of an opening, a one-year appointment at the Université de Perpignan for tourism students who needed practice in English conversation. Would I be interested? It wasn't Shakespeare — heck, it wasn't even composition — but it was a job, and I gladly accepted. Who knows, maybe I could turn that one-year appointment into a permanent post. And I did need the teaching experience, even if it was just conversation.

After that, I was unemployed again. And then I wasn't. I had done well in France. I had made some friends among the English faculty, who wrote glowing letters on my teaching. I had attended and presented at a few conferences and even published a review in the French Shakespeare journal *Cahiers Elisabéthains*. I wasn't setting the world on fire, but I was trying. The Perpignan contract was over, but those letters from my Francophone colleagues helped me to secure a one-year appointment at the Chinese University of Hong Kong, and the job was for a Shakespearean. However, I was no closer to a tenure-track job. I was, aside from some contract work, going nowhere fast.

More Advice: Stay Sane, Move On

The proposal was out there, but I just couldn't stomach the wait. So I began other publishing projects. And, like any tourist in Hong Kong, I walked the markets: flower markets, pet markets, fruit markets, software markets. And I saw something else that surprised me: dildos. In virtually all the markets, I repeatedly saw stalls with tables covered with dildos and other sex toys for sale. And then one day, on my way to teaching my classes, I saw a poster for an upcoming conference in Beijing — the first Women and Literature Conference. I had already attended one academic conference, and it had not gone well — I have already discussed it in my last chapter. Still, I had never been to Beijing. So I had a thought and wrote a paper on Renaissance dildos, where they came from, and what they were made from; I cited plays and poems, including Shakespeare's, in which they were mentioned. (The Chinese University of Hong Kong has, in all regards, a superb English collection.)

Not only were the conference organizers interested, so too were all the participants, among them Ward Elliot, a great English scholar teaching at the University of California at Riverside (UCR). He heard and liked the paper, took me aside, and asked me what I was doing in Asia. I told him I was on a one-year contract. He asked for my details; what hotel was I staying at? I was staying in the student dorms, on the kindness of the University of Beijing. Elliot was surprised. Why wasn't I staying in the hotel with the other foreign academics? I explained that, as a contract worker at the Chinese University, I had no access to conference funds. I was there on my own dime. He then asked if there was an extension at the dorm to get hold of me. I thought he wanted to meet for breakfast or something. I asked a grad student with whom I had become friendly for the dorm phone number, and he kindly gave Elliot the requested information. (This was all well before the explosion of cell phones.) And that was that, or so I thought.

The next day, the phone rang. It was John Ganim, the chair of English at UCR. He asked if I was the person who had given a paper on dildos. I said I was. He asked, "How did it go down?" Go down. Dildos. I thought it was a joke, so I replied in kind: "The subject is like the object; stimulating, but infertile." There was a pause and then a huge, roaring laugh! "Send me the paper," he said, "and your vitae." And that's how I got a job at the University of California at Riverside — because of a dildo joke!

I was at last teaching at a major U.S. university. True, I was yet again merely a contract worker, surviving on ten-week contracts, but the secretaries liked me and passed on to me whatever course openings came up. I had no health care and no benefits, I was teaching composition, and I was only ten weeks away from unemployment at any given point during the semester. I was renting a room in a house filled with grad students. Still, though the movement was glacial, I felt I was making progress. I continued to write a few small things, nothing of great importance. Most of my early work ended in rejection, but there were a handful of acceptances. I had published a one-page note for *English Language Notes* (*ELN*), a short note for *Notes and Queries*, and yet another note for *American Notes and Queries* (*ANQ*). I had an article accepted by an online journal.

While I was in Hong Kong, I met a Japanese director who was performing a Noh version of Shakespeare's plays. I did an interview with him, which was accepted by *Shakespeare Bulletin*. My paper on dildos was published in the Seattle-based journal *Para*Doxa*. I wrote a few unsolicited reviews for *Renaissance Quarterly*. I had also recently written a new paper on Thomas Nashe and *Romeo and Juliet*. It had been rejected by *Shakespeare Quarterly* and *Shakespeare Yearbook*, but Clemson University's *Upstart Crow* accepted it. Best of all, the second proposal, the one concerning the play *Vortigern*, was at last ready. I had made many changes and added a ton of new material, including a biographical statement. Let's see what I was doing right or wrong:

Dr. Jeffery Kahan
1 Wood Avenue, Suite 306
Westmount, P.Q., Canada, H3Z 3C5
Email: Vortiger@navel.ucr.edu

30 May 1998

Submissions Department
Northern Illinois University Press
Re: A Critical Edition of *The Tragedy of Vortigern*.

Dear Editor,

I have enclosed my proposal for an edition of the 1796 Shakespeare forgery, *Vortigern*. The play, as you may know, was recently staged at the Bridewell Theatre in Chancery Lane, London, England, and received national press coverage in the *Times, Independent, TLS, Guardian,* and *Telegraph*. The play's official patrons include Alan Ayckbourn and Kenneth Branagh.

I've enclosed a brief synopsis of the project along with a sample from the edition. I have also enclosed a brief biographical note covering my education and publications.

If interested, I'll send you the complete manuscript.

Yours respectfully,
Jeffrey Kahan.

[Biographical Note]

In the last 4 years, I have worked as a full-time lecturer on a contract basis for the Chinese University of Hong Kong, the City University of Hong Kong, the University of Marborough, Gibraltar, the University of Perpignan, France, and Dawson College, Montreal, Canada. Since September 1997 I have been teaching at the University of California, Riverside.

I have published articles on Shakespeare, Chettle, Jonson, and Nashe in some of the most distinguished journals in Western academia, including *Shakespeare Bulletin, EMLS, Upstart Crow, Notes and Queries, The Ben Jonson Journal, ELN* and *ANQ*. I have a series of reviews appearing in *Renaissance Quarterly*. My first book, entitled *Passions and Poisons*, an edition of Canadian poetry, was well received.

[Proposal]

[*The Tragedy of Vortigern*: Subject and Importance.]

1. Why should your press be interested in this edition?

Vortigern was the most controversial Shakespeare production of the entire eighteenth century. The play was staged on April 2, 1796, at Theatre Royal Drury Lane with some of the greatest Shakespearean actors of the day, including John Philip Kemble. The play was attacked by Shakespeare scholars such as Edmond Malone, George Steevens, and Joseph Ritson. Among the play's supporters were the Prince of Wales, the Duke of Clarence, James Boswell, and many other leading figures of eighteenth-century England's political and intellectual elite. *Vortigern* was a forgery. The intricate details of this impressive and at times bizarre history are set out in my book, *Reforging Shakespeare: The Story of a Theatrical Scandal* (currently under review at Lehigh University Press). However, the text of the play itself, due to the exigencies of space, received short shrift. After receiving what at times seemed a flood of letters expressing interest in the play itself, I began the arduous task of preparing this edition.

2. All right, the play *is* historically important. But this play was hissed off stage. Is it really worth reading?

On the occasion of *Vortigern*'s premiere, Edmond Malone, the top Shakespeare scholar of the day, had the play hissed off stage. He even convinced actors in the cast, including the lead actor, Kemble, to give purposefully shabby performances.

There is no doubt that this has colored the perception of the play's theatrical merits. All too often, the play has been dismissed as theatrically unworthy simply because it failed on its opening night. Yet drama scholars do not condemn Ben Jonson's play, *The New Inn*, though it too was hissed off stage. Indeed, Jonson's play has been redeemed by subsequent, more open-minded audiences. The recent performance history of *The Tragedy of Vortigern* may also redeem a play that was never truly given a fair trial.

On two recent occasions, excerpts of the play were staged. Both times actors, directors, and this writer were pleasantly surprised by the text's theatricality. On November 25, 1993, a reading of excerpts of *Vortigern* was given at the Theatre Museum, Covent Garden. The lead actor, Gilles Bryon, thought the part was bold and powerful. He compared it favorably to playing Tamberlaine.

On October 16, 1994, the BBC aired a prime-time special, "The Irresistible Rise of William Shakespeare." Having heard about this "lost" play, the BBC interviewed me and staged parts from this critical edition. The major newspapers, having seen the show in preview, focused favorable attention on the play. And there has been one full production. In February 1997, Tour of Force, a London company, agreed to stage the play. After contacting several leading actors and playwrights, we secured the patronage of Alan Ayckbourn and Kenneth Branagh. The play was performed at the Bridewell Theatre from October 19 to November 19. The production has received national press coverage in the *Times, Independent, TLS, Guardian* and *Telegraph.*

3. Has the play ever been edited before?

Yes. Originally, the play was rewritten, edited, and published in 1799. This 1799 edition was used as the copy-text for a second quarto published in 1832. A facsimile of the 1799 edition was published in 1970. However, the 1799 and 1832 editions and the 1970 reprint do not resemble the original play as staged.

Until recently, it was thought that the original manuscripts were housed in the Shakespeare Memorial Library in Birmingham and destroyed by fire in 1879. In fact, I have rediscovered seven manuscripts, collated them against copies of the extant 1799 and 1832 editions, and recorded over 3,000 variants and several hundred cut lines. *No modern scholarly edition has ever been undertaken.*

4. What does this study contain?

This book consists of a introduction to the play, which covers the play's authorship, sources, and textual and performance history, and a scholarly edition of the play, complete with textual apparatus, collations, and appendices, including all cut lines, parallel passages from Shakespeare's plays, preliminary prologues and epilogues, and the play's musical score and bibliography. The manuscript is 315 pages in length.

5. Sample Materials Enclosed.

I have enclosed the plot synopsis, Prologue, and Act 1, Scene 1, of *The Tragedy of Vortigern* for your perusal.

Reprinted with my comments:

Dr. Jeffery Kahan [I did not add academic affiliation or credentials.]
1 Wood Avenue, Suite 306
Westmount, P.Q., Canada, H3Z 3C5
Email: Vortiger@navel.ucr.edu [Using a UCR email address but a different
mailing address implies that I was a graduate student at UCR, not a former
graduate of another university. The problem stemmed from my part-time
status. Despite the fact that I was working at UCR, I had no idea how long
I'd be working there, so I used UCR letterhead and my home address in
Canada for correspondence. After all, it might take some time before I
heard back from these publishers, and who knows where in the world I
could be by that time?]

30 May 1998

Submissions Department
Northern Illinois University Press
Re: A Critical Edition of *The Tragedy of Vortigern*.

Dear Editor,

I have enclosed my proposal for an edition of the 1796 Shakespeare for-
gery, *Vortigern*. The play, as you may know, was recently staged at the
Bridewell Theatre in Chancery Lane, London, England, and received
national press coverage in the *Times, Independent, TLS, Guardian,* and
Telegraph. The play's official patrons include Alan Ayckbourn and Kenneth
Branagh.

I've enclosed a brief synopsis of the project along with a sample from the
edition. I have also enclosed a brief biographical note covering my education and publications. [Much of this is good, but much isn't. On one hand,
I suggested that the play is a living, breathing document with patrons,
while on the other it is a historical and little-known document. In fact, the
play was both. However, stating this was likely to be confusing. Also, I said
that the play had been staged recently but did not include my own role in
that staging. I had none. A university friend from my Birmingham days,
Joe Harmtsen, used the 1799 text, not my 1796 authoritative version,
which I was now peddling.]

If interested, I'll send you the complete manuscript. [The phrase "If
interested" implies that I had no idea why any press might be interested. I
should have searched for a press that only published rare or forgotten plays
of the Romantic era and then approached them, arguing that readers and
buyers of a forgotten Coleridge play like *The Remorse* were likely to be
interested in *Vortigern*.]

Yours respectfully,
Jeffrey Kahan.

[Biographical Note]
    In the last four years, [I did not mention my education or my disserta-
tion supervisor.] I have worked as a full-time lecturer on a contract basis
for the Chinese University of Hong Kong, the City University of Hong

Kong, the University of Marborough, Gibraltar, the University of Perpignan, France, and Dawson College, Montreal, Canada. Since September 1997 I have been teaching at the University of California, Riverside. [It was a mistake to list a variety of places I had worked. I was trying to show my experience, but instead I conveyed the instability of my career. I was also padding. I worked for City University of Hong Kong for one summer, teaching one class; same for Dawson College. As for the University of Marborough, Gibraltar, I had, in 1996, signed a contract to teach a correspondence course. I was to be paid per student, but no one enrolled in the class. The work at Riverside was on a term-by-term basis.]

I have published articles on Shakespeare, Chettle, Jonson, and Nashe in some of the most distinguished journals in Western academia, including *Shakespeare Bulletin, EMLS, Upstart Crow, Notes and Queries, ELN,* and *ANQ.* I have series of reviews appearing in *Renaissance Quarterly.* [This is radically overdone. I had, at that point, written one article on Shakespeare, Chettle, and Nashe, not various articles on all three. *EMLS* is an online publication, and while that medium is rapidly gaining in reputation, that was not the case circa 1998. As for *ELN* and *ANQ,* these journals publish only notes, and while perfectly respectable, don't come to mind as among "the most distinguished journals in western academia." Lastly, why would any of these publications assure the editor that I was a credible author on a Romantic forger? The genres of the articles and notes (Renaissance) don't jive with the genre and period (forgery, Romantic era) of the book.] My first book, entitled *Passions and Poisons,* an edition of Canadian poetry, was well received. [My "first book" was not a monograph but an edited collection. Also, I was co-editor and the company was created as part of a creative writing project in a Master's-level class in Canada. The book was "well received" by those who bought it — family and friends. As far as I know, no journal or press reviewed the book.]

[Proposal]

[*The Tragedy of Vortigern*: Subject and Importance.]

1. Why should your press be interested in this edition?

Vortigern was the most controversial Shakespeare production of the entire eighteenth century. The play was staged on April 2, 1796, at Theatre Royal Drury Lane with some of the greatest Shakespearean actors of the day, including John Philip Kemble. The play was attacked by Shakespeare scholars such as Edmond Malone, George Steevens, and Joseph Ritson. Among the play's supporters were the Prince of Wales, the Duke of Clarence, James Boswell, and many other leading figures of eighteenth-century England's political and intellectual elite. [This sounds good, but I can forget about those publishers that do not specialize in obscure, eighteenth-century plays.] *Vortigern* was a forgery. The intricate details of this impressive and at times bizarre history are set out in my book *Reforging Shakespeare: The Story of a Theatrical Scandal* (currently

under review at Lehigh University Press). [It's not a book if it's not published.] However, the text of the play itself, due to the exigencies of space, received short shrift. [Coherence problem. It was so important that I ignored it in a full academic study.] After receiving what at times seemed a flood of letters expressing interest in the play itself, I began the arduous task of preparing this edition. [A flood of letters written by whom? Also, why should an academic press care about a populist movement?]
2. All right, the play *is* historically important. But this play was hissed off stage. Is it really worth reading?

On the occasion of *Vortigern*'s premiere, Edmond Malone, the top Shakespeare scholar of the day, had the play hissed off stage. He even convinced actors in the cast, including the lead actor, Kemble, to give purposefully shabby performances.

There is no doubt that this has colored the perception of the play's theatrical merits. All too often, the play has been dismissed as theatrically unworthy simply because it failed on its opening night. Yet drama scholars do not condemn Ben Jonson's play, *The New Inn*, though it too was hissed off stage. Indeed, Jonson's play has been redeemed by subsequent, more open-minded audiences. The recent performance history of *The Tragedy of Vortigern* may also redeem a play that was never truly given a fair trial. [Not quite. Productions of Jonson's *New Inn* are rare indeed, and, while the play is considered worthy of study, there was no restaging for the academic purpose of judging its aesthetics.]

On two recent occasions, excerpts of the play were staged. Both times, actors, directors, and this writer were pleasantly surprised by the text's theatricality. On November 25, 1993, a reading of excerpts of *Vortigern* was given at the Theatre Museum, Covent Garden. The lead actor, Gilles Bryon, thought the part was bold and powerful. He compared it favorably to playing Tamberlaine. [This is in reference to the title character of Christopher Marlowe's play, which should be spelled "Tamburlaine."]

On October 16, 1994, the BBC aired a prime-time special, "The Irresistible Rise of William Shakespeare." Having heard about this "lost" play, the BBC interviewed me and staged parts from this critical edition. The major newspapers, having seen the show in preview, focused favorable attention on the play. And there has been one full production: In February 1997, Tour of Force, [The company was called "Tour de Force."] a London company, agreed to stage the play. After contacting several leading actors and playwrights, we ["We" is a vast overstatement. A friend of mine had produced and directed the play. I flew into London to attend a dress rehearsal and to see its opening night.] secured the patronage of Alan Ayckbourn and Kenneth Branagh. The play was performed at the Bridewell Theatre from October 19 to November 19. The production has received national press coverage in the *Times, Independent, TLS, Guardian,* and *Telegraph.* [I should have included the press clippings.]

3. Has the play ever been edited before?

Yes. [No. An edited book today, especially in a letter written to an academic press, suggests a modern scholarly edition. While I correct myself a few lines later, the damage is already done.] Originally, the play was rewritten, edited, and published in 1799. [How can a work be "originally"—that's to say, "initially" "rewritten"?] This 1799 edition was used as the copy-text for a second quarto published in 1832. A facsimile of the 1799 edition was published in 1970. However, the 1799 and 1832 editions and the 1970 reprint do not resemble the original play as staged.

Until recently, it was thought that the original manuscripts were housed in the Shakespeare Memorial Library in Birmingham and destroyed by fire in 1879. In fact, I have rediscovered seven manuscripts, collated them against copies of the extant 1799 and 1832 editions, and recorded over 3,000 variants and several hundred cut lines. No modern scholarly edition has ever been undertaken.

4. What does this study contain?

This book consists of a [Grammar!] introduction to the play, which covers the play's authorship, sources, and textual and performance history, and a scholarly edition of the play, complete with textual apparatus, collations, and appendices, including all cut lines, parallel passages from Shakespeare's plays, preliminary prologues and epilogues, and the play's musical score and bibliography. The manuscript is 315 pages in length. [This section is good, aside from the grammatical gaff, but I should also have mentioned images, which would better indicate the cost of book production. I should have also mentioned whether I had any university or institutional grants or subvention funds available.]

5. Sample Materials Enclosed.

I have enclosed the plot synopsis, Prologue, and Act 1, Scene 1, of *The Tragedy of Vortigern* for your perusal.

As the reader can plainly see, my approach had evolved quite a bit between 1996 and 1998, but I still had no idea what to include, and, worse still, who to pitch projects to. In those days, my idea when submitting was simple: carpet-bomb everyone. After all, even if a publisher did not normally publish on Shakespeare or theater or eighteenth century aesthetics, who knows what lies ahead? They might be starting a new product line. I was wrong. The rejections for the edition started coming within a week and kept on coming, first week after week, then one a month, then one every two months.

But I had other worries, like finding work. Riverside had been good to me—far better than it needed to be. The Department of English employed me on a term-by-term basis for two-and-a-half years, but it no longer had room for me. The coming term would be my last. While there, I had not only worked on getting published, I had also continued to send out my vitae for traditional tenure-track jobs. It was the fall of 1997. I had been on the market for 4 years at that point, and I had received no offer, not even for an interview, for a tenure-track job. I was about to become unemployed — again. I phoned my mom with the news: Get the couch ready, I guess I'm coming home. But I never got the words out. She was so excited — Lehigh had written. The book had been accepted! The reports came within a week. No major revisions were required!

Lessons Learned

As we close this chapter, I'd like you to keep in mind a question: Why had Lehigh accepted my book when all other presses had rejected it out of hand? In the excitement of the moment, I had not bothered to give the query enough thought. As I was (years later) to learn, the Lehigh Library Special Collection has a small but important bundle of William-Henry Ireland forgeries. I should have known that, but I didn't. Back in the late eighties and early nineties, finding out what was in a library's special collection was impossible without a visit. The World Wide Web was still in its infancy. Heck, many computer users had yet to make the change from DOS to Windows. The point here is that Lehigh published the book because the school, in very small part, already knew of, collected, and was interested in Ireland's forgeries. That important lesson has never left me. The academic press and its home institution share intellectual interests.

And, as I was later to figure out, I had still made some key errors in my query letter, especially in not addressing the editor by name. That was really dumb. First, I didn't know the name of the right editor and just assumed that some secretary would read the materials first and figure out who would be lucky enough to get my extraordinarily interesting proposal. That was wrong. As with a job application, you want to make an immediate, personal connection as a way of rising above the pile of other applicants. Second, by treating editors impersonally, I was inviting them to do the same to me. By writing to "Sir," "Sir/Madam," or "To Whom It May Concern," I was tipping them off to the fact that I was, in fact, carpet-bombing publishers. I now realize that even if a publisher were interested, the press would probably shy away on the principle that it had limited resources and could not afford to work, however briefly, on a project which might have multiple presses vying for the same manuscript. Oh, and I probably irritated the presses that were *not interested* by making them reply via mail or e-mail, which takes both time and resources away from viable projects. So, I wasted money, wasted the publishers' resources and time, insulted the very publishers I needed, alienated the press editors, and put a black mark against my name for any future projects. I had been extremely efficient. Look how many wrong things I had done in one letter!

If You Think You're Done When You Sign a Contract, You're Not!

Somehow, despite all my disadvantages and errors, I had succeeded. Lehigh had accepted by book. Pop the champagne! But no, I now learned that I had to put off that celebration. As I was about to find out, my work on my first book was about to begin. As odd as this sounds, I had not yet written a book. I had typed out a book-length manuscript, which had been accepted for publication on the condition that I modify per my readers' reports. The next 6 months or so were dedicated to working with the press in an attempt to turn my book-length manuscript into an actual book. This is not nearly as simple as it sounds, as is evident from the following:

Step 1. I still needed to revise my manuscript along the lines suggested in the readers' reports. If you, dear reader, are lucky enough to be at this phase, you will notice that you likely have deletions or additions to make, both or either of which may in turn affect the flow and logic of the entire manuscript. In my own case, there remained one section of the book — let me correct myself here, not book but book-length manuscript accepted for publication — that I did not like. In addition to other suggested changes, I sought and received permission to make some changes in that one chapter. Even after I relentlessly polished the new manuscript, I later learned to my shame and surprise that this latest version still contained an unconscionable number of infelicities — typos, some grammatical faux pas and the like. I also had to check a number of facts and fix some issues in my bibliography.

Step 2. The academic press sends the manuscript out to a proofreader. In the old days — i.e., the 1990s — an academic press proofer was a full-time, in-house employee. Nowadays, that is almost never the case. The proofreader of today is usually a freelancer or works for a firm that has secured the proofing tasks that had once been done in-house. The proofreader corrects your copy, which is then typeset and sent back to you, along with your original manuscript. You then have the crazy-fun task of seeing what changes and corrections the firm has made to your manuscript and you either approve or override them. Oddly, proofreaders and typesetters speak in a language all their own, developed in the Victorian era, and it is incumbent upon you, the writer, to learn this lingo and to respond in kind. (You are usually given a cheat sheet with a number of arcane editing symbols which you have to master.)

Step 3. You get another set of proofs to go through, this time to make sure that your last set of correction notes were all understood properly. Depending on how well or how poorly your proofer worked on your manuscript or how well or poorly you learned the anachronisms of editing symbols, you can expect your proofs to be somewhere between perfect and utterly unrecognizable. One overzealous proofreader took it upon herself to change my use of commas, which, while perfectly correct, did not meet her modern ear and eye. (I do tend to add, if I feel it necessary, a variety of commas and, rather daringly, parentheticals and dashes — a result of reading too much Tacitus in my youth.)

Step 4. You make sure you have secured all rights to images and the like. If you are as I was, these fees come out of your pocket; if you are as I am, this is no big deal, as your home institution will pick up the bill.

Step 5. The sales and marketing arm of each press sends a variety of forms. These forms usually ask which journals should get freebie copies of your book for review — though given the hostile nature of many reviews, you might want to think carefully about this. A bad review can do more damage than no review at all. On the other hand, you want to promote yourself and your work.

Step 6. A last set of proofs arrives. Any changes you make to this set will incur a charge, even if those changes stem from a misreading of the proofer's changes. By now, the thinking goes, you should have caught everything, no matter the origin of the fault. These charges for changes will be paid by you and must be paid almost immediately — i.e., you must write a check within a few weeks. (Yes, you will be sent an invoice for your tax records.) The point is, these last changes and the charges stemming from them will not be not deducted from any future royalties. There is a very good reason for this; in all likelihood, there will be no royalties. On why this is so, see Chapter 4.

Step 7. Indexing. Along with the final manuscript, you will now be asked to index the typeset manuscript, or you can sign off on a professional indexer to do this menial task for you. If you decide to leave it to the pros, expect another bill ranging from $300 to $1000. These professional indexers are, like proofreaders, usually freelancers. Given the choice, I have always indexed my books myself. It takes about 300 hours to complete and is about as much fun as a root canal. Oh, and for some reason, the press is now in a hurry. Generally, last proofs and indexing must be completed within two weeks. (The press has now queued your book for production and shipping. A lot of people are suddenly dependent upon you to complete your tasks in a timely manner.)

Step 8. The press has farmed out the book design, cover design, front and back flap copy, and cover artwork to yet another freelancer. You will have some modest say concerning the image and font on the front cover and you will be asked to supply a biographical blurb for the back cover. If this is your first book and you have yet to secure a tenure-track job, this blurb will be, in most instances, brief. You will also be asked to supply an authorial photo. In my case, I had some fun with it. Since my book was about Shakespeare forgery, I had my head superimposed on a picture of Shakespeare's body. Lehigh agreed to the unconventional approach, though I had to argue hard for it by pointing out that Shakespeare's image in the First Folio has a caption which reads, "according to the true original copies." My image, I argued, suggested that forgery played with the definitions and distinctions between true, original, and copy. If there are costs involved for the front-cover image or your back-cover author photo, you can expect another bill.

Step 9. You will be asked to write a short description of your book—now in press!—for the thousands of catalogues and flyers about to be printed and sent to academic libraries and individual scholars in your field.

Step 10. Ten copies, sometimes less, of your book are mailed to you! When that happens, it is always a good idea to email your editor, the various sales and marketing people, the kind secretary who has patiently fielded your queries, and all the freelancers involved in the making of your book, thanking them for all their hard work.

My box of books for *Reforging Shakespeare* came during my last week of classes at UCR. I brought one copy with me to show my students. They were in awe, and so was I. I had done it. I had published my first book. I updated my vitae and, that summer, sent off my resume with a great deal of optimism. The year was 1998, and the rejection letters came in just as quickly as before. It would be another three years before I would land a tenure-track job.

Ten Things You Need to Know

1. A doctoral dissertation and a book are each created with functions and audiences in mind.
2. It is natural to be emotionally attached to your dissertation, and that makes revisions even more difficult.
3. A good dissertation does not necessarily make a good book.
4. A bad dissertation might well make a good book.
5. Typically, you need to cut down your dissertation and revise your entire approach for the publishing market.
6. A strong query letter is key—explain how your project fits in with their product line.
7. Having a job helps a lot, but don't pad your qualifications.
8. A proposal needs to cover some basic information but should also state your experience and sources of funding.
9. There remains a great deal of work to be done, even after your book is accepted for publication.
10. Don't expect a job just because you have a book out.

Chapter 3

Readers' Reports, Replies, Rejections, and Writer's Block

That first book nearly killed me. Not the revisions, mind you, but the near constant stream of form-letter rejections, almost all of which offered no explanation. There were days that I dreaded opening that mailbox; each letter confirmed my status as an out-of-work academic, a failure, a fraud. This is another great reason for adopting my system. It will cut down — radically cut down — those dismissive and heart-crushing letters. By targeting presses that want your work, you will no longer have to dread opening up your mailbox only to find endless form letters from journals and publishers, all of whom thank you for your submission but don't find that it fits their product line, or some such.

Once you understand how to target journals and presses and understand what is required of you in the submission process, things go much easier. Why shouldn't they? Almost all of your competitors are submitting to the wrong journal, don't even know the name of the editor to whom they are writing, or both. Your submission will now stand out simply because it's not as poorly conceived as those of your competitors. Your submission will now go into a pile of manuscripts that will be given some attention. The editor will read it and, if she thinks it valuable, send it out to an external reader for consideration.

We have already discussed targeting board members as readers in Chapter 1, but here we might note the real upside. Instead of endless rejections, what you should be getting are acceptances — either blanket acceptances or acceptances contingent upon revisions, and, on rare occasions, a rejection letter or two. Here, too, there should be a marked change. Instead of form-letter rejections, you can now expect something far more thoughtful and useful. I once received a rejection on a proposal and sample chapter of one of my books, *The Cult of Kean.* Along with the standard rejection letter was a detailed critique of why the project was rejected. I found the critique of my sample chapter so persuasive I rewrote sections of it as a result. Remember that I was here responding to a rejection that pointed out my failings. Was I stung by the rejection? Yes. Was I devastated? No. Why? Here is one of the secrets to surviving in academia: it's not personal.

Learning from Readers' Reports

Remember when we looked at book review writing and we said that it is far easier to write a negative review than a positive one? Well, the same is true for the reader who receives your manuscript. Even if the reader loves the book, she will still feel compelled to point out some of its failings. That is just part of the business we are in. We shouldn't bear the reader any ill will. It's just what she has been trained to do — look for flaws and attack. Those attacks may be unfair in that they are often inflated. If you make a minor error on, say, page 15 of an article, the reader should in good conscience point it out but not hammer on the point for paragraphs on end. Yet all too often, a reader will pound on negatives simply because it is easier to do that than to talk about positives.

That may be unfair since the editor trusts the reader to be reasonable and dispassionate, but let's face facts. All criticism is negative, so much so that when we have something positive to say we have to note it with an adjective, as in, "I have some *positive* criticism for you." Recall also that when your friends ask you about the movie you saw last week, it is easier to wax on the negatives: "Oh, the movie sucked; the acting was horrible; the script made no sense." Heads nod. The conversation moves on to another topic. In such instances, we are rarely asked to elaborate on *why* things are bad. The opposite is true of positives. "Oh," you tell your friend, "I loved Emma Thompson in that movie!" And then your friend asks, "Really, why? Tell me more." Now you are forced to go into specifics, citing a line, a look, a gesture, her motivation, etc. The comparison is telling. The negative view carries the weight of wisdom without the weight of incidents or arguments. It is true of water cooler discussion; it is true of readers' reports.

Sometimes, the report seems to have been penned by someone who didn't bother to read your paper thoroughly. There is a reason for that. Each press usually has a list of outside readers, experts in the field. But, because of their national and perhaps even international prominence, these scholars often have their own robust research agendas and teaching. Doing reports is merely a small part of their overall activities, and, since it is a small part of their work, it can sometimes seem as it if receives short shrift.

It is sometimes the case that you get a report that suggests the reader did not read your manuscript with the attention you feel it deserves. Keep in mind that these are busy people. Your project, while the world to you, is last in a long line of projects for them. The reports they write may sometimes seem rushed because, well, they *are* rushed. Nor can readers dedicate multiple revisions to their reports. I am not impugning any particular reader; rather, I am pointing out that the system depends upon cheap labor, which, even if the scholar means well, must take as little time as possible. Readers' reports are not meant to be polished literary masterpieces.

To my mind, the most annoying sorts of report goes something like this — and here we will keep to our cinematic water cooler discussion. "Emma Thompson was good, but then, she's always good. I'd love to see her in something totally different." The academic version of this is to point out what you didn't write about. Here, for example, is a letter one scholar wrote to me on a paper submitted and eventually published. Since I don't have the author's permission, I am revising the critique, but the substance remains intact. The essay concerned the possible use of castration myths by a major author:

> I agree that the authors sometimes used a variety of myths and legends, but Kahan suggests the author had a thorough, rather than passing, knowledge. Kahan might have made a stronger argument had he used the author's letters to make his case.
> Another troubling aspect with Kahan's essay is that he ignores the dichotomy found in many of the author's stories. Where he sees a myth of castration, I see a simple case of effeminization and urbanization.

The tone is distinctly negative — that's to be expected — but let's really look at the argument. The reader argues that myth is present in the story but wishes I had gone beyond the story to the author's letters as evidence. Does it follow that because I did not cite the letters I was wrong in my analysis of the story? Of course not! Would the article have been strengthened by the inclusion of the letters? Possibly. Are countless published analyses of stories based entirely on close readings of the text? Yes! Yet somehow not doing what my reader wished I would have done is now "another troubling aspect." A "troubling aspect" of what? Not of argument, but of approach. I read on. Now the reader disagrees with her own words: There is no borrowing from myth; rather, we have an analysis of urbanization.

Personally, I don't see that our views are utterly incompatible. While it's clear that the reader sees it otherwise, to my mind effeminization is a form of cultural castration. Again, the criticism shows not so much interest in what I wrote as what the reader wishes to write. These sorts of reports remind me of a seriocomical statement Anthony Burgess made: "The trouble with Chesterton is that he is not Kafka." True, but what of it? Shouldn't Chesterton be read as Chesterton, not as Kafka? Likewise, shouldn't the reader put aside personal dislikes and read the article on its own merits?

In the above-cited instance, I was lucky. The editor requested I make some changes, and with a few easy patches, it was published. I was happy to make those changes. Did I, at the time, offer any critique of the reader? Absolutely not. There was no need. The editor had already given me a way forward, and, without looking back, I took it. In your writing, I'd advise you to be flexible. The goal is to publish. Further, you should not be upset or angry when asked to make changes with which you disagree. The critic who wrote the negative report is not losing sleep over the report, and you shouldn't over the negative assessment. Instead, try to see what the reader is seeing. If the paper has been rejected outright, then you might want to consider the reader's negative assessment and contemplate what you might do to improve the paper before sending it out to yet another journal.

Replying to a Reader's Report

So far, we have dealt with the negative view of an article. A reply to a negative reader's report of a book is a more complex task and should be undertaken only under the right circumstances. There are, you might remember, three readers: the press' editor, who saw something in the project, and the two readers your editor selected to read your manuscript. If you have one hostile reader, then the other reader must be very encouraging. If not, drop the matter and move onto another press. But if you do have a split decision among your readers, you have an excellent chance of getting your project published. Why? Because the editor liked your manuscript. If she didn't like it, the manuscript would never have been sent out for review. However, you don't want to dismiss the negative assessment, nor do you want to be confrontational. You need to be careful in discussing the views of a hostile reader, who, very likely, has a very good relationship with your editor.

When writing your reply, don't dwell on the differences in the readers' reports. Instead, you want to find as many positive points of agreement between the encouraging and the hostile readers. Next tip: Don't respond to all negatives, especially if you think one is unfair or overemphasizes a small point. As stated, almost all criticism is negative; no one expects you to fall into lockstep on every single point raised. Instead, find some salient points that address important issues that can be easily corrected. Show flexibility by conceding that you may not have been as nuanced as you could have been, and thank the reader for pointing out the underlying issue. Next: Demonstrate professionalism. Write out a formal report. Besides looking professional, it demonstrates the mechanical, nonemotional, and constructive way you are processing the negative comments. If you feel that the negative reader's critique stems from a misunderstanding of what you wrote, then show a bit of (extremely polite) backbone. If applicable, note that in one instance the hostile reader *may* have misinterpreted the manuscript and that you think your argument is sound, though you now recognize that if the reader has misinterpreted the point, some minor retouching of tone and pace is probably necessary. Lastly, set goals. The report should outline what you are willing to do and how long it should take you to complete the project.

Here is an example from my newest book, *Bettymania and the Birth of Celebrity Culture*, which had one very positive and one very negative report. My reply is reprinted here with the kind permission of Lehigh University Press:

> To: Scott Paul Gordon, Editor, Lehigh University Press.
> Re: Readers' Reports concerning manuscript
> *Bettymania and the Birth of Celebrity Culture.*
> Response Prepared by Jeffrey Kahan, Professor,
> University of La Verne, January 11, 2009

Dear Scott Paul Gordon,

I want to begin by thanking you for your supportive and encouraging emails, which culminated on December 23, 2008 with the delivery of the Readers' Reports concerning my book on Bettymania. As you know, this is the first thorough and scholarly investigation of that event. I find the reports to be detailed, reasonable, and appropriate.

Most of the suggested revisions deal with (A) degrees of tone and argument and (B) suggestions for supplementary research. Many of the suggested changes in both Readers' Reports are page and passage specific and, therefore, can be undertaken systematically and without undue difficulty or delay.

In the following, I want to address, point by point, the Readers' main concerns.

Table of Contents

I.) Reader A

Reader A's report was overwhelmingly positive. Two suggestions were made to improve the manuscript:

Issue 1: The Title and Focus

Reader A writes:

First off, I would suggest a change of title from "Bettymania and the Birth of Celebrity Culture" to simply "Bettymania and Celebrity Culture." Designating a moment of "birth" would enmesh the book in a Foucauldian dynamic that is neither called for nor fulfilled. Second, I would ask the author to decide whether this is a work of cultural criticism or of archival historical research. I think its claim to the second is much stronger. "Bettymania" fills in some important historical gaps in the history of theatre and comments intelligently on the cult of the child in its history. I think that the cultural studies framework is much weaker and diverts the reader's attention from the principal story that the book wants to tell. Thus, I would say that the author needs to decide either to significantly strengthen the introduction and coda to really focus on existing scholarship about celebrity culture or significantly cut the coda, in particular, to focus more on the significance of Bettymania itself. I think particu-

larly that the claim for a coincidence of political conditions and celebrity culture, although probably correct, cannot be sustained by the present study and would require an entirely different study as proof.

Reply: Agreed. And I think this might be easily accomplished. All but the last paragraph of the Introduction focuses on Betty himself. The Coda can be easily revised in keeping with the general drift of both Readers A and B. Alternative titles will be offered to General Editor Scott Paul Gordon, and I will comply with his selection.

Issue 2: Narrative Pacing.
Reader A writes:

I'd start at the end, with Betty's ultimate fate and even his charitable work for children as a conceptual starting point and then work back through his career. Tell the story dramatically, not chronologically.

Reply: Re: chronology. The narrative, in its present form, begins at the height of Bettymania, and then tracks it to its origin and then to its conclusion. Along the way, the story "breaks" at important moments to delve into Romantic issues of revolution and sexuality or pauses to situate Bettymania within the differing cultural contexts of Ireland, Scotland, and England. I carefully wrote and rewrote section after section to make these cessations in narrative pace as circumspect as possible. The reaction of the reader suggests that I have been successful. That being said, once I begin the enhancements, the process of refinement may well allow for a number of narrative rearrangements in keeping with Reader A's considered remarks.

II.) Reader B
Reader B agreed that "this project has tremendous potential," and suggested some areas worthy of revision. Among the suggestions — shared by Reader A — is that the finished version downplay connections to our own celebrity-driven culture. Many of the other germane suggestions are page and passage specific. I appreciate the thoroughness of Reader B's remarks and will respond to the most important of them individually:

Issue 1: Further Connecting Manuscript to Current Scholarship.
Reader B remarks:

In its current form the manuscript would appeal to theater historians as well as literary scholars interested in the Romantic period.... [however, the] author's general engagement with current work in theatrical history and theory could be significantly stronger. I've listed below several of the project's major concerns; for each of these I have mentioned some of the scholars who represent the current state of the field.... I do not mean to hold the manuscript to account for what it does not set out to do, but some real engagement with the theoretical questions engaged through this scholarship would strengthen the book's claims considerably.

Reply: The remarks are shrewd: Although much of the Introduction is dedicated to mapping out the systematic dismissal of Bettymania, there is no doubt that the more connections I draw to recent criticism, the more I situate the narrative within ongoing academic discussion and debate. I welcome this opportunity to improve the book, and I will make every attempt to follow Reader B's suggestion. Most of the titles cited by Reader B are known to me. None, so far as I recall, mention Betty *per se*. In its present form, the study already cites over 300 articles, books, unpublished letters, and contracts, but I am willing to look for broader secondary and tertiary connections to recent scholarship. I have already ordered the half-dozen or so books suggested by Reader B — as well as another half-dozen newly-issued books on Romanticism — and stand ready to bolster my arguments where appropriate.

Issue 2. Methodology/Use of Sources.

Reader B remarks:

At too many points in this narrative, we find lack of attention to the complexities of the historical realities.... [O]ften the author seems to take archival sources too readily at face value. A few examples: ...can selections from memoirs and reminiscences, such as the exchanges from Murdoch and comments from Anne Mathews on page 159, all be taken as actual accounts of a conversation? On page 199 we are told that "John Philip Kemble himself was spreading the rumor" that Betty was a woman. The footnote points to a letter from Sheridan (hardly a disinterested observer) supporting the anecdote.

Reply: We agree that there are issues of authority here that need to be better articulated. Reader B's specific attention to tone here is very valuable. We can, however, debate some of Reader B's specific examples: Sheridan, while not a disinterested observer, had no reason to lie or to exaggerate his account, which is found in a private letter to his wife. Anne Mathews' letters and memoirs are often cited directly and unproblematically in many accounts of the period.

Issue 3. "Re-ordering" Statements in a Quotation.

Reader B takes brief issue with p. 19, note 73, in which I write that I reordered the statements found in the accompanying quotation.

Reply: This is easy enough to remedy. I can simply remove the quotations and keep the citation, which should be perfectly acceptable.

Issue 4. Further Accommodations.

In the following, I note Reader B's page specific criticism, and how I might clarify the narrative:

(4.1) Concerning pp. 74–75, Reader B writes:

On pages 74–5 we find a tenuous connection between Betty's nursing a mortally wounded man and the Napoleonic wars. Is there archival evidence to suggest that audiences actually connected the scenes to the political realities the author mentions? If so, it would be helpful to see it.

Reply: Some repointing here, as well as including an image, already in my possession, of Betty as Napoleon, should clarify. At present, I do point out both in the Introduction and in Chapter 2 that many Londoners, in their mania over Betty, put aside their fear of Napoleon. I further cite James Boaden's first-hand account that "the spectators ... applied the lines [of the play] to Buonaparte," which occasioned "the most vehement applause."

(4.2) Concerning pp. 144–45:

Reader B takes issue with the discussion on page 144–45, particularly my focus on (Reader B's words) "Kemble's rivalry with Betty (whom he engaged)." In Reader B's view, the manuscript "doesn't provide the textual evidence to support a claim that he [Kemble] 'hated the boy.'"

Reply: As stated in Chapter 3, Kemble was a minority shareholder in Covent Garden but was still very much an employee of the theater. Saying that Kemble "engaged" Betty is, therefore, imprecise. Additionally, all of Chapter 3 discusses Kemble's openly hostile actions, including his refusal to act with the boy. (Sarah Siddons and Mrs. Jordan approved of his actions and followed suit.) Kemble also attempted to destabilize Betty's standing as a serious performer by casting and billing him with clowns, tightrope walkers, and other panto performers. Still, I agree that the language here can be more nuanced. I will revise the passage with a more restrained expression.

(4.3) Concerning p. 210:

Reader B wonders whether the discussion of Thomas Lister Parker's interest in Betty warrants a charge of "pedophilia" (page 210).

Reply: I understand Reader B's objections and will modify to suit. I would note, however, that the word "pedophilia," in or out of quotations, *is not employed* on page 210, nor is it used in the chapter. I do, on pages 208–211, state the facts concerning Parker's "pedophilic tendencies." Parker was obsessed with the boy, traveled up and down the country to see him, threw posh parties for him, and commissioned two very expensive portraits of Betty, which he personally supervised. (One of the portraits depicts him as a scantily-clad shepherd boy — an accepted gay motif dating to ancient Greece and Rome.) Further, Parker wrote a highly inappropriate letter to Betty's mother complaining that the boy was not sufficiently affectionate. In the same letter, Parker reiterated his desire to spend time alone with him in the country. Behavior may not, I grant you, reveal intention, and Reader B is quite right: Parker's intention remains a matter of conjecture. As such, I have already revised the passage to underscore the unidentified nature of his purpose.

(4.4) Concerning p. 86, Reader B writes:

On page 86, the author argues suggestively that "political expressions of Bettymania exposed the sheer exhaustion of the old political elite." But that point is reduced on the next page to a remark about the (87) "generally worthless lot in charge of Britain."

Reply: Reader B's word "reduced" is perhaps too strong here. I was offering a summation after a long passage. I quote here at length, underlining both the opening and closing passage cited by Reader B. **N.B.** I have, for the purposes of this report, excised the footnotes found in the manuscript:

Political expressions of Bettymania exposed the sheer exhaustion of the old political elite: In 1804, England's King George III was sixty-six years old and insane. His eldest son, the future George IV, was forty-four years old, a dissolute wastrel who had a habit of vomiting in public. He was legally married to one woman, Princess Caroline of Brunswick, illegally married to another, Maria Fitzherbert, and, notoriously, cheating on them both. His brother William, the Duke of Clarence, kept a married woman — an Irish actress no less! — Mrs. Jordan, as his mistress. Frederick, Duke of York, age forty-one, also had a long-term mistress, Mrs. Clarke, who accepted cash and, some said, traded sexual favors in return for influence with her royal lover. Another brother, Edward, Duke of Kent, had been the governor of Gibraltar, until his own soldiers mutinied against his authoritarian rule in 1802; thereafter he returned to London in disgrace. Yet another brother, Ernest, was rumored to be having an incestuous affair with his sister Sophia and having a homosexual affair with his valet, Joseph Sellis, which culminated in Sellis's attempted assassination of the Duke on May 31, 1810. George III's seventh son, Prince Adolphus, Duke of Sussex, had married Lady Augusta Murray in Rome on April 4, 1793; the marriage was annulled sixteen months later, which was scandalous in itself, though the fact that Adolphus continued to live with his ex-wife until 1801 was still worse. His younger brother, Prince Octavius, died on May 3, 1783, at Kew Palace, London, age four years old. The last of George III's sons, Alfred, died in the same year, at the age of three. As for George III's daughters, Augusta Sophia never married; Elizabeth would eventually end up with the malodorous German Frederick, Prince of the petty state of Hesse-Homburg; Mary eventually married her cousin, the feeble-brained Duke of Gloucester, known commonly as "Silly Billy"; as stated, Princess Sophia was allegedly involved in an incestuous affair with her brother Ernest, who may or may not have impregnated her; Amelia had tuberculosis, the disease which would claim her life in 1810; Charlotte married the paunchy Prince of Württemberg, who, at the height of Bettymania, was collaborating with Napoleon. Putting the Royals aside, Britain's chief political players included the Prime Minister, William Pitt, who first served that post in 1783 at age twenty-four; by 1804, he was only forty-four years old but addicted to drink and dying of liver disease. His political rival, the grossly overweight Charles James Fox, was a notorious lecher and gambler.

With this aging, ill, and *generally worthless lot in charge of Britain*, it is not entirely surprising that her citizens were seeking a symbol of juvenescence, for, as Alan Richardson has recently noted, their intensified interest in youth culture stemmed from their fears of and longing for their own version of the French Revolution.

III.) Timeline for Revisions

Clearly, all revision work depends on a degree of self-supervision. I think that, in this respect, I have a strong record of publication. My first book, *Reforging Shakespeare* (Lehigh, 1998), was the first comprehensive study of the Ireland forgeries of 1795. *Reforging Shakespeare* argues that the time may be ripe to re-examine the W.H. Ireland forgeries as a decisive case history in the development of our current respect for antiquity, our appreciation of authenticity, and our understanding of bardolatry. My other recent books include *King Lear: New Critical Essays* (Routledge, 2008), *The Cult of Kean* (Ashgate 2006), *The Poetry of Robert Southey* (University of Gloucester, 2006), and *Shakespeare Imitations and Forgeries 1710–1820,* 3 vols. (Routledge, August 2004). I am the author of some 50 scholarly articles, book reviews and notes, and serve on the board of *Shakespeare Yearbook.* I can rigorously address all the aforementioned Readers' concerns by July 1, 2009.

The report was read by the board and enthusiastically endorsed, on the condition that I complete my promised revisions in a timely manner. Of course, I agreed.

Note the time lag. It had been over four years since I had begun the Bettymania project. It took two years to write the book, a year to get a publisher interested, another year to receive the readers' reports, a month or so to reply, another month to receive their cautious acceptance, another month to undertake changes deemed necessary for acceptance, and then 9 more months of proofing and indexing before I held the finished product in my hands. I discussed this in Chapter 1, but it is worth repeating: The delay in publishing is enormous. You need to diversify your academic output to ensure you have enough publications in hand when you submit your dossier. A bunch of projects "under consideration" just ain't gonna cut it.

Develop Strong Writing Habits

My own trials and tribulations, as well as my modest successes, in academia have convinced me that my system is practical and effective. But it won't work unless you, dear reader, are willing to write every day and to engage in a multiplicity of publishing projects. Why every day and why more than one project? The two are actually integrally related. Obviously, the more you do something, the better you get at it. This applies to weight lifting, painting, and, yes, writing. Remember, we want a steady output of varying publications for tenure. And steady is the key.

We don't want a feast or famine approach. Many of the most prolific writers of the modern era are also some of the most disciplined people you will ever meet. In an article on the habits of seven successful writers, author Leo Babauta notes that, commonly, the most successful writers approach their craft mechanically. More often than not, some of our most famous writers (a) write or wrote every day, (b) write or wrote at a set time, and (c) often have or had a ritual associated with writing — walking, a cup of tea, sometimes a shot of booze, etc. I've here cited Babauta's findings and rounded out his list with some other famous writers:

1. Stephen King, in his book *On Writing*, says that he writes 10 pages a day without fail, even on holidays. King goes through these motions when he sits down to write: "I have a glass of water or I have a cup of tea. I have my vitamin pill; I have my music; I have my same seat; and the papers are all arranged in the same places."

2. Ernest Hemingway wrote 500 words a day. He woke early to avoid the heat and to write in peace and quiet. Interestingly, though Hemingway is famous for his alcoholism, he said he never wrote while drunk.

3. Vladimir Nabokov, the author of such great novels as *Lolita*, *Pale Fire*, and *Ada*, did his writing standing up and all on index cards. This allowed him to write scenes nonsequentially, as he could rearrange the cards as he wished. His novel *Ada* took up more than 2,000 cards.

4. Truman Capote, the author of *Breakfast at Tiffany's* and *In Cold Blood*, claimed to be a "completely horizontal author." He said he had to write lying down, in bed or on a couch, with a cigarette and coffee. He would switch the coffee to tea, then to sherry, and then finally, as the day wore on, to martinis. He wrote his first and second drafts in longhand in pencil. And even his third draft, done on a typewriter, would be done in bed with the typewriter balanced on his knees.

5. Philip Roth, one of the greatest living American writers, works standing up, pacing around as he thinks. He claims to walk half a mile for every page he writes. He separates his work life from his personal life and doesn't write where he lives — he has a studio built away from his house. He works at a lectern that doesn't face the view of his studio window in order to avoid distraction.

6. Isaac Asimov, who published nearly 500 novels as well as less fanciful studies on subjects ranging from bicycle repair to Shakespeare to nuclear physics, was an obsessive writer whose various phobias included a fear of flying and travel. He woke at 6:00 A.M. and wrote all day, sometimes until 1:00 A.M.

7. Joyce Carol Oates, an extremely prolific writer (see her bibliography on her Wikipedia page!), has won numerous awards, including the National Book Award. She writes in longhand, and while she doesn't have a formal schedule, she says she prefers to write in the morning, before breakfast. She's a creative writing professor, and on the days she teaches, she says she writes for an hour or 45 minutes before leaving for her first class. On other days, when the writing is going well, she can work for hours without a break — and has breakfast at 2 or 3 in the afternoon!

8. Charles Dickens, at peak production, wrote 2,000 words a day, every day except Sundays. He began work at 7 A.M. and wrote until about 2 P.M. He also placed objects on his desk in exactly the same position, always set his bed in north/south directions, and touched certain objects three times for luck. He also walked twenty to thirty miles a day.

9. Anthony Trollope wrote 47 novels (and worked full time at a government job) by penning ten pages a day, completed in three hours. He started promptly at 5:30 A.M.

10. Jack London published a book called *John Barleycorn*, which his wife suggested he call *Alcoholic Memoirs*. In it, he tells about the first time he got drunk. He was 5 years old and drank some of the beer in the bucket he was carrying to his stepfather at work in the fields. In his teens, he learned to drink strong men under the table. For a long time after he turned to writing, he refused to drink until he had done his thousand words a day. Soon he learned to get a "pleasant jingle," as he called it, after the 1,000 words were on paper but before lunch.

11. Immanuel Kant would begin his day with one or two cups of weak tea and a pipe of tobacco. While smoking, he would meditate. He would then prepare for his lectures, teach from 7:00 to 11:00, write, and then have lunch. Lunch would be followed by a walk and time with his friends. The evening would consist of a bit more light work and reading.

12. Writer and thinker C.S. Lewis had a very clear schedule of his day, with activities such as work, walking, meals, tea, and socializing down to the very hour they should be done. He even describes when beer should be enjoyed (not at 11:00 for fear of running over the allotted 10 minutes for the break).

Of course, you may be the sort of writer who can pen nothing for months at a time, then sit down and pump out a chapter of a book in a day or two. If so, then you are exceptional, and the truly exceptional probably don't need a self-help book like the one you are reading. My advice: Write the same amount 5 days a week. Be reasonable in the amount you select, but stick to it. Personally, I bash out 1,000 words a day. If it takes me an hour to do it (rare), then I am done for the day. If it takes me 8 hours (very rare), then I am done for the day. Usually, it takes me about 2.5 hours. I begin writing every day at the same time: 8.30 A.M. My mind is clear, I am rested, the house is quiet. I have already walked my dog and checked my email. I have already eaten a bowl of cereal with fruit and drank 2 cups of coffee. The phone is off. The mail truck won't come by for three hours. My neighbor will begin playing his stereo too loudly at 1 P.M. This is my window to write.

When I first began writing my 1,000 words a day, I really struggled, but then I'd hit a stride. Sometimes I'd get overeager and write 2,000 or 3,000 words, but then I'd be exhausted the next day. After a few months of the process, I found that as I approached my one thousandth word of the day, I was automatically leaving notes and clues as to what to write the next day. What I think happens is that the brain doesn't like working so hard, so it finds ways of doing the work in the least taxing way. For example, I think all of us would like to write sequentially, but my brain has already decided otherwise. Sometimes the 1,000 words will go into, say, Chapter 2; sometimes it goes into what eventually becomes the conclusion. Although I keep trying to write an introduction first, all my writing experience tells me that my introduction will be penned last. I don't know why; I guess that's just the way I work.

I should really do some sort of survey on this because, unless I am truly bizarre, I am coming to the conclusion that almost everything we have been told about essay writing is wrong. We have all been told that you should do an outline, begin with an introduction, then write the main body and then the conclusion. Somewhere along the line we learn to revise, smooth narratives with transitions, and then proof the bejesus out of the paper and —*viola!*— it's done. The reality, especially when it comes to writing books, is almost the opposite.

What I am saying at heart is that your writing relies on trust. You have an outline, but if the paper starts going somewhere else, let it. When I write, I really don't *know* what the project will end up saying. I will discover that in the doing. I just have to trust the process. Writing, we have been told, is a mechanical process — but it's not. It's organic. Let the paper grow into what it wants and needs to become, then see what you need to do to make it suitable for submission.

Another piece of advice: Write while you are researching; don't wait until you have mastered the facts. You will never completely master the facts. Going back to my own work habits, after I write my 1,000 words for the day, I then begin to read things that I hope I can use the following day. Once I dog-ear or post-note the salient points, I close the book, shut off the computer, and then get on with my professorial responsibilities, including grading papers, preparing lectures, writing applications for research funds, attending meetings, and teaching classes. My writing is only a small (but important) facet of a long day.

Don't Spend Too Much Time on Campus!

In the opening chapter I described the difficulties all of us face when going through the tenuring process. A job evaluation lasting half a decade or more (5 to 7 years of "tenure-tracking" is the norm) can cause sleepless nights, strains on relationships, weight gain or loss, and premature graying. It's terrifying to recognize that every day you step onto your home campus you are being evaluated; that no matter how strong your last class was, you need only to make one inappropriate comment, perhaps a joke that doesn't go over well, and a formal complaint can be lodged that in turn may begin an inquiry that will end with your dismissal; that every meeting you have with a departmental colleague may pull you into a political alliance, which, if not strong enough, may doom your chances of receiving a letter of departmental endorsement. I have had enough emotional turmoil in my pre-tenured years to last several lifetimes. Some would call my post-tenured life regimented, routine, boring. Sometimes boring is good.

Of course, you can take some steps to lower the stress of the tenuring process. In terms of student interaction, you can be friendly with students

but not engage in banter. And you can take some steps to protect yourself
from your colleagues. Newbie faculty often are "asked" to serve as secretaries in committees, recording comments and writing up meeting minutes — a thankless and time-consuming task. Committees may be asked
to prepare long reports or to make recommendations on issues such as
diversity, salaries, recruitment, etc. You need to prioritize your commitments. Departmental and committee politics burn time — time you need
for writing.

In addition to departmental and campus-wide committee meetings
and the preparatory work for lectures — not an inconsiderable task, since
it's likely that the freshly-minted Ph.D. does not have a deep reservoir
of prepared lectures from which to draw — there are the many assigned
and unassigned contact hours, office hours, emails, tweets, and the like.
Then there is the grading and departmental paperwork, the selection of
course materials, the writing of new course proposals, and so on.

In addition, there are formal and informal functions which take up
a great deal of time: Arts and sciences meetings, campus-wide meetings,
or a variety of formal and informal events. Your campus probably has
some or all of the following clubs and celebrations, all of them (potentially) a drag on your time: the African American Student Alliance
(AASA), the Essence of Fortitude, the Brother's Forum, the International
Student Organization (ISO), the Kanaka Hui Ohana, the Latino Student
Forum, the Rainbow Alliance, the Sister Circle, the United Hermanos;
the Black Alumni Dinner & Black History Month Awards; Cesar Chavez
Day Celebration; the Engendering Diversity and Community, Women,
Gender & Sexuality Studies Conference; the Diversity Forum on Grad-
uate Education; Asian American Heritage Month Speaker; the Annual
Bienvenida Celebration; Cinco de Mayo Carne Asada Celebration; the
African American Graduation Celebration; the Latino Student Graduation Celebration; the Pacific Islanders/Asian American Graduation Celebration. There are, too, research lectures by visiting poets or political
personalities, art exhibits, and open lectures which might interest you.

On top of all of that, you are likely required to participate in a
number of programs and mentoring relationships, put in place at many
universities to help you through the tenuring process. You are probably
meeting with other new hires as a group two or three times a year; you
probably have to attend library information sessions; your IT department
probably wants to discuss online security and issue you passwords; the
dean of your college has put you in touch with the people who handle

applications for course release or research funding. All goodwill measures to insure that you have adequate resources to meet the expectations of publication — and all time-consuming.

Then there are activities you may feel pressured to attend. For example, this very day I received a letter from Student Housing and Residential Education asking whether I would like to serve as a faculty fellow, a post in which I would have to hang out with students once a month or so at the dorms. While there is no pay involved, the letter stated that, at the conclusion of the academic year, my dean, departmental chair, and university president would receive a report regarding who participated in the program. An untenured faculty member doesn't need a black mark of any sort and would likely feel compelled to participate. (But I am now tenured and politely declined the offer.) In all likelihood, untenured members at other campuses are being asked to join similar clubs or activities in an effort to demonstrate school loyalty. Heap on top of all that the pressure of working in a new city, finding a place to live, balancing the checkbook, and, oh ya, your personal life — which may include raising children, feeding pets, spending time with your life partner, making friends, maintaining relationships with family members in various cities, etc. — and you can see quite quickly that time management is an all-important issue.

Being unable to write because you are tired and being unable to write because you are not committed to the task at hand are radically different issues. Time can always be managed better. It simply means sacrifice. At a recent Alpha Chi event, I met the mother of one student who told me that her daughter got up every morning at 3:00 A.M. to do her homework, then worked all day for a busy trucking company, then went to school in the evenings. We may applaud these sorts of Herculean efforts, but we think of them as worthy of praise simply because they are so exceptional. Not sleeping for five years — or however long your tenuring process is — is not a reasonable solution to the problem, nor is simply cutting back your attendance at the above or like events. After all, while you are certainly not required to attend all functions, you do need to attend some. Most new hires quickly establish a set number of committees and functions that they feel are necessary to maintain an adequate profile at their place of business. Virtually all new hires understand that teaching classes and teaching them well is a priority; research follows a close second; formal functions and committees are a distant third.

My advice: Cut down to a minimum the number of committees on

which you serve, turn off that TV, ignore on-campus lectures, stop peo-
ple-watching at Starbucks, grade papers rather than go to the movies —
then find a way to give yourself 2 to 3 hours a working day to write and
stick to it. Academia is a job, and you can no longer afford Romantic
notions of wafting from one Platonist symposium to another. Many academics will find this counsel difficult to follow because for years they
have thought of academia as an opportunity for personal growth. I share
in your disappointment. Speaking personally, I imagined that when I
became a professor I would continue taking classes and earning credits.
I had a heady daydream that my wall would be, by the end of my academic career, covered in doctoral degrees. The reality is that I spend
much of my time roaming from committee to department meeting while
answering emails, entering Facebook updates, reading instant texts and
tweets, preparing lectures, jumping through the paper-hoops of grant
applications and new course designations, and, when time allows, cor-
recting misplaced commas in my students' papers.

I now understand why my old professors looked old, worn out,
beleaguered. I once thought that they did nothing but talk about books.
I am now beginning to recognize that teaching is only a small part of the
job. Many hours of writing go into the creation of that seemingly effort-
less lecture, but still more hours are wasted in committees and campus
activities, and even more go into the creation of an article or a book. If
you need a mantra, here is one for you: The less committees, the less
commitments. If you have to sit on a committee or two, sit, smile and
think about what you need to write tomorrow. Remember, no one is
going to grant you tenure for taking great notes in a meeting.

Academic Writing Is Work, Not Art

The rhythm of your daily activities is now far different from when
you were a grad student. Then, you could devote a set time every day
to writing and had only a handful of duties to perform as a teaching
assistant. The change of pace can be jarring. A colleague of mine who
sailed though graduate school reported that the pressures incumbent
upon the job were too much for her. She eventually left her otherwise
desirable tenure-track post at New York University to work in the educational outreach division of a local theatre. It was not that she hated
the job or the campus life; it was that she knew she simply did not have

the time to publish and, knowing that her tenure was going to be denied, politely stepped away from the job, her dignity intact.

It's easy to say that life goes on. For my friend in New York, life did go on, and it went on just fine. But for some, failure is not an option. After all, you have so much riding on your writing—your tenure, your ability to repay student loans, your career. Your life hangs in the balance. What advice do I offer to cope with the stress? The prolific mystery writer Lawrence Block argues that self doubts are common to writers and suggests a series of self-affirmation mantras, including "I'm a terrific writer," "I have something to say," and—get this one!—"Rejection won't hurt me." What guff. It is all well and good to tell yourself that you are great, but to say that "Rejection won't hurt me" is, in the context of your tenuring process, professionally irresponsible. Sure, none of us wants to spend years on a book that might get rejected, and if you are an academic fighting for tenure, rejection will hurt *you*—thus my repeated advice that you need to think very carefully about what you are going to write and for whom. Moreover, it is perfectly natural to feel some trepidation every time you sit down to write.

I get all that.

But I believe we need to readjust our thinking. We have been told that writing—any writing, even academic writing—is a personal journey or an expression of personality. In *Passion and Politics: Academics Reflect on Writing for Publication*, authors Carnell, MacDonald, McCallum, and Scott interviewed a variety of academics and came to the conclusion that most of them referred "to writing as central to the identities that they willingly inhabit: writing is a part of the core that makes them who they are" (9). This form of writing, stylishly referred to as "I-Writing," champions the notion that writing is a form of self-expression and discovery. If you have personalized every paper you have submitted, then every acceptance or rejection is a referendum on your self-worth. After all, at the heart of "I-Writing" there remains an undeniable truth: We all want recognition for what we do. We would all like to write a paper or a book that will be lauded, that will place us at the very forefront of our discipline. And, of course, we want the praise of having accomplished something significant, something that will sit on a library shelf forever.

Yes, that would be nice, but that isn't the task at hand. The task is to get published in forms that are recognized and deemed acceptable by your tenuring committee. I say again, your job here is not to change the world or to feed your ego. Yes, it is true that it is easier to write about what interests you than what does not; it is also true that intellectually, as well as physically, you are what you eat. If you spend 10 hours a day reading about teen crime stats, then more than likely your conversations will be about that very topic; the conferences you write for and attend will be geared to your topic, and so forth. But a curious and clever mind can become interested in just about anything.

The truth is that academic writing *can be* a personal journey, perhaps even a therapy; it can be an expression of self—thus a true art form. It *can be*, but it doesn't *have to be*. When you set up a factory-like writing schedule for writing you are not only being practical about diversifying your opportunities, you are also reminding yourself that what you are doing and what you are producing is just work. Rather than seeing yourself as an artist, think of yourself as an artisan, conforming to the dictates of the market. You are making things for a publishing house. It's a publishing *house*. What does this house need? A coffee table, a new desk, maybe a few shelves for the wall. As was discussed in Chapter 1, you need to figure out what publishing houses want and what you need to do to craft objects for those houses. That does not mean that the maker has no sense of pride in the finished work. It means that you see writing as factory work, with various projects of various sizes in play.

Writer's Block Demystified

This sounds as sensible as someone saying "eat right, exercise, and you will lose weight." Yet there are many of us who struggle with our weight. Sometimes common sense is not enough. Even for those who have prioritized their teaching and research, even for those who have set aside time to write every day, even for those who write well, the pressure of having to write for publication can be trying. And that's when the writing goes well. What of those days, or, God forbid, weeks or months, when we don't seem to write well at all? We even have a word for it— writer's block. The condition has affected the brilliant and the not so brilliant. Yet the more one explores the phenomenon, the more it seems we are discussing disparate forms of writing problems that we can conveniently, perhaps even unthinkingly, dump into a one-fits-all term. In Ernest Hemingway's classic tale "The Snows of Kilimanjaro," the narrator discusses Harry, an author suffering from writer's block: "He had destroyed his talent by not using it, by betrayals of himself and what he believed in, by drinking so much that he blunted the edge of his perceptions, by laziness, by sloth, and by snobbery, by pride and by prejudice, by hook and by crook.... It was never what he had done, but always what he could do." Hemingway's feelings of inadequacy were clearly deep-seated. Years later, when publishing "The Dangerous Summer" in *Life Magazine,* he confessed that he felt "ashamed and sick" to have written so poorly (Baker, *Ernest Hemingway: A Life Story,* 554). Around this time, Hemingway was treated with electric shock for his severe depression, yet he still wrote voluminously; he just wasn't happy with what he wrote. So argues Raeburn in his biography *Fame Became of Him:* "The right words simply would not come.... When he could no longer write well enough to satisfy his own high standards, his fame, instead of sustaining him, mocked him, and the disparity between what he was to his public and what he was to himself may have been finally too great to bear" (John Raeburn, *Fame Became of Him,* 166). What we have here is not so much writer's block—*not so much the inability to write*—as an artist who is so critical that he is disgusted with himself.

Likewise, the novelist Tillie Olsen suffered from the sort of writer's block many writers would envy: "Absences of creativity where once it had been ... though the books may keep coming out year after year" (Tillie Olsen, *Silences,* 9). In Olsen's case, production was not the issue, nor was quality—what was produced was clearly good enough to convince her editor and publisher of its overall value. The issue for Olsen was one of personal esteem, of whether or not the writing met her own lofty goals. Olsen had created a stern taskmaster; to make sure that she was goaded to write still more, she told herself that what she had done thus far was worthless. She was, in effect, a "normal" workaholic—someone who does quite enough work but thinks she should do more or do it better.

Other forms of writer's block can be intellectual rather than emotional. Each of us may think that we possess a great idea only to discover in the research phase that we have it wrong or that the idea itself isn't complex enough to sustain us for a book. Yet, because we are more apt to discuss projects that are going well, we rarely mention those (many!) projects that we have worked on and then abandoned; we might even think that we are alone in having failed in our projects. But nothing could be further from the truth. Every writer will have a project that fails. Indeed, as Martin Amis has recently observed, for everyone who succeeds, some will "fail, some will lose. And we will find new ways of failing and losing" (*The Pregnant Widow*). That is true for even the finest of writers. Henry Miller, for example, spent a great deal of time on a biography on D.H. Lawrence only to conclude that what he had to say was half-baked: "The further I got into the book, the less I understood what I was doing. I found myself in a mass of contradictions. I found that I didn't really know who Lawrence was, I couldn't place him, I couldn't put my finger on him, I just couldn't cope with him after a while. I got completely bewildered.... So I abandoned the work" (http://www.parisreview.com/media/4597_MILLER_H.pdf). Here, the issue isn't Miller's ability to write — the words come out fine, page by page. But when reading the biography as a whole, Miller found a variety of intellectual observations that clashed with each other and which ultimately he could not resolve.

One wonders why he didn't turn his book into a series of essays, or, especially given his talents, into a novel. The point here is to get something from everything, even from failed work. After all, even the most seasoned academic gets rejection letters; but as you get better at academic writing, they come more and more infrequently. That's not to say that everything a veteran academic writes is publishable. Every academic has a drawer of junk essays, but even those junk essays may have some nugget of value. A failed book may have some sections that will make a good article; a failed article may have the makings of a good note.

Of course, we don't want to waste years writing a book only to end up with an article that might have been penned in a few months, but sometimes the brain needs to do what it needs to do. As we all know, failure is endemic to the writing process. Ben Jonson says that Shakespeare "never blotted a line," but we are not Shakespeare. Our essays, even our emails to friends, often go through laborious drafts, spell checks, second and third thoughts, elaborations, and reconsiderations; and, even after we complete the process and send our email off, we may still regret the way we phrased a line or two. Likewise, we can't expect everything that we write to be perfectly acceptable to all. Given time, we often learn from our writing mistakes; we learn that some of our ideas need more refinement, that our stylistics need further polish, that we haven't fully gauged the journal or the market when submitting our project. In short, we are always learning about the craft of academic writing, even when we fail to publish one of our writing projects.

Writing consistently, though not brilliantly, and deliberately halting production are not, most would agree, scenarios that spring to mind when one mentions writer's block. For most, writer's block conjures up something akin to Gustave Flaubert's confession to George Sands: "You don't know what it is to stay a whole day with your head in your hands trying to squeeze your unfortunate brain so as to find a word" (Sand and Flaubert, *George Sand-Gustave Flaubert Letters*, 29). Yes, we have all been there, struggling with various sentences, reordering paragraphs, wracking our brains for the right word, staring at the white word processor screen waiting for that magical sentence to emerge. We can all, I think, understand the anger and confusion of writer's block. Here we are, professional thinkers and writers, and our very skills seem to have impishly deserted us.

But beating yourself up leads to trouble — unproductive trouble. We may here keep in mind the Candle Problem, also known as the Candle Task, a test created in 1945 by Karl Duncker, a Gestalt psychologist. In Duncker's original experiment, two groups were given a complex task to complete. Duncker's study was conducted several times, often with new twists added. In one variation of the original experiment, one group was told that it would get a cash prize if it completed the task first; the other group was just told to complete the task. Surprisingly, the group offered no cash reward completed the task 25 percent faster than the motivated group. Reiterations of the experiment with other groups produced roughly the same result. What are we to take from this? We might say that money makes us dumber, and in a sense it does. By allowing money to be the focus, group members shut down the creative side of their minds to focus on the reward rather than the task. I suggest that the fear of losing tenure and, quite possibly, the prize of tenure itself may be slowing the cognitive skills of many academic writers.

We may take heart in knowing that writer's block is, at worst, a condition, not a disease or an infection. It's not like cancer or hepatitis or influenza. It isn't communicable. The American Psychiatric Association's *Diagnostic and Statistical Manual of Mental Disorders* (1995) ignores writer's block; the Website "Phobia Dictionary" does not cite the condition. After all, it's not like we have permanently lost the ability to spell, to conjugate verbs, or to put pen to paper or finger to typewriter. The mechanical ability to write is rarely lost. Indeed, all of the writers cited above continued to write; often they wrote about their inability to write!

Don't Wait for Inspiration

We may further keep in mind that academic writing, unlike, say, penning a novel, does not have to be overly creative. Most of us, especially in the humanities, understand that much of our work has a mechanical component. Saint Augustine, in his introduction to *De Viris Illustribus* (*On Illustrious Men*), laid down the artistic rules of scholarship. In his view, the point of scholarly reading and writing was to locate and to record passages in one book that were of particular interest to the scholar, then to reorder those passages in a new sequence. This reordering would create an original chain of argument. In short, Saint Augustine was exhorting his reader to reorder knowledge according to personal interests. Criticism does exactly the same thing, although instead of creating a new narrative out of one work, it does so by linking and reordering the notes taken from many works. This is not quite fully creative work in that it relies upon the examination of existing documents, novels, stories, myths, etc., but it is *re-creative* work.

Yes, many aspects of criticism — for example, reading and taking notes, restating essential ideas, or tracing essential themes — can be handled mechanically. Yet few who have written an essay would argue that there is no inspirational side to critical engagement. I have no doubt that all of us have begun writing an essay, come upon a problem in the argument or in the structural presentment of the idea, and been stymied. Sometimes the solution comes when one is doing something mundane like vacuuming or walking the dog. Sometimes the solution comes in the middle of the night. Sometimes we happen upon just the right passage in an old book, one seemingly designed for our writing purpose. Sometimes writing is like magic: It just happens. When I was an undergraduate in Canada I read Colin Wilson's *The Occult*. Thirty or so years on from my first reading, I still vividly recall a section wherein he discussed his writing of the book. When he hit a wall on one particular narrative section, he rose from his desk and approached his bookshelf, grabbed one book, and inadvertently knocked over another book, which magically opened to a page that gave him exactly what he needed to continue writing. I'll bet that each of us has had a similar experience, as if some unseen hand were guiding us, willing us to write our essay. But those incidents are a rare gift.

More likely, writing is difficult and tiring. And in almost all instances our theses are intellectual puzzles, not artistic conceptions. More often than not, writing is about work. It is about making. Sometimes it is about failure. But it should never be about being afraid to work. After all, when everything is said and done, writing is just an occupation. It does not have to be your life story. That is not to say that you don't have a great deal riding on the acceptance of your research, but your work does not need to be, *per se,* autobiographical. The sooner you realize this critical distinction, the sooner you will see that publication is often a mechanical process. As discussed in Chapter 1, it begins with conferences, wherein you float new ideas; it continues with research, some of which you can turn into book reviews; it includes turning deleted passages from articles into publishable notes; it culminates in the targeting of a press or a journal, wherein your academic wares can be displayed. And even as you bring those wares to market, you should be turning your attention to yet other projects still in need of refinement and assembly.

The approach I am advocating may take the fear out of your writing, and that is certainly my intent. But it may also take some of the fun out of your writing. After all, we tend to be more engaged in projects that interest us personally. Yet there are many aspects of our academic careers that don't particularly thrill us, that we find boring or demeaning — in my case, committee work comes to mind — but we do it as part of our professional responsibilities. It is sensible to practice the norms of your vocation matter-of-factly and professionally. The method advocated — writing 1,000 words a day, varying and rotating through projects to avoid emotional attachment — does not preclude the notion that the maker has no sense of pride in the finished work. I'll bet that many factory workers take a great deal of pride in their work, but then go about their day. And the very next day they will fashion yet another object and so on and so on. Just so, we as academic authors should write on whatever we think can be used for our professional benefit in a timely manner.

Ten Things You Need to Know

1. By targeting publishers, you can expect more acceptances or useful comments for revision.
2. Readers' reports are often negative, but they are rarely personal.
3. A reader may misread, but there is rarely anything you can do about it.

4. If you have a "split decision"—i.e., one positive and one negative report—the editor may ask you to respond.
5. Minimize distracting on-campus activities and committee work.
6. Write the same amount 5 days a week, no matter how much or how little time it takes.
7. Forget the outline—writing is organic.
8. Writer's block is not a medical condition.
9. Rotate projects—it will help create a sense of detachment.
10. Writing is not art—it is work.

CHAPTER 4

Contracts, Cash, and Other Queries

I hope that you will agree that I have been straightforward and clear with you, my readers. Certainly, I have tried to be. Over the course of writing this book, I have presented bits and pieces of its contents to various groups of struggling, young academics, many of whom are working to create a portfolio of publication for tenure. I have noted that questions raised in discussion often center on the same topics. I have, in this chapter, picked the most representative of those concerns and my responses to them.

Question 1: Realistically, what are my odds of getting a book deal?

Not all manuscripts can be published, and many good ones will not be. That is a fact. Just how lucky do you have to be to get a book published at an academic press? Well, that would depend on the press' finances, and what else has been submitted that year. It's not just the number of books a press publishes that must worry you. For example, let's say you wrote a great book about Shakespeare but the press usually only publishes 5 books on Shakespeare a year. If they already have 6 really good Shakespeare projects signed up, it is unlikely that your book will be published with this press, no matter the book's genius. That means that your brilliant book on Shakespeare may be turned down but a rather mediocre book on the politics of East Timor may be accepted. Given these factors that you cannot control, you want to have a strong

119

relationship with your editor and as clear a query letter as you can possibly craft.

So, all else being even, just what are your chances of success? Let's begin by looking at the number of presses. From 1920 to 1970, new university presses opened at a rate of about one a year. But between 1970 and 1974, only ten more new presses were founded, and only five more were started between 1975 and 2000. A decade later, the publication landscape is pretty much unchanged. There remain about 70 active university presses, though the number of titles published by each press varies widely. Some may print no more than 5 or fewer titles per year. Others, like the University of Chicago, maintain an enormous back catalogue. In 1998, the University of Chicago Press published 46 journals and 272 books in addition to the 4,600 titles it already had in print. More typical is the University of Colorado Press, which published 22 books in 2008.

So there seem to be thousands of books published a year, but most of those are back catalogue stock. How many new books are published a year? In 1989, Paul Parsons did the math. While 1989 is some time ago, we can assume that the numbers have not improved. His findings are as follows: American university presses generally receive around 32,500 inquiries. They will generally ask to see the finished manuscript of about 10 percent of these letters of inquiry; of the 3,200 or so manuscripts examined, about 600 will be published. So your odds of getting your book to press are about 2 percent (Paul Parsons, *Getting Published*, 54). However, if you have read Chapter 3, you know that it is my contention that a huge number of submissions are mailed to the wrong sort of presses and/or are ineptly presented. So, if you follow my advice, you should have a far greater chance of success. As you'll read in the next chapter, I have never written a book or edition that has not been published. I have, to be fully forthcoming, written more than a few papers that were duds, but I knew they were duds and never submitted them for review.

Question 2: There are plenty of bad books out there. But I have a good book. Why are my chances of publishing so poor?

Again, it's a numbers game. A university press generally puts out the same amount of material year after year and usually publishes in the same sorts of product lines. This means that a press that prints books on Shakespeare one year is likely to do the same the year after. Likewise, unless the acquisitions editor is starting a new field, a press that has never published on Native Americans is unlikely to do so. (This, by the way, is not a new phenomenon, nor is it limited to the humanities. In 1967, Carroll G. Bowen, the former director of MIT's press, commented, "We can't publish broadly in biology, for example. We're interested specifically in microbiology, in biophysics, and in biochemistry" [Gene R. Hawes, *To Advance Knowledge*, 48].) To continue that logic still further, a university press that publishes narrow (i.e., scholarly) studies of Shakespeare is also unlikely to publish a popular or entry-level book on Shakespeare, even if it is likely to make money. In the words of one editor, "When I run into an author with a book that has commercial possibilities, I tell him so, and I have done this many times" (William B. Harvey, former director of New York University Press, in Gene R. Hawes, *To Advance Knowledge*, 19).

Question 3: Why are academic press runs so low and prices so high?

Blame Thor Power Tools. Really! Until 1975, university presses generally stayed afloat through revenues generated by a "balanced portfolio" approach to publishing — a mix of volatile but potentially lucrative stocks with some less sexy corporates and stable, low-risk government bonds:

Class 1. Books of Limited Interest: Sales ranging from 75 to 300 books over the first 4 or 5 years.
Class 2. Books of Limited Interest: Sales of 300 to 1,500 copes over the first 4 or 5 years.
Class 3. Borderline Books (books with potential crossover mass-market appeal): Sales of 1,500 to 3,000 copes over the first 2 or 3 years.
Class 4. Semi-Popular Books: Sales of 3,000 to 10,000 over the first 2 or 3 years. (Chester Kerr, *A Report on American University Presses*, 105–106.)

The logic for this approach was outlined in Roger Shugg's *The Two Worlds of University Publishing* (University of Kansas, 1967), in which he noted that a stable, though slow-selling, backlist — common among older presses — was the defining feature "that makes a press a growing concern. A press with a thousand or more books on its backlist can naturally do a bigger volume of business and go much farther toward supporting itself every year than can the smaller press that is still struggling to accumulate backlist resources" (Roger Shugg, *The Two Worlds of University Publishing*, 19–20).

The difficulty with the approach was the warehousing of this backlist, but those costs were "written off as a loss in a certain amount of years ... [for] the books that remained unsold" (19). So a large backlist allowed presses to have stable sales and thus cash flow, and the dead back catalogue was written off or depreciated on a year-by-year basis against the profits shown by popular titles. The most obvious example of this approach was the University of Chicago's canonical *Chicago Manual of Style*, now in its fourteenth edition. The book was and remains a big money generator for the press, which continues to use its profits to fund other academically useful but economically challenging projects. Nonetheless, "even large and well-established presses like those at Harvard and Yale are frank to admit that they could not make ends meet without the benefit of their endowments and subsidies," according to Roger Shugg's *The Two Worlds of University Publishing*, 20 (on this point see also the findings of Chester Kerr's 1949 report in *The American University as Publisher*, 14–16).

As precarious as that older model was, it died a swift death not because the press was losing too much money but because the government found a new way to tax publishers. Oddly, the case that changed the publishing industry had nothing to do with publishing. In fact, it was a court case involving a tool company. No joke! Here's what happened. Thor Power Tools had an accounting trick. You see, the IRS, always interested in getting as much money as it can from American business, has a rule by which it charges companies for unsold goods. Let's say you have 100 hammers and they cost you a buck a piece (never mind what you sell them for — their base value is, for the purposes of this explanation, a buck). That means you have $100 worth of hammers in your inventory. That's an asset. If, for example, you were to sell your business, you'd count the $100 worth of hammers as part of the value of the business. If you had a million hammers, then your business would be worth 1 million bucks. So the IRS charges you a percentage based on the value of your hammers. So far so good. But Thor Power Tools argued that if its tools remained in stock, that was because no one wanted them and, thus, they were not worth a buck. So they tried to depreciate the value of their inventory. In other words, Thor Power Tools was saying that it wanted to keep its valuable stock but at the same time write down the value. The IRS argued that Thor was being silly. After all, why store what was worthless? Why not just throw the tools away? The Supreme Court agreed with the IRS: unless Thor Tools sold its stock at a loss, it had to pay tax on the value of the unsold items sitting in its warehouse.

Now, what does all this have to do with academic publishing? Quite a bit. In the late 1960s, all universities had warehouses and shipping facilities wherein they stored book inventories worth, in some cases, several million dollars (Gene R. Hawes, *To Advance Knowledge*, 86). But the Supreme Court's ruling now made the warehousing of intellectual property a taxable asset. The immediate result was that book publishers, who had been warehousing thousands of unsold books but writing down their value, suddenly found themselves facing whopping tax bills. As a result, academic publishers could no longer afford to carry large inventories. The mixed selling approach outlined above, in which presses counted on both fast and slow sellers, was scrapped. University presses now have low print runs, often about 300 to 500 copies per book, and thus don't carry massive inventory. At the end of the year, even these slow sellers are cleared away. That's why you find those liquidation bookshops with brand new books for a buck. The publishers need to unload their old inventory on an annual basis, and do so, often at a loss, to offset the profits that they have made on books that they have sold at full price. (The rise of flash publishing, the printing of books only after they have been ordered — preselling — is also a result of this 1979 Supreme Court ruling.)

The rise of e-publishing has obviously complicated this model; for more on that, see Chapter 1. For the here and now, to ensure survival, academic presses have added fail-safes: (a) high costs and (b) vanity-press–style subventions. A 1960 study, *Production and Manufacturing Problems of American University Presses* (Richard G. Underwood), noted that its books regularly sold for $4 to $5. Factoring for inflation, the price in today's money would be $29.41 to $36.76 (Federal Reserve Calculator found at http://www.minneapolisfed.org/index.cfm). Yet the average university press book today retails for about $100 to $120.

Question 4: If the profit margin on academic books is high, may I infer that academic presses, accounting tricks to the contrary, make money?

Sadly, not only do most university presses not make money, they have been losing for a very long time. The obvious issue is the cost of manufacturing a book, which is then priced beyond the means of the consumer.

The basic question a commercial press asks itself is, "Will it sell?" However, a scholarly press may not ask that same question for all of its books. For one, subventions by the scholar or by the scholar's university may make profit a moot point. Second, the press may and likely does have its own guaranteed sales in the form of libraries that regularly buy up everything on offer by that press. Still, those sales may not be enough to cover costs. In the recent *Handbook for Academic Authors* (2002), Beth Luey calculates that the average academic book has a production cost of anywhere from $27,000 to $31,000 (252). Thus, if the publisher were to print 1,000 books, every single one would have to be sold for $27 to $31 just to break even. If only 500 copies were printed — which is, in my experience, the likely press run — then all the copies would have to sell at a price of $54 to $62. Consider, however, that it is unlikely that the press will sell all the books for the full price. Most academic books will find their way to remainder tables in a variety of book outlets. Thus, out of a print of about 500 books, the press probably expects to sell about half that number and then dump the rest for cost or at a slight loss. This explains why academic books, which cost about $30 to make, must sell for about $120. Selling about 250 books for double their actual production cost is the only way the presses can break even (Beth Luey, *Handbook for Academic Authors*, 254–255).

Obviously, this is a failed business model. As Chester Kerr, former director of Yale University Press, puts it, "We publish the smallest editions at the greatest cost, and on these we place the highest prices, and then we try to market them to people who can least afford them. This is madness" (Chester Kerr interviewed in Gene R. Hawes, *To Advance Knowledge*, 5). Things today are a bit better than they were. In the 1960s, for example, it was common for the wives of university professors to work for free at university presses as copy editors (Gene R. Hawes, *To Advance Knowledge*, 6). I know of no press that engages in that practice today. Still, there can be no doubt that most presses operate with little room for error. And that is all the more surprising, given the obvious advantages university presses have. Many university presses, particularly those with buildings on their parent campuses, likely get free office space; they probably have access to student workers or interns who are willing to work solely for the experience (thus, no payroll); their Websites may be serviced by the university's IT department and run on the university's server;

their phone, electricity, heating, mail service, etc. are also likely funded in part or in full by the university. Further, press fund-raisers are usually on the university's dime.

So university presses lose a bit of money, which is usually offset by the university. So what's in it for the university itself? Mostly prestige and a bit of marketing. David G. Brown, in his book *The Mobile Professors* (1967), furnished statistical documentation in support of the notion that universities derive prestige from the reputation of their faculties and, in turn, the reputation of the faculty depends upon academic publication (101–102). In short, both parent institution and press need each other. We fully recognize that any item with Harvard's name attached to it has instant credibility. In return, Harvard University Press acts as an intellectual billboard for the university.

Question 5: If universities subsidize academic presses, why do I need to pay a subvention?

Subventions are part of the new reality of academic publishing. Many presses now charge the author for publication, a fairly new phenomenon, and one that flies in the face of the original intentions of academic publishing, as described by W. McNeil Lowry, director of the Ford Foundation, a nonprofit that often subsidizes academic publishers. In 2008, for example, this foundation gave Columbia University $149,100 to help lower publishing costs. The justification for these foundation grants is based on the longstanding belief that "scholars in their early teaching careers should feel that their work can be made available in durable form, without having to finance it themselves. Unless they have some hope of this, the habits of careful research and writing learned in graduate school may be forgotten" (Gene R. Hawes, *To Advance Knowledge*, 14). Foundation subventions may aid some presses, but, overall, there just isn't enough money to go around. It is now up to the author — or, where applicable, the author's university — to help pay for publication costs. These costs may cover rights and reproduction fees for cover images or, color printing, for high-quality paper, or for proofreading and indexing services.

Today, there are still other, hidden forms of subvention. While I did not have to pay for paper and publishing costs, I have always been asked to cover the publishing costs of the various images included in my books and even the rights to the images on their covers. This makes some sense. Presses usually use a higher-quality paper for pictures and have to use a still higher-bond paper for color reproduction. If your book has photos, a press charge is likely. In addition, if your images come from a research library, the library itself may demand a fee before allowing the images to be reproduced. Again, it is the norm in academic publishing that the author carries these costs. On average, a library will charge about $100 per color image, and the press will charge you about the same for color printing. A book with 10 images, therefore, will run you about $2,000.

For newer faculty, many of whom are still paying off student loans, this news is discouraging. But consider the bigger picture: Some universities give substantial pay raises for publishing a book, so your $2,000 investment is likely to be recouped within a few months of publication. Further, the cost is one time only, but the raise lasts forever. As the years pass, that $2,000 will seem cheap. Better yet, many universities have funds for publication and printing costs; applying for these funds may mean that a large portion or even all of your costs will be covered by your employer. Lastly, an academic book with a reputable academic press virtually guarantees that you will meet your publication goal for tenure.

Some may wonder whether a subvention of any sort turns the publication into something akin to a vanity press book. After all, if both vanity presses and academic presses are now demanding ready cash for publication, then what's the difference? Quite a bit. A university press vets your work with experts in the field, provides readers' reports on ways to improve your manuscript for publication, promotes your book through catalogues, and likely places your completed work on display at regional, national, and even international conferences. A vanity press is unlikely to do any of these things.

Question 6: Why are so many university presses dedicated to highbrow jargon yet also publish books concerning everyday regional issues?

This goes back to whether the university press can meet its financial obligations. Let's give the presses the benefit of the doubt and assume that their costs, even with these various subsidies and subventions, are rising and that in a good year they break even. What can we learn from these changes and what does it mean when we think of publishable ideas?

To begin with, we might contemplate the short run of these books and their pricing, both of which suggest that they are marketed specifically for university libraries. Not many regular Joes or even academics have the funds to shell out $100 for a book. Given that these books are aimed towards libraries and geared for specialists, there is no longer an adequate need to use everyday language. This is a fairly new development and one, I think, that links to the Thor case. Prior to 1975, when academic books were aimed primarily at a wide literary audience, the language of a given specialization had to be tempered to the literary norms of the population at large. But with small press runs and books marketed specifically to academic libraries, specialists found themselves writing not for the dilettante but for the like-minded professional: "College instructors have become less and less preoccupied with educating young people and more and more preoccupied with educating one another by doing scholarly research which advances their discipline" (Christopher Jencks and David Riesman, *The Academic Revolution*, 13).

Secondly, many academic presses are now interested in regional issues (i.e., university presses in Texas seek and publish books on Texas history, culture, and geography, etc.). As such, university presses have developed into important disseminators and preservers of local culture; they act as buffers against encroaching urban homogenization. And, since large commercial presses don't normally deal in regional offerings, university presses enjoy a near monopoly in such offerings. Regional publishing has sometimes been dismissed because it has a provincial flavor to it (i.e.,—and this is a purely fictitious title—*Thirty Years on the Ponderosa: Reminiscences of a Texas Cowpoke*). But as Frank Wardlaw, director of the University of Texas Press in the 1960s, argued, "It is a narrow view of scholarship indeed which holds that the Medici banks of Florence are legitimate subjects of scholarly inquiry but that the operation of a big cattle ranch in the Texas panhandle is not" (Shugg, *The Two Worlds of University Publishing*, 11). Putting aside cattle brands, we may, I think, admit that it is logical for a press in, say, Detroit to publish a work on the history of the automotive industry. We might, however, raise an eyebrow if the same press were to publish on the caste system imposed by Genghis Khan when he conquered India.

Just as importantly, a university press' regional books can be surprisingly lucrative. Presses from the South, Midwest, and West—Louisiana State University Press, University of Texas Press, University of Nebraska Press, Oklahoma University Press, University of Arizona Press, and University of New Mexico Press are examples — often expand past the purely scholarly and may also include memoirs, celebrations of cultural heritage (including, for example, cookbooks), or more weighty analyses of immediate and local social and political issues. The acquisitions editors for these presses may also publish fairly affordable fiction. On far rarer occasions, a university press may also publish a regional author but release the book nationally in hopes of larger profits. For example, the University of Nebraska Press recently issued a series of paperbacks anthologizing the writings of the Texas writer Robert E. Howard, best known for his sword-wielding hero, Conan the Barbarian. The books retailed for less than 10 bucks each and, likely, made the press a nice sum of money.

Question 7: How do you know which press is interested in a given topic?

Simple! Every department gets catalogues from the major university presses, and you would do well to study them carefully. For example, on the day I typed this paragraph, the new catalogue for Duke University Press arrived. I noted that the press has a significant number of titles dedicated to cultural studies, but I also noticed that Duke is expanding its interests. According to the 2010 catalogue, there is one book published under the category "Gay and Lesbian Studies." There are two new titles published under "Political Theory" and one book each published under "Urban Studies" and "Theater." If Duke is interested in publishing one political theory title, and has already created a subject heading for it, then it is logical to conclude that Duke will now accept like studies to fill out or to expand that new product line. Thus, anyone writing on political theory, urban studies, or theater would probably do well to put together a proposal for Duke.

Flipping through other recent catalogues, it is equally clear that University of Notre Dame Press does not publish on psychology; Georgetown does not publish on drama; Syracuse does not publish studies of ancient history; Hawaii Press is not interested in Latin American Studies; Texas Tech shuns education and the social sciences (for more on likes and dislikes, see Paul Parsons, *Getting Published*, 33). Don't assume that a press will create a new product line because your book is so brilliant. If Cambridge University Press doesn't publish on the history of the American car wheel, don't think you're going to convince them otherwise. You are not.

Question 8: Will e-publishing revolutionize the economics of the industry?

Probably not. Since the costs of the book have far more to do with the editorial side of production — i.e., the considerable amount of time the industry dedicates to reading, proofing, editing, and formatting the text for print — there is no reason to assume that e-publishing will significantly lower the overall cost of book production.

I have heard people say that *if* e-publishing is one day adopted as the one and only format across the industry, profits will flow like wine at a Hollywood wedding. But that is merely hypothetical. The fact is, we are not yet there — and we may never be. To begin with, there are a variety of competing platforms. Amazon's Kindle uses "MobiPocket"; Barnes & Noble's e-reader, the Nook, along with various devices offered by Sony and Apple, use something called "Epub"; other digital readers use "PDF." Assuming that there is an e-war of one sort or another and one winner emerges, then publishers might be more inclined to offer their academic titles on the winning e-platform. But we are a long way off from that day. As it stands right now, presses that e-publish usually do not e-publish in more than one or two of these formats, a deliberate strategy which suggests that reformatting for e-readers is expensive and time-consuming.

Worse yet, readers have to make a choice between these formats. Kindle buyers are stuck with MobiPocket texts and can't use Epub. The same limitations are faced by Barnes & Noble, Sony, and Apple users, who can't used Kindle-ready files. (Amazon now offers an app that makes reading MobiPocket files on Apple products possible. So far as I can tell, MobiPocket files still don't work on Sony or Barnes & Noble devices, and Amazon's rivals have yet to offer an app which renders their Epub files Kindle-ready. Full transferability between all platforms may be coming, but when that will happen remains a key unanswerable.)

There is, too, the price of these e-reader devices to consider. Amazon's Kindle, the most popular of the e-readers, goes for $79; a higher-end Wi-Fi-ready device is available for about $40 more. While prices remain in flux, unless your buyer is an avid reader, price-wise these devices make little sense. While Amazon advertises that its e-versions go for just under ten bucks, academic fare, if available at all, goes for closer to $15. So you could buy the e-version of Stephen Greenblatt's *Hamlet in Purgatory* for around $15 or buy it used from Amazon for about $15 or buy it new for about $21. However, Greenblatt's seminal work, *Renaissance Self-Fashioning*, is not available to Kindle users at any price. The availability of academic titles might improve, but, as of this writing, at least so far as English literary criticism goes, expensive university press Kindle-ready material is more of an intellectual debate than it is an economic reality. (We should further note that e-publishing is changing the way we as authors negotiate with presses. See Question 15, below, on the differing pay scale for traditional and e-related sales.) There are still other factors working against an academic e-publishing revolution. Paper and ink is cheap. Maintaining and constantly upgrading banks of servers is costly; electricity is costly; air-conditioning for those servers is costly. So, too, are the salaries of the software and hardware specialists now added to the payroll to service the e-side of the publishing business.

One area in which e-books win hands down is the cost involved in pre-binding or rebinding. As I am sure you have observed, libraries often send out softcover books and even journals to be hardbound. Pre-binding or rebinding has its costs. The following figures are based upon Marcia I. Canibe's 1988 study. I have updated the numbers by way of the United States' Federal Reserve Inflation calculator:

1. A book up to and including 8 inches in height costs $8.17 to bind.
2. Over 8 inches and up to and including 10 inches in height costs $9.47 per book.
3. Over 10 inches and up to and including 12 inches in height costs $11.14 per book.
4. Over 12 inches and up to and including 14 inches in height costs $13.00.
5. Over 14 inches and up to and including 16 inches in height costs $16.71.
6. Books over 16 inches in height cost $20.43 per binding.
   (Marcia I. Canibe, "Economics of library binding," 15)

Given these high prices, we can assume that there is more than simply aesthetics — making the books look pretty on the shelves — going on here. A national survey by the American Library Association (ALA) found that the average softcover book might last only 20 to 25 circulations, "but books prebound or rebound according to the LBI standard will last at least 100 circulations" (Marcia I. Canibe, "Economics of library binding," 1). However, the shelf life of a book also depends upon the quality of the original binding.

The following details are based upon an inspection of a variety of books in my own library. I have noticed that most books published in England, whether softcover or hardcover, are perfect-bound. That is to say that the pages are glued. The British seem to be expert at this, and the size of the book doesn't affect the quality of the binding. However, American libraries generally rip the soft covers off and rebind them as hard covers. The removal of the soft cover generally weakens the spine, so rebound softcover books from the UK have a limited shelf life. In the States, hardcover books are still stitched and bound in signatures and quires, the same system of binding used in the Renaissance. This system works well unless a book is over about 400 pages. After that seemingly magic mark, I have noticed that the book's binding becomes weak, and the hardcover spine of the book eventually peels off. That being said, most new academic books do not run to 400 or more pages. Most run to about 200 pages, making some of the spine wear and tear of hardcovers a moot point. (On why 200 pages is now the norm, see the end of this chapter.) In any case, the salient point here is that e-books don't have any limitations on length and will save academic libraries the costs of rebinding. So we can say that, although there are some savings to be had in switching over to an electronic format, most of the savings occur in the afterlife of the book — i.e., after the book has been sold to a library.

Question 9: Is building a relationship with your editor *that* important?

Absolutely! Keep in mind that university presses generally pay little or no royalties; you will never be able to acquire an agent whose job it is to secure you a publisher. You are on your own here. Consequently, your editor is your agent. It is up to you to cultivate that relationship, to make your editor feel as comfortable with you as possible, and to assure your editor that your submitted project is a good one. Remember, that pile of manuscripts on the editor's desk will, for the most part, be dismissed as so much flotsam and jetsam. But when the editor sees your name attached to a project, you want the editor to have every confidence that what is on offer is worth a careful look.

To that end, you should find the name of the editor in the specific field for which you are writing. You might want to call the editor and introduce yourself. A good relationship with an editor during the various phases of one book deal will put you in good stead for your next. You have a relationship and a bond between you. Nurture it. Editors need writers and writers need editors, but there are tens of thousands of academics and only a handful of editors. We're not dealing with a relationship of equals here. You want to be polite, helpful, friendly, honest, enthusiastic or, if necessary, deferential, and, above all, brief. Remember, your typical editor is overworked and underpaid. Their annual salary is somewhere between $20,000 and $40,000. Usually, the editor has no more than a B.A. in a given discipline. Yet this poor drudge wields enormous power and regularly receives groveling letters from otherwise high-powered and well-paid academics all over the world.

We should also be clear about what your search editor does not do. Search (or acquisitions) editors are not press editors. They don't offer suggestions for improvements; they don't circle typos, correct grammar, double-check facts, or reformat the manuscript for publication. They serve as gatekeepers for the press in the sense that (a) they are the first to see all proposals and, therefore, the first to reject projects, and (b) they create and maintain the specialties of the presses.

OK, but how does a search editor search? On rare occasions, the editor may reach out to an academic for a project, although this practice is disappearing. Roger W. Shugg, a former director of Chicago University Press, once boasted, "We solicit aggressively and widely. We have five men who are house editors, and that's all they do" (Gene R. Hawes, *To Advance Knowledge*, 10). Today, it is far more likely the a university press' acquisitions editor finds projects by combing through voluminous letters of inquiry, which detail projects that might be of interest to the editor and press — thus the importance of the query letter.

In Chapter 1, I outlined some of the dos and don'ts of query letter writing. I want here to add some more thoughts on the subject. Your query letter to the publisher is the first glimpse your publisher will have of your materials. Even if it is just passing through the hand of a clerical worker, you need to be specific about what kind of project you are offering and why it fits that specific publisher. Citing the name of the editor who handles your type of project is vital. Other tips:

1. Don't make your query letter too long. Most of the information covering your project will be in the proposal itself.

2. On the other hand, don't make it too short. You need to entice the editor to move on to the proposal.

3. Don't insult other listings already published by the press: "Your catalogue of books has some shortcomings my own project will address or mend."

4. Don't deprecate: "I would be honored to receive your opinion on the following project."

5. Don't apologize or aggrandize: "I realize you must receive hundreds of project proposals. Let me outline why I think mine is a good fit for your prestigious publishing house."

So what should your query letter do? Essentially, it must name the editor, establish the subject, point out why that particular book would be a good fit, point out distinctive features, and recite your other accomplishments. (I have provided examples in the Appendix.) One last word of advice: You should check the press' Website and follow any special instructions concerning formatting. For example, does the press use only one type of footnoting? Does the press prefer MLA or *Chicago Manual of Style* for citation forms? And so on.

There is yet another reason to build a good relationship with your editor: your external readers. You see, your editor will be sending your manuscript out to be read by an expert. The selection of the expert is not at all straightforward. To begin with, let's remember that the editor probably does not have an advanced degree or specific knowledge beyond baseline interest in the proposal you have submitted. If the editor isn't an expert in that small subfield you are writing on, how is that same editor to select a good reader? Logic dictates that the editor will go with someone trustworthy, either a famous person in the field or someone that the press already has a relationship with or both. Note, however, that the reader may know little or nothing about your specific topic. To return to my own first book, I can safely say that there was but one expert in Shakespeare forgeries, Samuel Schoenbaum, who could rival me in knowledge of the Ireland forgeries. But he was dying of cancer at the time I was penning my dissertation, so another reader was brought in.

Continuing on the subject of external readers, there is an unwritten rule I have discovered, and that rule is that the press will not recruit a colleague from the author's own department to write a report. (I suppose this is due to personality-driven issues and internal departmental politics; you would not want a colleague who has it in for you selected as your "objective" reader.) In the case of *Reforging Shakespeare*, I met one of my readers, who then revealed herself—ten years after the fact. Who she is really isn't important to this narrative, though I am eternally grateful for her kind and generous report. The point here is that the reports are anonymous, but once the book is accepted readers will know who you are and may reveal themselves any time they feel like doing so. In my own case, I don't think there was any harm in the reader revealing herself, but I can tell you that—now that I am a reader on a variety of journals, none of which demand blind submission—were I to receive a manuscript from her, I'd be more likely to accept her work for publication. I'm not suggesting that readers do their reports looking for a favor years down the line, but it is human nature to be kind to those who have been kind to you.

You can't, of course, handpick your readers, but if you have a good relationship with your editor, you might pick up the phone and point out that one of the reasons your book will be an exciting addition to the field is that the topic is a contentious one: some critics, such as Professors A, B, C, will like the approach, while others, like Professors X, Y, Z, will not. What you are doing is notifying the editor that it is essential that some care be taken in the selection of readers. In some cases, the over-worked editor will simply ask you to draw up a list of potential readers. Obviously, this must be done with some delicacy. You don't want to pick someone who has already looked at the manuscript, nor do you want to pick someone who is unfamiliar with the topic. When asked for a few names, what I do usually is draw up a list of potentially hostile readers and outline why I think this small group might react with hostility to the project. Editors are usually grateful for your input. No one wants to waste time here and no one, whether editor or author, likes reading harsh reviews. I'd even venture to say that the writers of those harsh reviews don't like writing them very much.

Question 10: Is there a best time of year or season to submit a manuscript?

Surprisingly, the answer is "Yes"! Most academics disappear over the summer months, either spending time on vacation or going to some research library to complete their own work. If you submit in the late spring or early summer, the press will have a difficult time finding two adequately qualified readers who are free and interested in your project.

Christmas break presents another problem. The editor is usually anxious to get away and might not give your project the focus it deserves. Coming back from break, the same editor is doubtless faced with a mountain of unopened mail, email messages, and various tasks. Therefore, the best time to submit a manuscript, I feel, is August. The editor is probably looking for new projects for the next year, and they have about a month to draw up a list of readers, who are, by September, returning to their campuses refreshed and relaxed.

Question 11: Does it matter where you teach or if you teach?

Again, yes! Academic presses represent the university and, within the sphere of academia itself, work as a publicity agent for both author and institution. Just as you are more likely to be impressed by an author whose book is published by Oxford or Cambridge, so, too, the editor receiving a book proposal, is more likely to give credence to a query letter that bears the Cambridge, Oxford, Stanford, or Harvard seal. This is not to say that there aren't good presses besides Oxford or Cambridge or that there isn't a wealth of fine academic writing outside of those ivoriest of ivory towers — it is merely to acknowledge the reality of prestige in the academic marketplace. Unfortunately, it also follows that private scholars carry no rank, have no research budgets, receive no salary for teaching or research, and are considered by many to be intellectual amateurs.

Question 12: Do academic presses prefer to publish their own scholars, i.e., does Oxford University Press prefer to publish Oxford's own faculty?

No! Were university presses interested merely in publishing their own, they would be no more than vanity presses promoting the academic production of their faculty. By publishing the work of academics from all over the world, the academic press acknowledges that learning goes on everywhere. Knowledge is now fragmentary; no academic, no matter the high quality of the home institution, can know or teach all there is to know or teach.

On a related note, the libraries buying academic books have also made a conscious decision to acquire your book for a specific purpose — not as part of its collection, but as an extension of the classroom. Does this mean that you should worry that your book is too specific, that you should, in effect, write introductory texts for undergraduate students? Absolutely not. For one, the university press is not really banking on your book having massive sales. Actually, it probably expects the opposite and is charging accordingly. Second, university presses are not interested in publishing introductory texts — otherwise known as textbooks. Since academic presses are reflections of their home institutions, they quite naturally want to publish important, groundbreaking studies. Textbooks rarely have anything but standardized information and many tenuring committees are not impressed by them. Many tenuring committees reject textbooks outright, on the grounds that they are not scholarly — i.e., textbooks summarize known research, rather than push the boundaries of the field. (We may here note that in this regard textbooks are closer to Ph.D.-level theses than to scholarly books. On the differences between these and published academic work, see Chapter 1.)

Question 13: Are multiple submissions a good idea?

I understand your need to publish and applaud your desire to be efficient, but I'd advise against multiple submissions. You are trying to cultivate a special relationship with your editor; the last thing you want to do is to come across as the horny guy who hits on every girl in the room. You should be honest in stating whether you are actively submitting your manuscript elsewhere. This is a tricky thing. You want to cast your net wide, but not *too* wide, as there are probably only a handful of publishers who deal with your narrow subject. But here's the thing. Because the fields are so narrow, the experts are very few and it is likely that two presses may well send out your manuscript to the *same* reader. If that happens, then one or both presses may back off. Trust me on this; it has happened to me. A very good press wrote to me that it had sent out my manuscript for review only to receive a note from the expert saying he had already reviewed the manuscript (favorably) for another press. Since I had not stated that I was doing multiple submissions, the press was no longer interested in my project. My mortification grew as I realized that my relationships with the acquisitions editors at both presses were now likely permanently frayed. I didn't just lose out on publishing that book but all future books with two major publishers.

Question 14: What if money is not an issue? If the university is paying for envelopes and postage, why not carpet bomb every press out there?

You are simply setting yourself up to receive a ton of rejections. These rejection letters are always polite, but we need to understand what they are saying. Sometimes a press will return your materials with a polite thank you and a suggestion for where you might appropriately send your manuscript, i.e., "Our press does not publish work concerning 5th century Greek architecture. We suggest you try [BLANK]." Naturally, this referral does not entail a promise that the suggested publisher may be interested. And even if it did, you would still need to know why that press might be interested. How does your book fit their product line? Who is the editor? Does this press publish material similar to your project? Even if you are not paying the postage, it is lazy and simply stupid to submit to a press without these considerations in mind. It is also a waste of your time.

In addition, it's also impolite to waste the time and resources of the press, which had to pass along your manuscript to the right editor, who had to read the materials and then reply via letter, which in turn was made heavy and expensive because it included the return of your submitted materials. You might not care about politeness here, but you should. Given the power of computers and data programs, every press almost surely has your name on file. And if you submit another project in the future, that, too, will be noted. The last thing you need is a file that suggests that you don't know what you're doing.

Question 15: What should I be looking for in a contract?

In most cases, the contract will seem very generous — usually 15 or 20 percent of gross. But don't assume you're on your way to a big payday. Many presses will begin to pay royalties only after their own costs are covered. And, since many books never cover their own costs, the author can expect zero income. Still other academic publishers offer royalties only above and beyond a set number of copies sold. (This set number may be the break-even point, but not necessarily; see my response to Question 3, above.) My first book, for example, sold only about 550 copies. I had to sell 600 copies to receive any royalties, so the university publisher never had to pay me a dime. That being said, there are some aspects of the contract that you may want to clarify or to change. For example, your book might have the potential to be turned into a play or film. You might want to add a clause that states that, aside from the print medium, the intellectual content of the book remains your sole property.

Many contracts differ in their drawing of geographical boundaries. Some presses, for example, lump together all English-speaking countries (i.e., the United States and all Commonwealth countries, including Canada, Australia and New Zealand). Still others may treat the United States as separate from other English-speaking countries. You may also, if your project deals specifically with a non–English subject, want to have a look at foreign rights. Germany has a population of 60 million people; Russia has roughly the same population as the United States. Depending on your subject, German or Russian translations may become very lucrative. And then there is China, with its population of 1.3 billion. Let's say, for example, that your subject deals with the macro-economics of China and that the book is available in Chinese — unlikely circumstances, but let's play along. If just 1 percent of China's population wanted to buy your book, you'd have sold 13 million copies. If just .01 percent shows interest, you'd have 130,000 potential customers. If just .001 percent of the population opened its collective wallet, you would have sold 13,000 books. (Keep in mind that many academic books available only in English sell less than 600 copies, or roughly .00004 percent of China's population.)

You might also want to have a look at reversion rights. Many academic presses know that your book is unlikely to sell out on its first run. Some presses include a clause stating, in essence, that if the book is out of print for a set number of years, the rights to the book revert back to the author. Other contracts might state that the author has the right to buy the rights. All this can be complicated, and also pointless, since your book is unlikely to sell out or generate much interest beyond the initial library market.

The Internet raises other issues. As we all know, e-books are the fastest-growing segment of the book market. Already, many academic books are available in full or in part through Google and other Internet-based businesses. Are your royalties for e-sales the same as for press sales? The answer is "no." Traditionally, published academic books sell for quite a bit of money and the author is compensated, usually for about 15 percent of face value, after the clearing of costs. Many new contracts, however, have a separate and higher remuneration for e-sales, sometimes as high as 25 percent. It should also be noted that the e-version of your book will sell for a lower price, so your take-home pay is probably about the same per copy — electronic or otherwise. (All this depends on whether your book is even available for sale in an e-format; see my reply to Question 8, above.)

What about your university and its growing Internet presence? Many lectures are now being filmed with digital cameras and put online with services such as Apple's "iTunes U." This is an affordable and easy way for universities to promote themselves to digitally addicted students. At my own university, we have a research lecture series that is recorded for exactly this purpose. I had to object to the filming of my own talk because it involved material culled directly from my book, which was still in progress. Without permission from my publisher, I did not think I had the right to give away intellectual content from my contracted book. No doubt contracts will become more complicated in the future as the outlets for content grow and change, but it is best to be as careful as you can with all of this.

Question 16: What can I do to boost sales of my book?

After signing a contract, each author fills out a detailed questionnaire, which, in turn, will be used to help promote the book. The questions for every press are pretty much the same: Contact information, a list of journals you'd like to have the press send out complimentary copies to, a list of conferences you'll be attending in the coming year to make sure that your book is represented. Although presses are unable to attend all of the many academic conferences and seminars that occur each year, they do try to set up a table with books at the major academic gatherings. There are a couple of things which you can do yourself to boost sales. If you are a member of any Listservs or mailing groups, you should mention the book on those. Also, you can add some comments on Amazon.com by clicking on the link labeled "I am the author and I want to comment on my book." If not exhibiting, you might still ask the press for promotional flyers, which you can usually leave on a table for your colleagues to peruse. For most academic authors, that is the full extent of their promotional involvement. There is good reason to trust in the process. Academic presses know what they are doing. Each press catalogue is produced annually and mailed to academics, librarians, and bookshops. Amazon, Barnes & Noble, and other online retailers will likely have your book in their warehouse or on special order.

Still, some authors want to be more involved. Bookstore signings are an obvious option. You can contact your local bookstores. They are often happy to have you appear for a reading and a signing. But, as with any book, price will be a factor. There is little point in having a book signing for a university press book that retails for $100 or more. No one is going to buy it. On the other hand, a book in the $30 range might generate a few sales. Be aware, however, that your book, published by a university press, will not exactly be a sexy sell. The look, weight, and language are all designed to confer scholarly learning. You have not written a bestseller and can't expect your subject or style to appeal to non-specialist readers.

Before agreeing to a book signing, there is another cash-related factor to consider. Barnes & Noble will be hesitant to order a book that, in some cases, it will have to buy outright whether you sell it or not. We tend to think that booksellers don't own the stock in their stores — that they can return unsold copies. This is, in my experience, not the case. If the bookseller orders 10 copies of your $100 book and fails to sell any, the bookseller is out $1,000. This case actually works in your favor. If you can convince a local bookstore to have a special promotional reading and signing, you can thereafter often buy the unsold copies by simply trolling the liquidation table a week or two after your reading.

Question 17: Why are academic books so dull?

One would think that a book written by a professor would be designed to speak beyond the hundred or so colleagues in the world likely interested in exactly the same topic. One would think that a book would be written for the tens of thousands who have Ph.D.s in that field or, better yet, for the hundreds of thousands of experts, experts-in-training —

i.e., grad students — or practitioners in a field. One would think that, with a little extra effort, the book might come with an index explaining key concepts so that millions of intelligent lay readers could follow along. One would think all that, but one would be wrong.

Typically, a scholarly book is written for other scholars in order to convey new information, to assess old information in a new way, or both. By their very specialization, these books are not meant for casual or lay readers, who may find much of the language incomprehensible. Indeed, these books generally do not explain terms; they simply use them on the understanding that their (very few) readers are already aware of the technical language of the given field. This is the kind of book you might find in a research library, but not on the shelves of your local bookstore. However, this does not mean that the press is obligated to publish only the obscure, nor does it work under the mandate that it must publish all manuscripts it finds publishable.

Question 18: Is it true that good publishers make the best teachers?

The jury is still out. Dean Harry W. Pearson of Bennington College argues that "the overwhelming evidence is that those faculty members who rate highest with the students are the most productive scholars in their field. There are exceptions, of course, but there is no doubt whatever of the predominant tendency" (Gene R. Hawes, *To Advance Knowledge*, 16–17). But I doubt that this can be proven statistically. Further, we all recognize that it is possible to be an efficient and excellent teacher, full of practical and esoteric knowledge, without having published a book. Writing articles and books is a skill unto itself, and there is no evidence to suggest that being able to write long chapters in any way makes you more able to deal with teaching, which remains a highly personal experience (unless you are unlucky enough to be lecturing in a hall of hundreds). Think of your own rationale for becoming a teacher. I'll bet that there was one teacher who inspired you, probably as much by manner and style as by sheer intellect. There are, too, many great scholars who lack the interpersonal skills to be effective lecturers or motivators. Still, we have to accept that the need to publish is here for the foreseeable future and adjust to this reality.

The real question is why do colleges and universities now seek out and favor researchers, rather than teachers, as candidates for tenure? As I have argued in my introduction, administrators like to know what their employees are doing, and publication offers a convenient way to track production and performance. Furthermore, departmental and even institutional respectability and, indeed, survival depend upon a steady output of scholarship. The university prefers those published to those not published because publication, if suitably innocuous (see next section), helps to promote the university and thus indirectly improves the university's ability to recruit new students.

Question 19: How come so many academics with major publications still fail to achieve tenure?

Publication is just one facet of tenure. Perhaps the academic in question is a bad teacher. Another possible answer is to look at the kind and quality of the publication. In the introduction to this book, I discussed the importance of reflecting the core values of your institution in your research. But there are other related issues that the tenure-track professor must be aware of. Let us imagine that a new hire in history has been recruited to teach and to research the American Civil War. The assistant professor is encouraged to use collaborative teaching models. Her mode of traditional research is archival, but her classes are too large and her research too complex, so she creates a new project for her class — one she might be able to later convert into a book. She has them watch Hollywood versions of the American Civil War and then asks them to write a cultural analysis of them. The professor then takes the best of the notes and expands upon them in book form.

She may now find that this book is difficult to place. Film studies editors will likely find that the book is too "pop" oriented; traditional history editors may be baffled as to why the book bothers with films at all. The difficulty is at once apparent. The scholar is working at a variety of cross purposes. Our young scholar-academic is told that student involvement in research is the new model. But the kind of students on hand inevitably limits the kind of projects possible, and the resulting research product may not fit into the traditional norms of academic discourse or subject matter.

But our young academic is brilliant and lucky. A contract is issued. But now another problem arises. Her Department of History refuses to accept the book as part of a tenuring dossier on the basis that the book is a "Cultural Studies and Media" project, not a "History" project. This may sound incredibly myopic, but that's exactly what the guidelines of many schools openly demand — research and publication decidedly *within the bounds* of the professor's primary field of discipline. A math teacher, for example, shouldn't spend time writing a novel; likewise, a theology professor shouldn't bother writing on topics that more suitably belong in psychology.

We might demur by arguing that the professor needs to get creative, that given the long odds of securing a book contract, the tenure-track professor needs to think outside the box. But tenuring committees are often composed of academics who published in a far less competitive era and don't fully understand the realities of the new paradigm. The simplest way to avoid this issue is to check with your chair and your tenuring committee on what constitutes an acceptable publication.

Question 20: Given the changes in academia, as outlined in Chapter 1, are things likely to get better?

The future is always an unknown. Some believe that the need to publish is overblown. In 2002, Stephen Greenblatt, the then-president of the Modern Language Association (MLA), wrote an open letter to the members of the association, arguing that since publishers are cutting back on books, it is unfair to demand a book for tenure: "[The] narrowing of publishing possibilities, especially in fields viewed as marginal, may not have bottomed out but may in fact become more acute in years to come" (http://www.mla.org/scholarly_pub). But Greenblatt is hardly one to talk. His career has been built not on articles but on books published with major academic presses. And while he might want his grad students to have an easier time of it, it is only natural that other academics who had to write books just to get an interview, much less to secure tenure, will expect new faculty members to prove their mettle by doing the same.

There is reason, of course, to despair. There always is. To begin with, we might consider whether publishers are interested in new names or are likely to go with established academics. Even if the economy picks up and there are suddenly publishing contracts aplenty, it's likely that young academics will still struggle to secure publishing deals. As in any business, a proven track record trumps inexperience, so getting a second book published is far easier than getting a first book into press. The established academic benefits not only from more writing experience but also from relationships with various editors that have been cultivated over many years. It is worse still for the young academic without a job. As we all recognize, academic presses now often demand publication subventions. Untenured academics are likely to pay these costs out of their own pocket. Tenure-track or tenured academics will likely ask their home institutions to cover this burden. So far as I am aware, no university press makes allowance for this difference of economic reality.

Here is another false hope. I have been hearing for years that a boom in jobs is just around the corner. This talk is based on the expectation that academics hired circa 1960 through 1980 will have to retire sometime. If this wisdom prevails, the need to publish might dissipate somewhat. Who knows, the bar for tenure might be lowered! But this "just around the corner" talk has been going strong for 20 years now and seems naïve. So far, the vast majority of slots once held by tenured baby boomers have been converted to part-time positions. My best guess: Jobs will continue to disappear and the pressure to publish will increase. The corporate and technical structure of the university now threatens to make much of what we do obsolete. Technology, already used as an efficiency tool, will make jobs still rarer. Recorded lectures can do our jobs for us. Machines can grade pop quizzes. All that is left to us is our ability to write and to communicate.

But, for those lucky enough to get tenure, it's not all doom and gloom. It's not like we have been left with the dregs of the job. Rather, we have been given a golden opportunity to really focus on what we, as teachers, should enjoy: personal connection to students and the ability to translate thoughts into articles and books that will add to the richness of the discipline we call our own.

CHAPTER 5

Conclusion: Have Faith

There comes a time in the life of every writer when the truth dawns — *Yes, I can do this*. In the case of professional novelists and the like, that dawning comes with the cashing of checks. Academic writing holds no such profits. I made zero in royalties with *Reforging Shakespeare*, nothing on my various articles, notes and reviews, and little or nothing on editions. On the upside, I have not received a rejection letter in years. Not that every publisher I have contacted offers me a contract, but I now know that if one says no, another will say yes — if I approach and package the right project to the right people.

Confidence comes with repeated success. Why shouldn't it? In composing your Ph.D. dissertation, you fulfilled a variety of academic demands; in readying that dissertation for academic press submission, you wrote or rewrote with an entirely different set of objectives in mind. I discussed all this back in Chapter 1. My point is that, as you continue to write books, you get better at it. You learn how to pace the narrative, how much research on any one area is necessary, how to involve your reader. Even if you are not yet at this point, all I want to suggest right now is that, in the course of your academic career, you will work on one publication and, magically, you will find the subject matter for your next project, either through the kindness of colleagues or through your own curiosity and instinct. So it was with me; so it is with every academic I have encountered at conferences, at the Huntington Library, at the British Library, at the Ransom Library, at the Houghton Library, at the Folger Library. So it will be with you. Have faith.

In reading this book, you may think that I was driven, demonically driven, to succeed. But I wasn't. I'd say I was manically depressed. I had, even after the publication of my first book, never been short-listed for a tenure-track job. Even with a half decade of teaching at various international institutions — which, I figured, demonstrated at the very least my flexibility with minority students of all backgrounds — the rejections came in just as quickly. And I was sick of it. I was ready to walk away.

More "Chicken Soup for the Soul"

The new goal was to buy a franchise of some sort, get some stability and build a life. In a way, the fact that I owned virtually nothing made this plan feasible. Remember that after I published my first book, I was still working as a part-timer at UC Riverside. I was renting a single room. I owned no furniture. I didn't have a cell phone. I didn't even own a computer. Riverside had computer terminals in its library and I just carried a bank of disks around with me. I only owned a few pairs of jeans and some T-shirts. I dressed like a grad student. I didn't earn much. My first year in California netted me about $17,000, but I had managed to save $10,000 of it. By the end of three years, I had raised that sum to $27,000. I figured if I could raise about $75,000 I could get out of academia altogether, open an ice cream store — something like that.

I was disaffected with teaching and academia. Why wouldn't I be? I had completed a doctorate under extremely difficult circumstances; I had been eking out a living as, essentially, an academic migrant worker; every time I moved I had to give away most of my possessions, which didn't amount to much. I had started my academic career in a strange city in a foreign land, and then, a year later, I had to do it all over again, and not just in another strange city, but on a different continent. In three years, I had been hired on a contract basis in Europe (Perpignan, France), Asia (Hong Kong) and now in North America (Riverside, California). If that sounds like I was living the adventure of a lifetime, I suppose I was, but in a very real way I was powerless. I had no control over where I would live, what I would be doing. This anecdote says it all: Even as I started my very first day at UC Riverside, I was already answering ads for the next job, which was — par for the course — in Argentina.

With the acceptance of *Reforging Shakespeare*, I thought that Riverside would want to retain me, but I was wrong. There was nothing wrong with my teaching assessments. No, the issue was purely administrative. According to UC's rules, had the university retained me for more than three years as a lecturer, the English Department would have to grant me full-time and permanent employment. These lecturer positions had, in the main, gone to graduate students and Ph.D. graduates who, like me, had failed to get a tenure-track job. Some had moved on, others had been retained, a smaller pool stayed for the three years, some stayed permanently. The point was, the job was never mine, and the permanent jobs went to their own Ph.D grads, who were in the same boat as me.

Not that I cared much. I had proven my point. I had gotten the Ph.D. into print. I knew it was a good book, in its own way a useful book. It helped me to think that I had enemies, which was far preferable to the more likely truth: that everyone I had known in academia — prior to and excepting John Ganim's generous offer to come to UC Riverside — didn't really give a toss about me. Anger had kept me fresh. Everyone had expected me to crawl off somewhere and die. I hadn't. I was still in the game, and, if I was now ready to leave it, I was leaving on my terms.

One of my favorite literary passages is from Nikolai Gogol's *Dead Souls*: "The fiery youth of today would start back in horror if he could be shown his own portrait in old age." It likewise follows that our older selves can look back on our younger selves with some sadness of time wasted or misused. I suppose there are two ways of looking at anything, but only in retrospect. In the moment, one's options are all too often obscured. We walk by doors that offer easy shelter from the cold, we fail to see warning signs, we don't see friends and family offering help or friendly smiles. We think of ourselves as alone and miserable. I had been to the south of France, to Hong Kong, and to sunny California. That's not exactly Siberia, Somalia, and Liberia. Yet, looking back on photos from those days, the unhappiness is palpable. I was miserable. If I could only go back in Mr. Peabody's Wayback Machine (from the cartoon *Rocky and Bullwinkle*), I would tell my younger self, *All will be well. There will be more to do. Much more. But you will be fine. You have strength, more than you know.* I didn't know that at the time, and I lived in fear. No, even that is not quite right. I lived, as it were, estranged from the self that should have been happy or fearful or alive.

Then, by what seemed to me to be a random act of kindness, my life changed. I had received an email from England. It was from some guy named Nick Groom, who had read my book and wanted to know more about the Ireland forgeries, particularly the play *Vortigern*. I kindly replied that I didn't have a copy of my bound dissertation but that he was welcome, if he lived anywhere near Bexhill-on-Sea, to visit the university, which had the full dissertation on file. I pressed send. I refreshed the browser. He replied that he had already done so and wanted to talk about it some more. Would I be coming to London any time soon? He was, he explained, a general editor for a new series at Routledge, and he wanted to discuss getting the play back into print. I began to think I was dealing with some nutcase here. So I did a search on him. He was a professor who had published a book on Chatterton and was completing another book on forgery. London. If I were a tenured or even tenure-track academic, I could have qualified for travel and research funds. But lecturers and part-timers, and I was both, got squat. I sat under a tree in the courtyard opposite the library, watching students come and go with books in their hands. I walked into the library and wandered through the shelves of the English Criticism section: PR2950 .K35 1998. My call number. *Reforging Shakespeare* was sitting there. Sometimes, I would take the book off the shelf to see if anyone had checked it out. No one had. I looked around. I was alone. Then I took out a pen. I wrote in the book: "I win."

The next day, I withdrew $2,000 from my bank account and booked a flight to London. I emailed Nick Groom and informed him that, as it happened, I was doing some research at the British Library and would be happy to meet in a day or two. I did not let on that I was coming especially for this meeting. And then I had a sinking fear. What if he wasn't free to meet me? What if he changed his mind? I spent a sleepless night on that one, but then, in checking my email at the university the next day, I read his reply. We would meet at his club, the day after next at 6:00 P.M. At his club. I had visions of Wooster and Jeeves, the deep-backed red leather chairs, the chandeliers aglow, sherry poured by boys dressed in Raj-period costume, in the next room the delicate clink of billiard balls. I remembered my unhappy experiences at Bexhill-on-Sea. I looked in the mirror. My hair was long, thinning, and now down nearly the full length of my back. I was wearing a Black Sabbath t-shirt. Not good.

So I got on the bus — I still did not own a car at that point — and went to the mall. I bought a white dress shirt, grey pants, a yellow tie, black shoes. Then I walked into a barber. "Cut it off," I said. Then I bought a bottle of shampoo and a stick of deodorant and headed to the airport. When I landed in London, I found a carpeted corner, used my bag as a pillow and fell asleep like a dog home from a long hunt. It was 6:00 A.M. I woke around noon, stretched, and went straight to the toilet, then to the sink. I took off my Black Sabbath t-shirt, which I then used as a washcloth. I unscrewed the shampoo, washed my hair in the sink, and dosed myself with deodorant. Travelers coming and going didn't take much notice of me. I then went into a stall and changed my clothes. I threw away the T-shirt, jeans, and shoes I had worn on the flight. I asked someone for the time. 1:00 P.M. I had 5 hours. I took the tube to Tottenham Court and floated through the British Museum for 3 hours.

Then I walked to the club. I was on time. But there had to be some mistake. I was not in front of some grave-faced Victorian edifice, but a rundown two-story next to a sex shop. I ascended the stairs. Up top, there was a near-empty room, strewn with makeshift tables and folding chairs. No cigars, no Indian boy-waiters dressed as the Raj's servants, no sherries. Empty beer bottles littered the tables. The stain of smoke was on everything. I asked if I was in the right place. I was. I asked for Nick Groom. The barkeep pointed to a table — and a guy no older than myself drinking a beer. The guy looked up and smiled. His tooth was chipped, I think. He had long hair and wore a Deep Purple t-shirt. Drinks followed. Then more drinks. We discussed a possible collection for about 10 minutes. He asked for my ideas not just on W.H. Ireland but on the art of forged plays and imitations. I told him that Ireland wasn't just a forger, that he was in his own way a scholar, that much of what he had written did not come from Shakespeare himself but from Shakespeare imitators such as Nicholas Rowe. He asked why that wasn't in the book. "No room," I replied. Would I be interested in doing a collection? Sure. And then he said no more. After the club closed, I said my good-byes and headed to the tube. It was closed. Newspapers fluttered in the streets. I sat on a bus bench. Fortunately, it was a warm night. By 5:00 a.m, London was astir. I bought some fruit from a vendor, plunked my coins down for tube fair and headed back to Heathrow. I was back in California in 9 hours. All told, I had been away a little less than 3 days.

Had it been a waste of time? For the three weeks that followed, I certainly thought so. Then an envelope arrived. It was an author's questionnaire with a note from Nick, asking for a list of plays I would like to edit. I knew that the Huntington Library, just down the road some 35 miles from Riverside, had the Largent Collection, the Lord Chamberlain's approved copies of all plays performed in the eighteenth century. The University of California's library had a brown, hardback copy of the catalogue. I went through it, comparing it to my list, which I had initially compiled for Nick. The Largent Collection had nearly every play that interested me in manuscript; the Huntington's core library collection had very early quartos of all the other texts I was interested in. I cited the titles and the sources — whether I was dealing with an old printed text or the original manuscript — and the unpublished materials I had found. (You can see this full proposal in the appendix.) Six months went by. Then a year. It was now the year 2000, and I was working part time at a number of universities. My days were long. I taught a class in basic composition at Loyola Marymount at 7:00 A.M. Then I drove to Rio Hondo to teach a 10:00 A.M. composition course, then back to Loyola for another class at noon. Then off to Cal State LA for yet another composition class at 4:00 P.M. Then off to Pierce College for a 6:30 P.M. class. Once a week, I taught a Shakespeare course at the University of La Verne. I had to buy a car to make this all work: a 1969 Volkswagen Beetle, for which I shelled out $1,000.

I was, again, feeling exploited and discouraged. On the upside, I was making and saving money, and I was looking through a variety of franchise brochures. *In a few more years*, I told myself, *I'll make my move.* But, God help me, I had an idea. It had come to me while doing research on Shakespeare imitations. I was checking out the performance dates of Nicholas Rowe's Shakespeare imitation *Jane Shore* to see if Ireland might have been in London while the play was performed at Drury Lane or Covent Garden. I kept looking at all the biographies on the era's chief actors for further references, and I noticed that there hadn't been a biography done on Edmund Kean since the 1970s, and that one had been a popular study, without scholarly documentation. Further, Kean was, like Ireland, a character. And if I had identified with fakes while living in England, I was now, despite my shorn locks, thinking more and more of— and like — Kean, an outsider who lived on his own terms.

By this time, I knew the dangers of writing a book and the limited return. The danger was that I would spend years of my life working on a project that might not get published. I would do so with no hope of financial return. When I confessed that I was contemplating writing another book and expected no money and perhaps a heap of abuse in return, my friends looked at me like I was some sort of idiot. "Why do it?" they'd asked. I couldn't really say. I mean, tenured associate professors receive different marks of distinguishment for publication. Assistants are granted tenure, associates rise to the rank of full professor, but for me, a part-timer, I'd get exactly what I got from my first book — nothing. "Yes," I'd reply to these well-meaning arguments, "you are right. I have wasted enough time. I'll just keep looking for a franchise and teach at these various universities until I pick one. Yes, I won't write that book." But, even as I said it, I had begun to take notes and plot the narrative.

It was now the summer of 2000. I was doing some summer school classes at Pierce College and teaching the SAT to Korean students in Torrance, California, when the phone rang. It was Nick Groom. I assumed there was some word on the collection, but no. He was guest-editing a journal and one of the contributors had dropped out. The theme was authenticity. Did I have anything on forgery that might fit? "Sure," I lied. "I've been working on something for months." Then he politely asked how soon it could be ready, for, you see, he needed it in 4 days. Today was Thursday. "No worries," I lied. I put down the phone and had a think. He must have been the guest editor of this thing for months, but he contacted me with 4 days to go. So, someone either didn't come through with a paper or had written one that was beyond salvage-able. I probably wasn't his first call; people must have told him that doing a full article in 4 days was impossible. So he had tried me in desperation. Oddly enough, I felt I could do it. My teaching in Torrance gig was done by noon, and I had a six-and-a-half-hour break until my Pierce class, just enough of a window to squeeze in a visit to the Huntington and to hunt up a topic. By Friday, I was sketching the outline and had 1,000 words. An all-night writing session brought it up to 3,500. More work at the Huntington on Saturday and Sunday followed, with two more all-nighters spent polishing, and it was ready to go by Monday. Right on time. I think the finished product was about 7,000 words. I had done it, and Nick was thrilled. Somewhere in my twisted pathology I thought, *Well, maybe it's a test of some sort, to see what I can do.* I wouldn't put anything past the English, but, no, I was just being silly.

More time passed and more work came my way. Nearby Loyola Marymount needed a composition teacher and hired me for one class for the fall term. Pierce College needed a composition teacher. I got the job. Rio Hondo needed an extra body. I took the job. And then the impossible happened: La Verne's long-time Shakespearean professor, Rhoda S. Kachuck, was contemplating retirement. Would I be interested in apply-ing? Of course! She was only *contemplating* retirement. Yes, I understood. Would I still be interested in part-time work? Sure! A year later, I was offered the job on a permanent basis. That was 2001. It had taken me eight years, but I had secured a tenure-track job.

And then the bad news. My book *Reforging Shakespeare* had come out before I had joined La Verne on a tenure-track appointment. While the book was impressive, it could not be counted as part of my portfolio submission, since my tenure submission had to include only work done while employed at La Verne. So the upshot was that all my work had secured me a job, and now I had to start all over again. The good news was that my years of writing and submitting had taught me a number of important lessons. I had certain advantages. I had already done everything wrong and knew what not to do. I now had access to conference funds, to research budgets. I had a desk and an office to work out of on a permanent basis — permanent meaning five years — my deadline to put together a reasonable teaching and publication portfolio.

And then, one month into my tenure-track job, a contract from Routledge came in the mail. I looked at it in astonishment. Nick had come through, but the due date nearly gave me a heart attack. The entire project was slated to go to press in 18 months. We're talking about a general introduction, 14 plays, specific, short introductions to those individual plays, and notes. In all, we're talking about roughly 1,000 printed pages that needed to be written in 18 months. But, if I was successful, I would have a multivolume edition to submit to my tenuring committee. I signed the contract and set to work.

Somehow, I came up with what was, in retrospect, an insane work schedule. I would rise at 4:00 A.M., transcribe 100 lines of text, set up the line numbers and write the notes on them. That took me to 10:00 A.M. Then I'd go to La Verne and teach a class and then rush over to the Huntington to collate the printed version against the original manuscript in the Largent Collection. I completed editing the 14 plays in 8 months. I now had another 8 months to write the short introductions to each play and the longer 40-page general introduction. As it turned out, the plays were burning far more pages than I initially expected. I had to ask Nick for more pages. He wondered if cutting back wasn't a better idea, but, no, I insisted, I had already edited the plays. He agreed to up the page count to 1,800 pages. And at the end of 18 months, I submitted 1,750 pages, comprising nearly 1,000 pages of text, 350 pages of introductory materials and 400 pages of notes. It really wasn't as bad as it sounds. Remember that I had already edited *Vortigern* as part of my doctorate, and the collation for that play alone came out to 100 pages. Writing the introductory material for the Ireland plays (*Vortigern* and *Henry II*) only took a few days. It wasn't creative work. It was just hard labor. And for my 18 sleepless months, I earned my first royalty check, an advance of $150. But I had a three-volume edition and, with further thanks to Nick Groom, a journal article.

Those projects were a huge plus for my tenuring file. But I was still thinking about that book on Kean. I set to work on a proposal. I also thought it might be a good idea to start going to conferences. So, in the fall of 2002, nine years after my graduation, I finally attended my first Shakespeare Association Conference. I had a miserable time. I didn't know anyone and everyone seemed to be interested in topics in which I had very little interest. I did strike up a conversation with Douglas Brooks, who had a new book out that I had read. He asked me where La Verne was — conference attendees write the name of their affiliation on a lapel sticker. I told him it was near the Huntington. He told me he was going to be spending the summer there. We agreed to meet up for lunch.

I must have intrigued him, because I saw him the next day at the conference and he said, "I looked you up on Yahoo last night. You wrote a book a few years back on the Ireland forgeries." I admitted that I had. He asked me what else I had been doing. I told him of my new collection with Routledge. He asked for the title. I told him, "Don't bother. It's retailing for about $750." He laughed and said, "No, I don't have to buy a copy. I'm the editor of *Shakespeare Yearbook*. I'm going to have it reviewed." I can't tell you how tense this made me. I had been getting published, but I knew from my own review system that negative reviews were part of the game. What would my tenuring committee think if I had been trashed by *Shakespeare Yearbook*? There was little I could do. I gave him my details and told him that I looked forward to seeing the review. If the collection was in fact reviewed, I do not know. I never looked.

Then, in 2002, more good luck struck. Nick Groom, who had already secured me an article and a three-volume edition with Routledge, came calling again. He had convinced his university to host a conference on Chatterton and he asked if I could attend. Now that I had university travel funds, I happily agreed. As it turned out, this trip to England was much like my original residency. Everyone seemed to be on a different page than I was. A collection came out of it, and while Nick was not the editor, I was not invited to submit my paper. Then why the good luck? I had met John Goodridge, editor of the University of Nottingham's Trent Editions, which specialized in working-class poets. The luck was not initially apparent, but, when I returned from the conference, I was informed that one of my colleagues would be taking sabbatical. Would I teach her Romanticism course? I agreed.

Rather than just using a standard anthology, I included Goodridge's edition of Robert Bloomfield and photocopied some other "minor poets," such as my forger W.H. Ireland and the now nearly-forgotten poet laureate Robert Southey. I was surprised that students really liked Southey. That got me thinking. I did some checking. No cheap, student-friendly edition of Southey existed. So I bought an 1848 complete works on eBay for 8 bucks and did some reading, selected some of his long poems, cut them down, cut them down again, and cut them down yet again, wrote a proposal and fired it off to John Goodridge at Trent Editions, who promptly rejected it. He was only interested in working-class poets, but he suggested that I contact Peter Widdowson at Cydar House Press, part of the University of Gloucester. I did, and, as it happened, Widdowson liked the idea and accepted the collection. (The proposal is included in the appendix.)

While doing the notes on Southey at the Huntington, I again ran into Douglas Brooks. Over lunch, he told me that he had spent a fair amount of time with my Routledge edition and thought highly of it. He asked me if I would come to Texas A&M to give a lecture on Shakespeare imitations and forgeries. I agreed, on the condition that I take him out for drinks. He agreed. So, the following term, I found myself giving a talk at Texas A&M. I also wanted to spend a day at nearby University of Texas at Austin, checking out the Ransom Library. I took a tour and learned about their generous grants. I had a look through their catalogues. There wasn't much that interested me, but they did have a folder of Kean materials. So I called it up. A folder? No, a cart was more like it. There must have been two thousand uncatalogued items in this "folder," ranging from images to letters, none of which I had ever seen quoted. I took the name of the reference librarian, the kind-hearted Helen Adair, and asked for an application for their visiting fellowships. Helen also counseled me to contact Betty Falsey, a theatre collections reference librarian at Harvard. I did, and Betty assured me they had lots of materials on Kean, much of it uncatalogued. I applied for two grants, won them both and flew to Austin and Harvard.

I began to look for a press. This time, rather than just fire off a proposal to everyone and anyone, I began to target my submissions. I collected the catalogues sent to the department from the various publishing houses. If the subject at all touched upon Kean's era, the early nineteenth century, I made a note of the press. I did the same for theater. I came up with two presses — Ashgate and a-press-which-shall-remain-nameless.

I fired off proposals to both and, to my surprise, both were interested in the project. I informed them that the manuscript was still in process — a polite way of saying I had yet to write the darn thing — but that I had secured funds through some grants in order to do further research at the Ransom and at Harvard's Houghton. I think, in retrospect, that this fact impressed them. Both stated their interest in seeing a finished manuscript. (The proposal is included in the appendix.)

All I had to do now was write the thing, and that was going to be tough because Douglas Brooks had come calling. His own mentor at Columbia was putting together an *Encyclopedia of British Literature* and would I be interested? Sure! So I submitted a vitae and the editor asked me to write on the poets laureate, I suppose because Southey had been one. I agreed, but the thing was, aside from Southey I knew virtually nothing on the subject or its rich tradition. It took me about a week in the Huntington to read, select, and assemble enough materials to write the entry. And then Brooks came calling yet again. He was working with a press on a new complete Shakespeare works aimed at high school kids. As I had already edited Shakespeare imitations, forgeries and parodies, and the poetry of Southey, would I be interested in editing Shakespeare's *Much Ado About Nothing*? Sure! I was now awash in editions, but I felt I still really needed to publish a book. I had only two publishers interested, but, I told myself, I need only one.

With the contract for *Much Ado* in hand, I applied for course release, which was granted — I had previously applied for similar releases for the Shakespeare imitations project and the Southey edition — and set to work on *Much Ado*, retyping 100 lines every morning and working on Kean in the afternoon. In 30 days, I had my *Much Ado* text. I would now write the notes to the edition, targeting a rate of 50 lines a day. (This was a high school edition, so the years scholars generally took for an Oxford or Cambridge edition of the play was not necessary.) Another month was taken to write the introduction. I wrote another request to my own institution asking for help to cover the costs of images for the book, and in three months I had an edition of *Much Ado* in press. I now wrote another course release request for Kean and, upon the approval of my chair, bunched the rest of my year's work of classes into one term. Once I had completed my course teaching, I now had a full eight months to visit the Ransom and Houghton libraries.

I had a month-long fellowship at the Ransom Library. The first of the two weeks, I assembled and photocopied materials; in the second week, I looked for more useful materials. In my third week there, while going through images of Kean, I came across an image of yet another actor, William Henry West Betty, a teenager who acted with Kean in 1808. There was something about that image of Betty as Hamlet, a 13-year-old-boy holding the skull of Yorrick, that intrigued me. But I had Kean to complete.

Then I had another fateful encounter. My friend Stanley Stewart had kindly introduced me to John Mulryan, editor of the journal *Cithara*. John was at the Huntington on a grant and we became close. John was doing research on Milton, but he was also looking for papers to publish in his journal. He was putting together a special theme issue on Shakespeare and the Judeo-Christian tradition, and he asked if I had anything at hand. I didn't, but I had an idea for a paper, generated by a discussion I had with my students on *Julius Caesar*. So, I lied and told him I had a paper nearing completion and asked for submission dates and details. My work on Kean was coming to a head and I needed a break. So I read some criticism on *Julius Caesar* that fit my topic and a week later had a paper ready for him. It was accepted. I thought no more if it. My Kean project was coming along. When I felt it was ready, I did not submit simultaneously to both presses but sent everything to Ashgate and waited on them.

I needed a rest anyway but, as it turned out, luck would come into play yet again. John Mulryan was returning to the Huntington and wanted to discuss a project with me. We met for lunch, and he explained that he was going on sabbatical and needed a guest editor for the journal. Would I be interested? Sure! The issue would be Shakespeare-based. The first thing I did was ask Stan Stewart if he had anything handy. He did, and, as usual, it was great. I then sent out a general call for papers on the cfp and received some queries. (On the difficulty of putting together and publishing essay collections, see Chapter 2.) Philip Kolin was among the many who replied to my cfp listing. For those who don't know the name, he is a writing machine. He's a writer's writer, having written whole library shelves on Tennessee Williams, Edward Albee, Shakespeare, and English composition textbooks. His paper was brilliant. But it needed, in my opinion, some minor retouching, so I wrote out a report and then worked closely with him on the revisions. He was really very grateful, which, for someone with his publication record, I found surprising. In any case, the journal special issue came out and, I thought, that was that.

And then Ashgate emailed me with some great news! They loved the book and wanted to issue me a contract. I thanked the gods. I then wrote to the rival press, thanking them for their interest and telling them I was going with Ashgate. The editor was very understanding, After all, I had not wasted her time and resources by sending her a full manuscript. She was disappointed but asked to see more of my work in the future. I promised her I would send more to her. I then began reaching out to various libraries to secure the rights to images for the Kean project. I also had some work to do on the manuscript (see Chapter 2 on the drudgery involved in turning your manuscript into a book). Only a few days after I completed the last of the Kean revisions, I received another email from Phil Kolin. He informed me that he was the general editor of a new essay series on Shakespeare. I thought he was returning the favor and wanted me to write a short article for one of the volumes. Instead, he asked me which text I would like to work on and, once having selected the text, which scholars I would then invite. I told him I was just fool enough to take on *King Lear*, arguably the most complex play in the canon. He stressed that I needed to write a proposal, outlining my knowledge of the play and which scholars I would select to write knowledgeably on the play's intricate reception history.

So I set to work and selected every major figure I could think of for the collection. I then contacted each of them. Of the 14, only two did not respond favorably. I then mailed the proposal off and tried to forget about it. (The proposal is included in the appendix.) Besides, the proofs for my Kean manuscript, *The Cult of Kean*, had arrived. While I worked on those, Douglas Brooks came calling yet again, this time asking if I could be a reader on an essay submitted to *Yearbook*. I agreed, read the paper the same day he gave it to me, and generated a 1,000 word report. He was thrilled with the report and even more so with my speedy turnaround. He asked me if I wanted to join the board of *Yearbook*. Sure! He then asked me if I would do a few reviews. So long as I didn't have to do them in a day or long weekend, sure!

It looked as though I could at last relax. My Kean project had been accepted. I had multiple editions to my name and a few articles, I had guest edited a well-known journal, and I was now a board member of *Shakespeare Yearbook*. But things have a momentum of their own. I had met Franz Potter, an expert in Gothic literature, who was the general editor of a series reviving forgotten authors. I mentioned that my forger, W.H. Ireland, had written four Gothics. Potter became excited. Would

I edit them? "No," I said, "I just don't have the time to write a proposal. I've edited texts before and they are a lot of work." He then asked me for a list of some of my editions. I rattled off the Routledge series, and said that I had edited Southey, that I had edited *Much Ado*. So he said, "Look, no proposals are necessary. If you've done all you say you've done, and you are an expert on Ireland, then we'll publish your editions." I replied, "But I just can't be bothered to scan and transcribe those novels. They are huge! And I have this *King Lear* thing...."

I imagine that if any grad student had been lunching with me he would have pulled out a gun and shot me then and there. But Potter assured me that the texts would be readied for me. All I would have to do would be to write the introductions and the notes. Well, I thought, the *King Lear* contract has yet to be issued, and it may not be issued. Why not edit Ireland's novels? I knocked each of them out. I used the same mechanical process I had with the other editions. I read the entire novel, making brief notes. I then reread each chapter, underlining passages that either needed clarification or clearly corresponded to some line in Shakespeare. That process took 40 days for each novel; I then took one month on each introduction. In six months I had completed three editions. While I was in the middle of those editions, the *King Lear* contract, courtesy of Phil Kolin, came through. I wrote a 110-page introduction and a short essay, and my colleagues wrote their essays. Financially, I had some help. The Huntington Library awarded me a summer grant; I secured another month of funding to visit the Ransom Center (my Ransom grant proposal is included in the appendix); my home institution gave me a grant to purchase the rights to all images associated with the project. It all came off without a hitch. The collection was issued in 2006.

My chair told me it was time to rest up. I had, he assured me, published more in 5 years than most academics had in a lifetime. But I disagreed. I had come to realize that research and writing is something I do, not just for tenure, but because I like doing it. No, "like" is not the right word. Much of my early writing was generated out of fear. That fear has now passed. I don't need to publish to survive; I publish projects that interest me.

I began that book on William Henry West. I wrote a proposal and targeted a few presses likely to be interested. Three showed real interest, among them Lehigh, which had, a decade before, published my first book. I wish I could say the editor remembered me, but the head of the press, Scott Gordon, was new to the job. However, his staff had been there some time and many still recalled working on *Reforging Shakespeare* all those years ago. Staff members at Lehigh told me that they remembered me well, that I was very excited, very earnest, and showed a great deal of kindness and respect to everyone I encountered. Being kind and respectful, I have found over the years, helps enormously. No one likes working with difficult people. Not only is it easy to be nice, but people put themselves out for nice people, at least in academic publishing!

By now, I was not only a nice guy, I was also a happy guy. The pain of the last dozen years was at last behind me. In 2006, I was granted tenure. I had job security and, picking up my head, I began to see that I had not done it alone. I had been helped by a variety of well-established academics, especially John Ganim, Nick Groom, Stanley Stewart, and Douglas Brooks. And one of these four scholars would invite me for yet another new project. In 2006, I had a tenure celebration party. Stan Stewart, who lives only 25 miles away, came down and, over a glass of wine, he told me that he had a new project going on contemporary film. He asked me if I would have a look. Somehow we drifted from cinema to comic books. I found myself convincing him that a book on comics might be more interesting. We agreed to have lunch and to discuss the project some more. During that lunch, he asked me if I would like to coauthor the book with him. Stan is a great guy, and I've worked with him before. *Maybe he just wants a bit of company,* I told myself. *An academic's life is a lonely life,* I reflected. *Maybe this is his way of strengthening our friendship?* So I agreed to come on board.

The change in subject matter, from cinema to comics, would still allow us to discuss pop culture subjects but would also create its own form of internal cohesion. For example, because *Batman* comics have been running for over 50 years, it is possible to discuss changes in that comic through the decades as reflective of certain historical and cultural themes. Next, we discussed who our target audience would be. We both decided that turning something that was exciting to kids and to young adults into yet another dry academic study made little sense. So a popular press was in order. We then discussed whether we might turn the book into a textbook of some sort, maybe using adolescent interest in comics as a way of fostering a love of reading. Perhaps we might transition an interest in comic books to subjects relevant to academia? All we needed to do was find a publisher. The hunt was now fairly limited. We needed a private press, specializing in composition textbooks aimed at high school seniors, or college freshmen. Because comics were so popular in film, we added film studies to our search list. So, ideally, we needed a press that had published on comics, film, and pop culture, and had books adapted for high school or college freshman composition classes. I hunted through my catalogues. McFarland out of North Carolina did all these things. We wrote a proposal and a few weeks later we had a contract. We set to work writing 1,000 words a day. We finished the first draft in 100 days and had the book completed in seven months. *Caped Crusaders 101* is now in its 2nd edition and has been expanded by another 40,000 words.

After *Caped Crusaders 101* came out, I received an email from Mark Hall, editor of the journal *The Dark Man*. He was looking for reviewers. Maybe I could do something on the recent spate of Conan comics released in hardback? Sure! So, I started buying and reading Conan comics. He liked the review. I wrote another. He liked it. I wrote a short article for the journal which was accepted. He then asked me to become one of the editors. I agreed. Then I received an email from Germany. A new press was starting up, specializing in Gothic novels. The General Editor, Norbert Besch, had read my introductions and notes to those three Ireland Gothics I had published with Franz Potter. Would I be interested in joining the editorial board of his newly-formed Udolpho Press?

Then Stan Stewart came calling yet again. We were by then (and we remain) very good friends. He asked whether I would be attending an upcoming Association of Literary Scholars (ALSC) convention in which he would be giving the keynote speech. Of course! The annual national meeting was in Atlanta, and he gave a great speech. Listening to him and watching the faces of the other academics in the room was really interesting. I knew that Stan had enjoyed a very distinguished writing career, but I was taken aback by the sheer respect (reverence?) his audience had for his decades of service to the profession. Over drinks with Thomas Hester, himself the editor of the *John Donne Journal*, I shared my thoughts. "Oh, he's been very important to the profession," Hester replied. Everyone around us agreed. So, I said, "We should do a feshrift for him." For those who are unfamiliar with the term a feshrift is a collection in honor of an important academic, usually a distinguished colleague who is about to retire or has just retired. Hester chimed in that he'd be willing to help. So we drew up a list of Stewart's closest friends. Everyone agreed to write something, and we brought the feshrift out with the University of Edinburgh as a special double issue of the *Ben Jonson Journal.*

Not only have I achieved tenure on time, but my university is now worried that I will leave them for greener pastures. That is unlikely, given the job market, but even if the market were better than dreadful, it would take a very sweet deal indeed to turn my back on an institution which has given me the tools (research funds and classes off) to achieve tenure. No matter how hard I have worked, I know that all of it would not have been possible had it not been for a lucky draw. If La Verne had not hired me, I would, in all likelihood, still be a part-timer; if I had not been befriended by Nick Groom, Stanly Stewart, Douglas Brooks, Phil Kolin, and others, some publishing projects would not have come my way.

Al Clark, the deputy provost of my university, has been one of my most vocal champions, and he has encouraged me to share my knowledge with new faculty. In the fall of 2009, I did a presentation on how to get published. In the question period that followed, one colleague said, "So, if you are right about one work leading inevitably to another and if you are right about building up a good reputation with presses and establishing friendships with editors, then you should be able to turn this lecture you are now giving into an article or a book." I liked and accepted the challenge. It took me three weeks to land a contract for what you are now reading.

The work continues. While I typed up this book, I readied another issue of the *Dark Man* journal for press, finished the second set of proofs for my book on Master Betty (now available for purchase), wrote two entries for the *Encyclopedia of Gothic Literature*, and had a proposal accepted for a new essay collection. A new edition of *King Lear* is coming out, and the publisher has asked that I take a look at it. It's hard to think of myself as one of those guys who gets asked to evaluate manuscripts, but it is beginning to happen. (I wrote a very positive report — no more negative bashing.) Last week, I was in San Diego for Comic-Con. As the coauthor of *Caped Crusaders 101*, I am now seen as an authority on comic books and was invited to give my views on the state of the industry. I argued that comics were our last and best hope to get a generation of gamers interested in the printed word. After my talk, I was approached by a woman who handed me her card. Nancy Silberkleit. She's the co-CEO of *Archie Comics*, and she wants to discuss how *Archie* can be used in the classroom. We're still talking. Maybe I'll write a textbook for elementary school teachers with *Archie* characters.

More projects are on the horizon. I am writing a short paper on Shakespeare for a conference in Prague, and I am also writing another grant proposal for a book. But in other ways, I am beginning to break from my own system of success. The book review editor for the *John Donne Journal* asked me recently if I would like to do something for them. "No reviews," I replied. "I don't need to write negative reviews anymore." "But they could be positive reviews," he reminded me. "No, only established scholars can do those. This is a Donne journal, and I am not a Donne scholar." "Well," he added, "we could send you stuff on Donne and Shakespeare." "No," I said, "it's time for me to start turning things down, to write every day, yes, but to write not just on projects that come my way, but to write something that will benefit, genuinely benefit readers, something that will help young scholars." This book does that. I sincerely hope it helps.

This book is designed to help you publish for tenure. But I hope you have ambitions beyond tenure. I know I do. The truth is that I have begun to look at the books I have written not so much as steps toward tenure — the impetus for their creation — but as indicators of how my scholarship will be viewed in the years to come. We have already noted that in the "old days" far less was required for tenure. But the works that were published in that era were, I suspect, far better than much of what is published today. There is no particular reason why this should be. After all, if one writes every day, one should, theoretically, get better and better at one's craft. While a first book might be only fair, a second or third book should be stronger and stronger still. Yet the reality of the tenure-track system forces scholars to write at a breakneck pace. The result is hasty and sometimes weak scholarship. Paradoxically, the upside of weak scholarship is that it allows you or someone else to write still more on the subject in the form of reviews, corrections, expansions or the like.

You can see the effect of tenure on the size of the books as well. Most books published in the 1980s were about 250 pages; that shrank in the 1990s to about 200 pages; more recent studies are less than 180 pages. Scholars in the 1960s often wrote books over 600 pages in length and so comprehensive no one needed to write about that subject again for a decade or more. Those books often took over a decade to write. Today's tenure-track candidate simply doesn't have that luxury. But once that candidate is tenured, it behooves her to think long-term about her work and her legacy. It is distressing and, at the same time, uplifting to consider that, after the hundreds of thousands of words already committed to the printed page in an effort to achieve tenure, the really meaningful work still lies ahead.

The One Thing You Need to Know

You can do this.

Appendix: Sample Proposals

I urge the reader to look at these proposals only after studying the lessons learned in Chapters 1 and 2. In brief: Always keep in mind that your editor is overworked. Find out the editor's full name; state your project clearly; state why your project is a good fit for the press; outline why the topic is important; describe what other work has been done in the field. Add something about your own qualifications. Include a sample chapter or a detailed outline of the book, or, if it's an edition, a sample page. Be businesslike but friendly. Check the press website for submission instructions. Do they accept e-submissions? Would they prefer that you enclose a return envelope with postage?

Sample 1: *The Cult of Kean*

Number of Publishers Contacted: 4
Replies for More Information or Full Submission: 2
Number of Months from First Contact to Contract: 18

Overview

Edmund Kean is a seminal figure in English theatre history. No actor before or since has so dominated his own stage. While many biographies ably cover Kean's life, no work has yet tackled the complicated and fascinating story of his literary appropriation, both in his own day and after his demise.

Recent biographies of Kean, particularly Harold Newcomb Hillebrand's *Edmund Kean* (AMS Press, 1966) and Raymund FitzSimons' *Edmund Kean: Fire from Heaven* (Hmilton, 1976), have attempted to separate fact from fiction, yet neither author pays any attention to the countervailing principle of appropriating Kean as a literary character. This is all the more surprising when one considers that Kean appears in the works of such diverse canonical figures as Hazlitt, Byron, Keats, Coleridge, Dumas, Twain, and Sartre.

The Cult of Kean traces a remarkable history of appropriation of the actor Edmund Kean by writers, artists, and audiences. Each chapter discusses how many of history's greatest figures viewed Kean and how these figures examined and discussed themselves in relation to — or projected themselves onto or into — Kean, or, rather, a series of Keans competing in various intertextual and extratextual dimensions of origins and alternatives. This study, therefore, is not a search for historical "truth," but for the meanings that others found in Kean or created for him — a system of endless representations, a study of a vital, ongoing process. He struts with Napoleonic zeal in the poetry of Byron, rages against the aristocracy in a play by Dumas, and confronts the existential riddle of mankind in Sartre.

Briefly, What Do the Various Uses of Kean by These Canonical Authors Signify?

Even anecdotal evidence suggests that the disappearance of Kean as a recognizable signifier is the chronological consequence of social performance at work on past eras and our own. Kean's fame was established in his own lifetime and spread rapidly after his death. By the early twentieth century, a fictional Kean had appeared in dozens of literary works, several long-running plays, and half a dozen early silent films. By the middle of the twentieth century his popularity had waned, except among some of the most important British actors (Gielgud, Olivier, Burton, O'Toole) and theater academics. But the time is now ripe for his rediscovery: Kean's effect upon acting and culture continues in what Baz Kershaw terms our "performative society" — a society in which we are crucially constituted as performers. Kean is a totem to our new social order in which the separation of reality and theater — or truth and fiction — has little meaning.

Structure

Kean's theatricality, and the uses his own and subsequent generations made of it, can be defined broadly as fitting three categories: political, philosophical, and religious. This unity is a synthetic arrangement, yet another organizing fiction. The chapters might have been organized in other, equally useful taxonomies: chronological or geographical, for example. The divisions as they stand are not meant to be proprietary. As aggregate narratives, these appropriations appeal to disparate but often overlapping images and echoes of Kean. Some of these appropriations seem to be independent; others work as semiautonomous studies. But as these sundry studies progress, they often intersect with each other; at other points they interject. Kean is not quite a blank signifier, but rather a product that is at once self-replicating and referential, one that replicates and refers to itself within finite variation. The variations of these creatively conceptualized Keans are conceived by his actions. In this sense, Kean's behavior, often bizarre, sometimes quite unthinking, can still reveal his values, personal idiosyncrasies, social goals, and their productive potential.

Approach

The intertextuality of appropriation suggests every author's work is built upon the sometimes unstable foundations of his/her predecessor. Reading one Kean, then, does not simply tell us about how one artist or one era views Kean, but points to the inescapability of historical process, a structured negotiation of exchange. Appropriations of Kean, and rewritings of these appropriations, call into question the idea of authorship, which is predicated on the notion of a work belonging to, and emanating from, one person. As these appropriations go on, a former incarnation of Kean is variously modified, conflated, rejected, corrected and/or incorporated into a new version. In the course of assessing these appropriations and reappropriations, it becomes hard to know at any given moment whether I am responding to a Coleridgean Kean, a Byronic Kean, Dumasian Kean, etc., or, to recall how each appropriation adds to the appropriator as well as the appropriated, a Keanian Coleridge, a Keanian Byron, a Keanian Dumas, etc., or a Dumasian Byron, a Coleridgean Sartre, etc. On some level, I am responding to all of them. Kean is now an aggregate of meanings. And while these meanings can be discussed, they cannot be discussed conceptually because the concept is unfinished, always being added to. Any attempt to describe these meanings is also a conscious or unconscious attempt on my part to conventionalize, stabilize, delimit, and disempower them. Each chapter, as I wrote it, seemed to have its own story, each its own implicit ideology that begged for expression. The multiplicity and interconnectivity of these chapters are reflected in the critical methodologies, which in the minds of critical readers may hopefully stimulate new multiple and changeable forms of the Edmund Kean narrative.

Prose Style and Tone

To reinforce the theatrical nature of Kean both as a form of practice and subject, I would like to discuss briefly the stylistic choices I have made in writing *The Cult of Kean*. All factual studies unavoidably involve imaginative tools and speculative techniques, such as narrative cohesion, descriptions, similes, and metaphors, all of which go beyond the simple display of facts or the search for "truth." Nonfictional narrative drives, which seek to tell stories, not explain them, tend to blunt academic analysis in favor of theatricality, and this text presented several challenges, some of which are not fully satisfying. The greatest challenge was Kean's recognizablity, which, as I have noted, has waned considerably, and only specialized critics may know much about him. Rather than suggest that the uninitiated situate themselves by reading some "factual" biographies of Kean, I have started each chapter with a short historical survey of some aspect of Kean's career. These introductions are not intended to replace a full biography. Whole areas of interest and importance have been selectively excluded. I note only those elements which illuminate the appropriation of Kean by the various authors involved. While these vignettes do not exhaustively probe the "facts" of Kean's life, they do set up the discursive conditions for my various analyses. The details selected are not in every instance striking or decisive events in Kean's remarkable life, nor are they random or haphazard. Kean's style of acting, both on and off the stage, was a direct critique of and response to the status quo. Kean's attempts to attract attention both on and off stage through his shameless and often vulgar behavior were the epitome of bad taste, but Kean's impression upon his audiences was indelible, unequivocally Kean. While I do not argue that these writers were attempting to "correctly" remember Kean, their repeated selections of certain motifs reveal varying interests and engagements with the historical or factual.

These "factual" introductions of Kean are in themselves a form of appropriation and fictionalization, for in selecting some facts over another, in choosing one form of characterization and organization over another and laying these details out in a conventionally and deliberately melodramatic fashion, I create a narrative that is fraught with elements of rhetorical expectation. A typical example is culled from the opening chapter: *His rise was unlikely, his success spectacular, his fall inevitable.* While the use of convention is true of all narratives, this study will, in part, attempt to explore what Adriana Cavarero has recently labeled "the relationship of 'dependency' between lives, stories and storytelling" (144). Indeed, many of my analyses, rather than simply relying on various forms of storytelling as convenient narrative principles of organization, use their narrative agents as self-conscious modes of exploring the changing dynamics of appropriation, representation, and recollection. As the practice of appropriation itself suggests, the relative authority of one Kean will differ from another. Given these discursive conditions, no two appropriations of Kean can be alike, nor any two readings.

Pictures

The Cult of Kean features many rare and interesting paintings of Kean and other important actors of the period, including Junius Brutus Booth, Ira Aldridge, and Charles Macready. The book also features examples of how the press used images of Kean to attack Napoleon or frame arguments concerning English cultural superiority. I have secured and paid for the rights to all of these prints, all of which might be reproduced in black and white.

Length, Documentation, and Ancillary Materials

The Cult of Kean is 345 pages, typed in double-space, Roman 12 font. MLA citations are used throughout. There are over 300 scholarly sources listed in my Works Cited.

Competition

There is no direct book on Kean like this on the market. However, the book does fit into a variety of new, well-received studies on other cultural figures: Gary Taylor's *Reinventing Shakespeare* (Oxford University Press, 1991); Julie Sanders' *Novel Shakespeares: Twentieth-Century Women Novelists and Appropriation* (Manchester University Press, 2002); Lucasta Miller's

The Brontë Myth (Jonathan Cape, 2001); Stephen Gill's *Wordsworth and the Victorians* (Oxford, 1998); and J.A. Downie and J.T. Parnell's collection, *Constructing Christopher Marlowe* (Cambridge, 2000).

Market

Because this book deals centrally with the way a variety of canonical authors appropriated Kean, its market is wider than an ordinary book on, say, Wordsworth or Shakespeare. Each chapter of *The Cult of Kean* will appeal to critics of different interests and theoretical interventions. Anyone interested in Byron, Coleridge, Keats, Dumas, Twain, and Sartre, English, American, Italian, and French Theater, postmodernism, and subversion has good reason to read the *Cult of Kean*.

About the Author

Jeffrey Kahan is the author of *Reforging Shakespeare* (Lehigh University, 1998). He is completing a three-volume edition of Shakespeare imitations, parodies, and forgeries for Routledge. The project will be completed in spring of 2003. His articles have appeared in *American Notes and Queries*, *The Ben Jonson Journal*, *English Language Notes*, *Early Modern Literary Studies*, *Notes and Queries*, *Para*Doxa*, *Renaissance Quarterly*, *Shakespeare Bulletin*, *Shakespeare Newsletter*, *Upstart Crow*, and *Women's Studies*, among others. He is Assistant Professor at the University of La Verne, California.

Sample 2: *Caped Crusaders 101: Composition Through Comic Books*

Number of Publishers Contacted: 2
Replies for More Information or Full Submission: 2
Number of Months from First Contact to Contract: 7

1. Proposed title and subtitle: *Crusaders 101: Composition Through Comic Books*
2. Authors: Jeffrey Kahan and Stanley Stewart
3. Brief description of project's scope and content

Comic book heroes have saved us from exploding stars, streaking comets, alien invasions, communist conspiracies, bank robbers, and terrorists. So why shouldn't they save us from illiteracy? After all, high culture notwithstanding, comic books are books. And they are, moreover, one of the few forms of print culture that children willingly pay to read. Nevertheless, as many jeremiads remind us, something happens to these voluntary readers. After years of assigned readings in traditional "children's literature," they give up reading books, comic books included, becoming what literacy specialists call "reluctant readers."

We believe that comic books can and should be used to recapture student interest in reading, and, further, to engage their interest in more traditional and canonical texts as well. With interpretive readings and class-room exercises, this textbook moves from inquiry into the social and spiritual significance of superheroes like Spiderman to that of heroes and antiheroes in the works of many of the most celebrated authors in the canon, such as Marlowe, Shakespeare, and Milton.

An array of questions, based on specific actions of comic book heroes and aimed at stimulating classroom debate and outside research skills, accompany each chapter.

4. Target audience

We have designed this textbook for use in advanced senior high school and college freshman English classes.

5. The market

Pearson Education, whose offerings consist largely of freshman composition readers, states that it educates (that is, sells to) 100 million consumers of their products worldwide every year. No one needs to tell you that there are hundreds of composition texts on the market. We believe this unique text, which engages many of the most intensely debated issues of our time by the device of the somewhat removed, but morally transparent, actions of comic book superheroes, will capture a significant part of this huge market.

6. Synergistic marketing

Each chapter links the reading or film treatment with a variety of other books offered by your press.

7. What makes our project distinctive?

There is no other book on the market that uses comic books as a composition reader, an amazing oversight when you consider the popularity of comics and adaptive offshoots in film and television.

8. What are the particular benefits offered by its content, scope, organization, and/or educational features?

The content of this project will naturally interest freshman students raised on comic books and their related movies and TV series: *The Hulk, Superman, Spiderman, Daredevil,* and *Wonder Woman.* Our aim is to harness this interest by returning the study of comic books to more traditional approaches.

The Composition Problem of the 1990s

Roger Shattuck, after studying literacy standards for the last 40 years, concluded that modern education is no longer interested in literacy and literature: "It is a simplification, but not a distortion, to refer to two categories of interests that tend to displace literature: politics (including race, class, feminism, minority and cultural studies, gay and lesbian studies) and theory (reliance on prior methodology or approach by which to read all works)."* Today, English departments are more likely to teach quasi-political science, New Historicism, Deconstruction, Cultural Materialism — schools of analysis that distain any meaningful articulation of aesthetics,

---

*Roger Shattuck, *Candour & Perversion: Literature, Education, and the Arts* (New York and London: W.W. Norton and Company, 1999), 4.

except in relation to economics or history. Freshman comp is usually taught by grad students who merely replicate the learning models they have experienced. These trendy critiques avoid discussion of the literary merits of the "work itself," which is held to be a "social construction" (that is, a pious fiction foisted on hapless, helpless victims).

Granted, anyone who has been involved in education (be it a parent, a student, or a teacher) is aware of the falling standards of our system and recent attempts to fix it. In a recent article in the *Los Angeles Times Magazine*, Richard Lee Colvin discusses a "model" taxpayer-funded program in which students are taught to be more concerned with "social justice" than with literacy. Thus, students are graded not on their ability to read or enjoy texts but rather on their ability to agree with the teacher's liberal-socialist agenda. A typical day now consists of discussions as to why the war in Iraq is wrong or why capitalism is evil; a class that may have been spent discussing Dickens' *Hard Times* is converted into a meet-and-greet with a drug dealer, who thinks that he has been unfairly jailed by the fascist U.S. government. The result is a curious mixture of militancy and apathy. Students discussed in the article regularly boycott Taco Bell as a class assignment, but are woefully underachieving in reading and writing.* This may seem like an extreme, isolated, and unfortunate example of a school system at least open to new methodologies; yet these examples tell us much about the kind of education presently offered in our programs and the kinds of professors we are presently hiring to do that professing. To call the current process "education" seems both misleading and self-serving. As anyone who has gone through graduate school in the last thirty years knows, the aforementioned political sophistry, or one very much like it, is not only indulged but embraced in the highest circles of academia.

As for those readers who sign on with English departments expecting to relive the excitement of their early introductions to literature, well, maybe college brochures should carry legal disclaimers, like those on cigarette packs and over-the-counter analgesics — warning: this text may induce drowsiness, headache, and boredom; long-term effects may include a loss of literary taste, a profound dislike of learning, and prolonged bouts of philistinism. Gone are the heady days of asking English majors to evaluate a novel or poem for its literary value. Nowadays, we (we are talking now about university professors) are openly hostile to such "frivolous" approaches. As Stanley Fish, chair of the English Department at the University of Illinois at Chicago, wrote not so long ago, "There is a great difference between trying to figure out what a poem means and trying to figure out which interpretation of a poem will contribute to the toppling of patriarchy or to the war effort."†

---

*Richard Lee Colvin, "But Teacher, My Homework Got Run Over at the Taco Bell Protest." *Los Angeles Times Magazine* 5 October 2003: 12-5, 31-2.

†Stanley Fish, "Why Literary Criticism Is like a Virtue" *London Review of Books* 10 June 1993, p.11.

A Return to Basics

This textbook is not interested in getting young students to think of English's recent shift towards theoretical paradigms. Rather, we want to spark a love of reading, debate, and research. We believe that comics, a multibillion dollar industry, hold the key. Whether we are dealing with readers of *Love and Rockets* or *Superman*, we are dealing with readers so passionate about books that they cherish them like treasures to be handed down to future generations. We are talking here of millions of readers, willing readers, habitual readers, readers hooked on character and plot, readers who weigh virtues not simply in terms of winning and losing but in spiritual and moral terms of good and evil, readers who discuss issues and concerns with other readers at conventions, online, and in coffee houses, readers whose pleasure in a suffusion of ethics and aesthetics, paneled in transitions of images and words, is drawn from the disparate vocabularies of cuneiform, the printed word, and the cinema.* They are comic book readers, and, we argue, each one has the enthusiasm, dedication, and imaginative skill to make a motivated English major and a competent reader of traditional academic materials.†

9. Chapter by chapter synopsis of the project's planned content and main argument(s).

Chapter One: **Black Heroes for Hire: Serializing Social Construction in the Comics**

Comic books, of course, are a business, one that is increasing and going through radical change. Marvel's mighty heroes include new film franchises like *Spiderman, The X-Men, Blade,* and *The Hulk.* However, since 9–11 Marvel in particular has renewed its focus of using heroes to address ideas of democracy and liberal egalitarianism. In this chapter, we argue that comic book writers have aggressively attempted to use their market among the young to politically reorient its readers, specifically towards embracing racial equality. Ironically, the idea of the superhero itself presupposes inequality and racial purity. Our argument relies upon a detailed study of Marvel's earliest "black" comics: Luke Cage and The Falcon.

>   **Materials Discussed**
>
>   *Comics* (listed in order of emphasis): *Captain America, The Falcon, The Hulk, Luke Cage: Hero for Hire, The Black Panther.*
>
>   *Canonical Texts* (listed in order of emphasis): Shakespeare, *Othello*;

---

*Hugo Frey and Benjamin Noys have argued that comics have been intellectually marginalized because the medium is a hybrid of text and image and thus defies easy categorization ("History in the Graphic Novel," in *Rethinking History* [London: Routledge, 2002], 255-60; 255).

†Anne Rubenstein argues that comics compete directly with video games and movies more so than they do with other forms of print media. See *Bad Language, Naked Ladies, and Other Threats to the Nation: A Political History of Comic Books in Mexico* (Durham and London: Duke University Press, 1998), 8. Nonsense. A comic book's direct competition is other comics on the same rack. Video games often feature comic book characters, and are, thus, an extension of the comic book reader's experience. Ditto films, which increasingly cater to comic readers: witness the blockbuster summer films *X-Men, X-Men 2, Daredevil,* and *Spiderman.*

Mark Twain, *Huck Finn*; Malcolm X, *The Autobiography of Malcolm X*.

Chapter Two: **Spiderman and Corporate Responsibility**

The largest-grossing movie of 2002 was *Spiderman*, an adaptation of the Marvel comic. The gross take on the film exceeded $800 million (a record $150 million for its opening weekend), a tacit approval of the movie's primary message: "With great power comes great responsibility." Ironic, since the comics, long blamed for moral decline in America, have taken a position akin to the gun lobby's: "It's not bullets that kill people; people kill people." The appeal of *Spiderman*'s message was in some ways bolstered by the events that formed a backdrop to the movie. 2002 was the year of corporate irresponsibility, falling stock prices, and the debacle of three huge firms: Arthur Anderson, Enron, and Worldcom.

Materials Discussed:

Comics and Films: *Spiderman* (comic and film), *Daredevil, Spiderman, Spiderman 2099, Batman, Batman Beyond* (TV series), *The Fantastic Four*.

Canonical Texts: Marx, *Das Kapital*; Adam Smith, *The Wealth of Nations*; Edmund Burke, *Reflections on the Revolution in France*; Hobbes, *Leviathan*.

Chapter Three: **Dr. Doom and the End of America's Manifest Destiny**

As the superpowers of America and the Soviet Union grappled for world domination, DC and Marvel Comics wrote story after story in which superheroes with superpowers fought supervillains with global ambitions. A case in point would be the Fantastic Four, who waged war against Dr. Doom and his robot armies of the East. But on many occasions, even at the height of the Cold War, Marvel found reasons to see Doom as a "Good Guy," protecting women and children, minority rights, and cultural values from American globalization.

Materials Discussed:

Comics and Films: *The Fantastic Four, Green Lantern, The Avengers, The Justice League, Doom 2099, Super-Villain Team-Up, Astonishing Tales, The Mighty Thor, Star Spangled War Stories, The Ultimates*.

Concepts: Manifest Destiny, American Imperialism.

Chapter Four: **The Comic Code and American F-agg**

Fredric Wertham's *Seduction of the Innocent* was among the most discussed books of the 1950s because it dealt so centrally with the youth of America and its perceived moral failings. It was clear why America's youth preferred premarital sex, marijuana, and rock 'n' roll. Their strong moral upbringing had been attacked — not by foreign commies but, more insidiously, by the very reading materials their doting parents had bought for them. In the pages of comic books, the child learned all manner of crimes. But Wertham's major axe wasn't against theft, physical violence, or even murder but ... (gasp!) homosexuality.

Materials Discussed:

Comics and Films: *American Flagg, Batman* (TV series), *The Hulk* (comic and TV series), *Superman, Smallville* (TV series), *Alpha Flight, Wonder Woman.*

    Canonical Texts: Henri Barbusse, *L'Enfer*; Robert Louis Stevenson, *Doctor Jekyll and Mr. Hyde.*

Chapter Five: **Dr. Strange, or How I Learned to Love Metaphysics**

Heroes are not merely an expression of power, and yet, in the comics, might makes right. Villains yield not to entreaties but to blows. What do the comics have to say about the nature of good in relation to power? Are they the same? This chapter will use Dr. Strange to introduce students to the basics of metaphysical argument.

    Materials Discussed:

    Comics and Films: Strange Tales, Dr. Strange (comic and TV movie), *Marvel Premiere.*

    Canonical Texts: Immanuel Kant, *Collected Works*; Nietzsche, *Beyond Good and Evil*; William James, *The Varieties of Religious Experience.*

Chapter Six: **9–11 and Daredevil, the Man Without Fear**

In a widely publicized and controversial book entitled *The Clash of Civilizations*, Samuel Huntington predicted a new cold war, one unlike the political conflict between communism and the West. This emerging conflict would be, and is already, a revival of a religious war that goes back to the Crusades of the Middle Ages, when men like Richard, Coeur de Lion, led armies to the Holy Land. Because this conflict emanates from religious differences, this new cold war has rendered recent ideology passé. Instead of Marxist determinism and Stalinist panzer divisions, Huntington argues, the West faces hordes of Muslims who think of Western ways with revulsion and resentment. America, worst of the worst, is "materialistic, corrupt, decadent and immoral." Moreover, the West is determined to spread its corrupt ways throughout the Muslim world through CDs, magazines, movies, and tight jeans.

    Materials Discussed:

    Comics and Films: *Spiderman, Daredevil* (comic and movie), *Captain America, Iron Man, Nick Fury: Agent of SHIELD, Batman.*

    Canonical Texts: Milton, *Paradise Lost*; Spenser, *Fairie Queene*; Marlowe, *Dr. Faustus.*

Chapter Seven: **Comics and the Prison System**

At the end of the *X-Men* movie, we see Magneto (Ian McKellen), who has the power to control anything magnetic, locked away in a prison made of plastic and glass. He warns his nemesis, Professor Charles Xavier (Patrick Stewart), that the prison will not be able to hold him; he will soon find a way out. Xavier concedes that Magneto will not be in prison forever; either the villain will break out, or he will serve his term and be released. Either way, Magneto is determined to impose his will on society, and all Xavier can do is "be waiting for him."

    Such cat-and-mouse scenarios are the warp and woof of comic book heroism. After all, without a villain, who needs a hero? At the same time,

Magneto's imprisonment raises interesting philosophical questions about the nature and value of punishment. Given the fact that the *X-Men* movie came out during a renewed debate over California's three-strikes law, it's hard to read Magneto's warning of future mayhem apart from one of the burning issues of our time: criminal recidivism and the death penalty.

Materials Discussed:

Comics and Films: *X-Men* (comic and movies), *The Hulk* (comic, TV series, and movie), *The Punisher* (comic and movie), *Judge Dredd* (comic and movie), *Batman* (comic and movies).

Canonical Texts: Michel Foucault's *Discipline and Punishment: The Birth of the Prison*; Alexis de Tocqueville, *Democracy in America*; Alexander Hamilton, *The Federalist Papers*; Adam Smith, *The Wealth of Nations*.

10. Study Questions: A Sample Culled from Chapter Eight: Thinking, Debating, Writing

1. Draft a letter to the UN outlining why you believe the United States has the right to respond militarily if it feels itself to be in danger. If you do not agree with this position, respond to a paper written by one of your classmates who does take that position.
2. The essay argues that religion is at the heart of the *Daredevil* movie. Rent the movie and then write an essay in which you disagree; use evidence from outside sources to back your arguments.
3. Write an essay on the history of America's Middle Eastern policy. When did it start? What changes has it undergone?
4. Did it surprise you that America sells its advanced weaponry to other nations? Look up the history of Lockheed Martin, Boeing, and other military contractors. Do American companies do America a disservice by selling weapons to other nations?
5. This chapter argues that New York is a "scary place." Look up the crime statistics for the city of New York and then contact your local law enforcement agency to see if New York deserves that descriptive.
6. Is Islam a misunderstood religion? Read the *Koran* and come to your own conclusions. Contact a cleric at a local mosque and get his view as well. Present your findings to the class.
7. All the examples in this chapter focus on military solutions. Research and describe what political initiatives have been offered to solve terrorism.
8. Research Oliver North and the Iran-Contra hearings. Did North subvert the Constitution?
9. How accurate is it to compare Guyon to Daredevil? Read Canto 12 of Spenser's *Fairie Queene* and compare.
10. Captain America and Nick Fury look back nostalgically to the "good old days" of the Nazis. Look up the history of World War II and discuss whether the current situation is more or less dangerous.

11. How long do you expect the project to be in printed pages?

We are aiming at 300 pages of typeset text.

12. Does the project require any illustration? Please indicate if you envisage including any images and, if so, approximately how many.

Yes, as you might imagine in any study of such a visual medium, this textbook does incorporate a variety of photos and pictures from both film and traditional comic books. Almost all of the pictures have been culled from press kits and require no payment. Other pictures have been downloaded from Corbis, a mainstream photo-content company, with licensing agreements with most textbook publishers.

13. When do you realistically propose to deliver a final typescript?

We fully expect to complete the manuscript by August 2004.

14. The authors and their track record

Jeffrey Kahan is the author of *Reforging Shakespeare* (Lehigh University, 1998), *New Shakespeare, Now with Nobler Lustre,* 3 vols. (Routledge, 2004), *Shakespeare for Children* (Shakespeare Millennium, 2004), *The Poetry of William-Henry Ireland* (Mellen, 2004), and coeditor of *The Compendium of Renaissance Drama* (Pro-Quest, 2004). His articles have appeared in *American Notes and Queries, The Ben Jonson Journal, English Language Notes, Early Modern Literary Studies, Notes and Queries, Para*Doxa, Renaissance Quarterly, Shakespeare Bulletin, Shakespeare Newsletter, Upstart Crow,* and *Women's Studies,* among others. He is an associate professor at the University of La Verne, California.

Stanley Stewart (B.A., M.A., Ph.D., UCLA) is the author of numerous books and articles, including *The Enclosed Garden: The Tradition and the Image in 17th-Century Poetry* (Wisconsin, 1966), *The Expanded Voice: The Art of Thomas Traherne* (Huntington Library, 1970), and *George Herbert* (G.K. Hall, 1976). He is coauthor, with Bernd Magnus and Peter Mileur, of *Nietzsche's Case: Philosophy as/and Literature* (Routledge, 1992) and, with James Riddell, of *Jonson's Spenser: Evidence and Historical Criticism* (Duquesne, 1995). Coeditor of *The Ben Jonson Journal: Literary Contexts in the Age of Elizabeth, James, and Charles,* he serves on the editorial boards of *John Donne Journal: Studies in the Age of Donne* and *Cithara: Essays in the Judeo-Christian Tradition.* His most recent publications are *"Renaissance" Talk: Ordinary Language and the Mystique of Critical Problems* (Duquesne, 1997), *"'New' Guides to the Historically Perplexed"* (in *Neo-historicism,* ed. Robin Headlam-Wells [Boydell & Brewer, 2000]), and *The Cambridge Companion to Ben Jonson* (Cambridge University Press, 2000), which he edited with Richard Harp, and to which he contributed a chapter on "Jonson's Criticism." A former Guggenheim and Mellon Fellow, currently working on "Philosophy's Shakespeare," he has been honored by the Academic Senate as a recipient of the Distinguished Teaching Award and as Faculty Research Lecturer, UCR (2000).

15. Contact details

Jeffrey Kahan, Dept of English, University of La Verne, 1950 3rd Street, La Verne, CA 91042

Stanley Stewart, Dept of English, University of California at Riverside, 900 University Avenue, Riverside, CA 92521

Sample 3: *The Poetry of Robert Southey*

Number of Publishers Contacted: 2
Replies for More Information or Full Submission: 1
Number of Months from First Contact to Contract: 5

Overview

In his collected works of 1837, Robert Southey, then sixty-three years old, wrote that his poetry "had obtained a reputation equal to my wishes: and I have this ground for hoping it may not be deemed hereafter more than commensurate with their deserts."* Today, Southey is the focus of renewed critical attention, but no reasonably-priced edition now in print adequately represents Southey's verse.

Southey's Verse: A Case of Misrepresentation

Although Southey stresses poetic morality, poetic feeling, and purity of expression and rejects — along with Wordsworth and Coleridge — the Augustan heroic couplet in favor of blank verse and experimental forms, his work doesn't really fit into the pastoral splendors of the English Romantics.

Jack Simmons summed up the rationale for critical dismissal: "If only Southey had written more of England, which he knew and loved devotedly, instead of dealing with remote subjects for which neither he nor we can really feel any deep sympathy, he might have been a major poet."†

There are two replies to this argument:

(1) Simmons is not strictly accurate. Southey could be topical and nationalistic, if not always militaristic or jingoistic. (See, for example, his "Ode, Written During the Negociations with Buonaparte, In January, 1814", "Ode, Written During the War with America, 1814," "Poems Concerning the Slave Trade," "Botany Bay Ecologues," and his collaborative play, *The Fall of Robespierre*.) As Mark Storey's archival work suggests, Southey saw his *Joan of Arc* poem as a commentary on the revolution in France.** His Madoc poems were also designed as suggestively topical commentaries: the Welsh bardic "Unitarian" escapes the Saxon Catholic tyranny of England in order to establish a Christian colony in the New World.†† That being said, there is no doubt that Southey's best poetry concerns half-forgotten legends and myths. His typical heroes are weapon-wielding Saxons, Saracens, Goths, Asians, and Aztecs.

(2) Southey *was* a major poet: Coleridge wrote glowingly of Southey's

---

*Robert Southey, Preface, *The Poetical Works of Robert Southey*, 10 vols. (London: Longmans, 1837), I:V.

†Jack Simmons, *Southey* (London: Collins, 1945), 210.

**Southey wrote in a letter, "Vive La Republique! My Joan is a great democrat, or rather will be." See Mark Storey, *Robert Southey: A Life* (Oxford: Oxford University Press, 1997), 32.

††Ibid., 56.

Thalaba; it was also one of Shelley's favorites. Scott esteemed Southey's *Madoc* poems. They kept Fox and his circle at St. Ann's Hill from their beds at night. And, in the Victorian era, Edward Dowden, the famed Shakespeare biographer and critic, justly sang the poet's praises.

The Market: Why Southey's Epics Speak to Us

Earnest Bernhardt-Kabisch (1977) lamented that Southey seemed too fantastical to relate to urban and urbane readers: "few ballads can still captivate us with their quick-paced renditions of supernatural or otherwise pathetic anecdote...."* Nearly three decades on, Earnest Bernhardt-Kabisch's perspective no longer seems to apply.

Given Southey's interests in foreign lands, his work is ripe for appropriation for anyone teaching Said's *Orientalism* or any class which looks at colonialism and/or post-colonialism. In *Madoc in Aztlan*, a Welsh prince of the twelfth century sails to South America, where he confronts demonic spirits appeased by blood sacrifice. In *Kehama*, Southey wafts us through the eldritch adventures of an Indian Rajah, whose greatest battle is between the conflicting impulses of his soul, represented by the Divine Preserver on the one hand and the Divine Destroyer on the other.

There are other factors that make a Southey collection an attractive proposition. Increasingly, American state school boards are mandating that teachers augment canonical texts with multicultural and postcolonial offerings. Given these constraints, it is Southey, not Wordsworth, who may well be the poet of choice for teachers who have only room for one or two Romantic poets on their syllabi. At the university level as well, a collection of Southey would make a sound addition to courses on Romanticism, postcolonialism, or even fantasy fiction.

Proposed Page Length

I intend to follow the standard edition format: short introduction (30 pages approx.), poems, including short commentary on each poem, and notes. (See below.)

Proposed Selected Material and Ordering

Religious Verse:
  A Tale of Paraguay II.15–20
  Madoc in Aztlan, XII
  The Curse of Kehama X.10–14.
  Roderick, the Last of the Goths: Book XX
  All for Love, VIII
  The Lay of the Laureate, stanzas 73–79–encourages collonization
Tales of Adventure and Horror:
  Madoc in Wales, Book VI
  Madoc in Aztlan, VII, XIV
  Thalaba the Destroyer, Book II, IV, IX, X
  The Curse of Kehama, I, II

*Earnest Bernhardt-Kabisch, *Robert Southey* (Boston: Twayne Publishers, 1977), 180

"The Old Woman of Berkeley, a Ballad"
English Wars:
Joan of Arc, Book IX — English abandoned, like the Aztecs
Metrical Tales: The Battle of Blenheim
Ode, Written During the Negociations with Buonaparte, In January, 1814
Ode, Written During the War with America, 1814
The Poet's Pilgrimage, Book II: The Evil Prophet

Notes

In his *Complete Works* (1837), Southey added an array of notes, some of which are undoubtedly arcane. I propose that we reprint only the most user-friendly of these notes. Some other passages concerning geographical locations, comparative influence, and source material will need light commentary. Further commentary on Southey will be excerpted from Lionel Madden's *Robert Southey: Critical Heritage* (London and Boston: Routledge & Kegan Paul, 1972) and a variety of up-to-date critical studies. As well, I have uncovered some hitherto unpublished Southey letters and drafts at the Huntington and HRC.

Competition and Previous Editions of Southey's Verse

Overview

The most successful of Southey's collections center on his epic verse. No such reasonably-priced collection is presently in print.

Verse

1. *The Poetical Works of Robert Southey*, 10 vols., London: Longmans, 1837.

Comment: This is a near-complete works, edited by Southey himself. His first long poem, *Joan of Arc*, is drastically revised. The emphasis is put on his most famous poems, his long verse narratives.

Status: Reprinted in 1977 by Georg Olms Verlag. This edition is out of print and, when still in print, was far too expensive ($75 a volume) for students.

2. *Southey*, ed. Sidney R. Thompson (London: Walter Scott, 1888)

Comment: A short selection of Southey's epic narrative; the editor agrees that Southey's sword and sorcery verse is his best material.

Status: Out of print.

3. *Poems of Robert Southey*, ed. Edward Dowden. London and New York: Macmillan and Co., 1895.

Comment: A short though affirming introduction, followed by a short selection of Southey's miscellany, and then selections from some of his epic narratives: the *Madoc* poems, *Thalaba The Destroyer*, *Roderick, The Last of the Goths, The Curse of Kehama*.

Status: Out of print.

4. *The Poems of Robert Southey*, ed. Maurice H. Fitzgerald. Oxford: Oxford University Press, 1909.

Comment: Fitzgerald bemoans the fact that Southey is hardly ever read and thinks *Thalaba, Madoc,* and *Cure of Kehama* are his best works. His collection also has a selection of short verse.

Status: Out of print.

5. *A Choice of Robert Southey's Verse*, ed. Geoffrey Grigson. London: Faber and Faber, 1970.

Comment: Aside from a short excerpt (some 40 lines) from *The Battle of Blenheim*, this is a selection of miscellaneous verse. The introduction and the selection misrepresent Southey as an unoriginal and unexceptional verser, capable of only imitating Coleridge and Wordsworth's *Lyrical Ballads*. The error is compounded by Duncan Wu's selection of Southey; see below.

Status: Out of print and nonrepresentative.

6. *Poems*. Oxford: Woodstock Books, 1989.

Comment: This is a facsimile of Southey's political collection of 1797. Almost all the poems are short miscellany.

Status: Out of print and nonrepresentative. When in print, it sold for $70, far too expensive for students.

7. *Robert Southey: Poetical Works, 1793–1810 (The Pickering Masters)*, eds. Lynda Pratt, Tim Fulford, and Daniel Sanjiv Roberts. Pickering & Chatto Publishers, 2004.

Status: In print, but it costs $750!!

Survey Course Compellations

8. *Romanticism, an Anthology*, ed. Duncan Wu. 2nd ed. Oxford: Blackwells, 1998.

Comment: Wu notes that Southey's fame rests on his epic fantasies but includes none of them. He opts for about 40 lines from Book III of *Joan of Arc*, *Hannah* (a minor poem, but among Coleridge's favorites), "The Idiot" (seemingly because of its parallels to *Lyrical Ballads*, a collection Southey disparaged), and "The Sailor Who Had Served in the Slave-Trade".

Status: In print but nonrepresentative.

Drama

While I am not discussing or selecting from his plays, I should note that there is a market for them:

9. *Wat Tyler* is available in *Five Romantic Plays, 1768–1821*, eds. Paul Baines and Edward Burns. Oxford: Oxford University Press, 2000.

Status: In print.

10. His collaborative play, *The Fall of Robespierre*, is also available. New York: Kessinger Publishing, 2004.

Status: In print.

Secondary Materials

Although there is no reasonably-priced edition of Southey's verse in print, his work continues to generate a significant amount of criticism, some of which I have already footnoted. Nonetheless, I think it's important to acknowledge that publishers continue to show interest in Southey's work and his life. (This list is representative, rather than exhaustive.)

Biography

11. Joseph Cottle, *Reminiscences of Samuel Taylor Coleridge and Robert Southey*. New York: Lime Tree Bower Press, 1970.

Status: In print.

12. Mark Storey, *Robert Southey: A Life*. Oxford: Oxford University Press, 1997.
Status: In print.
13. *The Contributions of Robert Southey to the Morning Post*, ed. Kenneth Curry. Alabama: University of Alabama Press, 1984.
Status: Out of print. When in print, it sold for $99, far too expensive for students.

Letters
14. *Life and Correspondence of the Late Robert Southey*, ed. Maurice H. Fitzgerald. 6 vols. Connecticut: Native American Books Distributor, 1912; reprint, 1970.

Criticism
15. Lionel Madden's *Robert Southey: Critical Heritage*. London and Boston: Routledge & Kegan Paul, 1972.
16. Christopher Smith, *Quest for Home: Reading Robert Southey*. New York: Intl. Specialized Book Service, 1997.
17. Andrew Pagett, *The Lakeland Poets: In the Footsteps of William Wordsworth, Samuel Taylor Coleridge, Robert Southey and Others*. New York: Chaucer, 2004.

About Jeffrey Kahan
Jeffrey Kahan is the author of *New Shakespeare, "Now With Added Lustre": Shakespeare Imitations and Forgeries 1710–1820* (3 vols., Routledge, 2004), *The Poetry of William-Henry Ireland* (forthcoming, Mellon, 2005), and *Reforging Shakespeare: The Story of a Theatrical Scandal* (Associated University Presses, 1998). He is editor of the ongoing series *Shakespeare for Children* (2004), coeditor of *The Compendium of Renaissance Drama* (Oxford Pro-Quest, forthcoming 2005), and coeditor of *Passions and Poisons: The Prose and Poetry of New Canadian Writers* (Nu-Age, 1987). In addition, Dr. Kahan has published some 50 articles and 17 book reviews in a variety of journals, including *American Notes and Queries, The Ben Jonson Journal, Critical Quarterly, English Language Notes, Early Modern Literary Studies, Notes and Queries, Para*Doxa, Renaissance Quarterly, Seventeenth-Century News, Shakespeare Bulletin, Shakespeare Newsletter, Shakespeare Yearbook, Upstart Crow,* and *Women's Studies,* among others. His present research concerns Shakespeare forgery, a book on the 19th century actor Edmund Kean, and a cultural study of comic books. Jeffrey Kahan is Associate Professor of English Literature at the University of La Verne (http://faculty.ulv.edu/~kahanj/).

Sample 4: *Proposal for Multivolume Edition of Shakespeare Imitations, Parodies, and Forgeries (Circa 1750–1850)*

Number of Presses Contacted: 1
Replies for More Information or Full Submission: 1
Number of Months from Contact to Contract: 21

Overview:

Editions of Shakespeare adaptations for the seventeenth through nineteenth centuries are readily available, but little or no editorial work has been done on Shakespeare imitations, parodies, and forgeries for the same period. This proposed edition would select works from circa 1750–1850, an era in which Shakespeare's plays reached an unprecedented height of critical and theatrical popularity.

Scholarly Interest in Shakespeare Adaptations:

Shakespeare — and his influence upon subsequent playwrights, critics, and actors — is of crucial interest to a growing number of scholars, including Michael Dobson, Jonathan Bate, and Gary Taylor. Perhaps what is more important from a publishing standpoint, books that republish Shakespeare adaptations from different eras are appearing with greater frequency. Montague Summers's *Shakespearean Adaptations* (1922; rpt. 1966) reprints the famous Tate version of *King Lear* and the Davenant and Dryden version of *The Tempest*. Christopher Spencer's *Five Restoration Adaptations of Shakespeare* (1965) includes Davenant's *Macbeth* and Grenville's *Jew of Venice*. In 1994, the University of Nebraska issued a single-volume edition of Dryden's *All For Love*, an adaptation of *Antony and Cleopatra*. In 1997, Everyman brought out *Shakespeare Made Fit: Restoration Adaptations of Shakespeare*. Routledge has just released *Adaptations of Shakespeare* (2000), a work that, along with the online resource *Editions and Adaptations of Shakespeare* (1997–2000), offers a wide selection of adaptations from the seventeenth century to the present. There is even a five-volume set of nineteenth-century Shakespeare parodies edited by Stanley Wells (*Shakespeare Burlesques*, Diploma Press, 1977).

Rationale of Multivolume Edition on Shakespearean Imitations, Parodies, and Forgeries:

A gap, therefore, remains in scholarly editions concerning Shakespeare imitations and forgeries, and — with the exception of Wells work — this gap extends into the field of Shakespeare parodies. All three of these Shakespearean subgenres are covered in my twenty-eight-play selection. The proportional breakdown for the edition is as follows: fourteen imitations, ten parodies, four forgeries. The editorial principles and critical rationale for this multivolume edition, and the quality of the plays selected, are herein summarized briefly:

I. Shakespeare Imitations:

The title pages to these plays more often than not state that they "are written in imitation of Shakespeare." These imitations reveal the biases of eighteenth-century stylistics, the influence of Shakespeare criticism, and the almost menacing dominance of Shakespeare in London theatre.

But these plays are far from derivative. Indeed, rather than simply rewriting Shakespearean situations, these playwrights often placed Shakespearean characters in neoclassical frameworks. As such, they, in fact, implicitly reflected the notion that Shakespeare was a gifted but imperfect writer in need of often-radical correction. These were not simply plays Shakespeare might have written. They were plays that Shakespeare might have written had the Bard enjoyed the benefits of a neoclassical education.

Although many of these plays are unfamiliar to us, within their own day these works enjoyed much critical and commercial success. For example, Nicholas Rowe's *Tragedy of Jane* was the most popular new play of the eighteenth century and the sixth-most performed tragedy, following *Hamlet, Macbeth, Romeo and Juliet, Othello,* and *King Lear.* Even William Shirley's forgotten play, *Edward the Black Prince* (1750), "was well receiv'd with great applause" and had a stage history spanning three decades.

The creative impulses behind these plays stemmed in part from the notion that a properly retooled Shakespeare — modernized in a French Neoclassical format — might serve as a useful cultural weapon against revolutionary and reactionary forces at home and abroad. This was especially true for plays written and/or performed during the French Revolution.

I have selected fourteen Shakespeare imitations and located manuscript copies and/or first editions for each. Where possible, this edition will base its text upon manuscripts reflecting the theatrical natures of the plays. No modern edition exists of *any* of these plays.

II. Shakespeare Parodies:

Parodying Shakespeare was not only a popular practice, it was a venerable one. The first parodies of Shakespeare date from the seventeenth century. The fact that these parodies were commercially viable projects is indicative of how familiar audiences were with his plays. These parodies are *paratexts,* compositions which recognizably relate — in various harmonies and disharmonies — to parent texts. The reader or listener then compares the original and the parody intertextually, realizes their differences, and appreciates their comic interplay. But parody is more than a cultural parlor game. Michael Dobson, Gary Taylor, and other theorists have linked parody to a subversive movement that through accident or design inevitably debases cultural icons.

Some preliminary editorial work has been done in this field. Stanley

Wells edited a five-volume set of Shakespeare burlesques in 1977. But
the edition, while valuable, has some critical inadequacies: Wells' edition did little to set out the aesthetic conditions that gave rise to parodies. Nor did he discriminate between the differing political and
cultural formations of American and British Shakespeare parodies.
Lastly, his texts were all based upon printed versions. This edition will
help address these critical and editorial shortcomings.

I have drawn up a list of ten Shakespeare parodies and located
manuscript copies and/or first editions for each. Where possible, this
edition will base its text upon manuscripts reflecting the theatrical
natures of the plays.

III. Shakespeare Forgeries:

During the eighteenth and nineteenth centuries, the subversive
impulses to forge Shakespeare were manifold. Significantly, most
Shakespeare forgeries were written when Shakespeare's cultural force
was arguably in most need: during the French Revolution. But not all
forgeries were necessarily overtly political acts. Some playwrights
forged to enhance their own reputations; others forged to undermine
the literary reputations of critics; still others forged as private jokes.
No matter the impulses at work, forgers, in the words of Samuel Ireland, "pollute the cultural repository from which they spring."

Jonathan Bate, Nick Groom, and Jeffrey Kahan have done some
basic research in this burgeoning field, but scholarship has hitherto
focused on critical discussions of plays and literary documents long
out of print and unfamiliar to most scholars and lay readers. No modern scholarly edition exists for even the most famous of all Shakespeare theatrical forgeries, William-Henry Ireland's *Vortigern*. Scholars
interested in the work have had to make do with the two early quartos
of the play (1799; rpt. 1970 and 1832). Invariably, scholars were
satisfied with these editions, as it had long been accepted that the
manuscript(s) to the play were lost. However, in 1993 I located no
less than six distinctly unique manuscripts of *Vortigern*. In collating
and recording over 3,000 variants, I made a startling discovery: The
1799 and 1832 variants bore only facile resemblances to the version
originally staged. In short, the play, as staged April 2, 1796, at Theatre–Royal Drury Lane, has *never been* printed. The same textual
problems plague Ireland's other Shakespeare forgery, *Henry II*.

As for Theobald's *The Double Falsehood,* it was last edited in 1967;
a reprint of the 1828 quarto is also available. Recent scholarship is
unsure whether Theobald really did base his play upon the manuscript of the lost Shakespeare play *Cardenio* or whether he forged the
play outright. Considering that Charles Hamilton has recently published what he believes is the manuscript for *Cardenio* (Glenbridge
Publishing, 1994), a new edition with a critical introduction examin-
ing the relation — if any — of *Double Falsehood* to *Cardenio* is an
immediate imperative.

In all, I have located manuscript copies and/or first editions to four Shakespeare forgeries. Where possible, this edition will base its text upon manuscripts reflecting the theatrical natures of the plays.

This Prospective Edition's Mandate:
I propose a multivolume edition of these eighteenth- and nineteenth-century Shakespeare imitations, parodies, and forgeries. The opening volume's critical introduction will serve the following purposes:
  (1) to map out the theatrical conditions of the seventeenth and eighteenth century from the perspectives of critics, playwrights, and audiences;
  (2) to provide a brief history of the development of the specific genres of Shakespeare imitation, parody, and forgery; and
  (3) to supply concise summaries of the central texts and their impact on theatrical, critical and editorial practice.

The second volume will also include the following information, placed in a series of appendices:
  (1) a suggested list of further readings;
  (2) a complete list of all imitations, parodies, and forgeries of the period, whether published in this edition or not;
  (3) a list of related sources, including online links for research sites concerning Shakespeare imitations, parodies, and forgeries;
  (4) a bibliography; and
  (5) a comprehensive index.

The plays I have selected meet the following criteria:
  (1) they must have been staged at a professional London theatre;
  (2) they must have been popular enough to have merited print; and/or
  (3) they must state in either the title page or prefatory material(s) that they:
      (i) are imitations;
      (ii) are lost works by Shakespeare; and/or
      (iii) include at least one of Shakespeare's characters.

Division of Volumes:
In discussions with Nick Groom, a two-volume format was decided upon. The volumes will be divided in the following manner:

Volume One: Shakespeare Imitations Written Circa 1750–1850

Volume Two: Shakespeare Parodies and Forgeries Written Circa 1750–1850

Individual plays will also have short prefaces covering the following facets:
  (1) biographical details;
  (2) a study of the elements the author considered essential when crafting a "new" Shakespeare;
  (3) a survey of each play's theatrical reception and history;
  (4) a survey of each play's critical history; and
  (5) the print history and the location(s) of the original manuscript(s), if extant.

Selected Plays for Each Volume:
Each play listed below contains the following information:
(1) Author;
(2) Title; and
(3) Proposed copy-text and, where possible, the location of the manuscript.

Volume One: Shakespeare Imitations (Fourteen Plays in Total):

Date: 1714
Author: Nicholas Rowe
Title: *The Tragedy of Jane Shore. Written in Imitation of Shakespear's Style*
Copy Text: *Bell's British Theatre*, Vol. III, 1791, for 1797, compared against *Inchbald's Theatre* X (1808), and *Cumberland's British Theatre* V (1826).

Date: 1715
Author: Nicholas Rowe
Title: *The Tragedy of Lady Jane Grey. Written in Imitation of Shakespear's Style*
Copy Text: Vol. XV. *Bell's British Theatre*, 1791, for 1797.

Date: 1721
Author: Edward Young
Title: *The Revenge*
Copy Text: *Inchbald's Theatre* XII, 1808 compared against *Inchbald's Theatre* XII (1808), *The Modern British Drama*, Vol. 2 of 5 Vols., London: William Miller, 1811, and *The British Drama* Vol. 1 of 2 Vols. London: Phil M. Polock, 1853.

Date: 1737
Author: William Havard
Title: *Charles the First. Written in Imitation of Shakespear's Style*
Copy Text: Vol. XIX. *Bell's British Theatre*, 1791, for 1797.

Date: 1750
Author: William Shirley
Title: *Edward the Black Prince. Written in Imitation of Shakespear's Style*
Copy Text: Manuscript Larpent 81—includes unknown prologue entitled, "An Appropriate National Prologue to the Rival of *Edward the Black Prince.*" Compared against Vol. IX. *Bell's British Theatre*, 1791, for 1797, *Inchbald's Theatre*, Vol. XIV, 1808, and *The Modern British Drama*, Vol. 2 of 5 Vols., London: William Miller, 1811.

Date: 1751 (performed 1753 according to *Inchbald's Theatre* XXI, 1808).
Author: Henry Jones
Title: *The Earl of Essex. Written in Imitation of Shakespear's Style*
Copy Text: Larpent 91—many differences compared to Vol. VI. *Bell's British Theatre*, 1791, for 1797, and *Inchbald's Theatre* XXX (1800).

Date: 1756
Author: John Home
Title: *Douglas. Written in Imitation of Shakspeare's Style*

Copy Text: Vol. III. *Bell's British Theatre*, 1791, for 1797, compared to *Inchbald's Theatre* XVI, 1808 and *The Modern British Drama*, Vol. 2 of 5 Vols., London: William Miller, 1811 and *Cumberland's British Theatre* I (1826), and *The British Drama* Vol. 1 of 2 Vols. London: Phil M. Polock, 1853.

Date: 1761
Author: John Delap
Title: *Hecuba*— Prologue notes that the character inspired Shakespeare and was written in the English style.
Copy Text: Manuscript Larpent 202.

Date: 1766
Author: William Kenrick
Title: *Falstaff's Wedding, a Comedy in the Imitation of Shakespere*
Copy Text: Manuscript Larpent 252; prologue 1382, compared to *Bell's British Theatre*, Vol. XXXI, 1797 and *The Modern British Drama*, Vol. 4 of 5 Vols., London: William Miller, 1811.

Date: 1767
Author: Dr. Franklin
Title: *The Earl of Warwick*
Copy text: *Bell's British Theatre*, Vol. XVII, 1792 for 1797 and *The Modern British Drama*, Vol. 2 of 5 Vols., London: William Miller, 1811.

Date: 1773
Author: Thomas Hull
Title: *Henry II, or the Fall of Rosamund*— epilogue makes reference to this as sharing Shakespearean qualities.
Copy Text: Manuscript Larpent 352 compared to *Bell's British Theatre*, Vol. XXVIII, 1792 for 1797 and *Inchbald's Theatre* IX (1811).

Date: 1795
Author: Francis Waldron
Title: *The Virgin Queen*
Last Date of Publication: 1795; reprinted 1970.

Date: 1800
Author: Joanne Baille
Title: *De Monfort*
Copy Text: Manuscript Larpent 1287 compared to *Inchbald's Theatre,* Vol. XXIV, 1808.

Date: 1818
Author: John Howard Payne
Title: *Brutus; or The Fall of Tarquin.*
Copy Text: Manuscript Larpent 2059 compared to *Cumberland's British Theatre* 11 (1826), and *Modern Standard Drama*, Vol. 8 of 12 vols. ed. John W.S. Hows. New York: Samuel French, n.d.

Volume Two: Shakespeare Parodies and Forgeries (Fourteen Plays in Total):
Parodies (Ten Plays):

Date: 1730
Author: Henry Fielding
Title: *Tragedy of Tragedies, of Tom Thumb* (a parody on Shakespearean tragedy)
Copy Text: *The Modern British Drama*, Vol. 5 of 5 Vols., London: William Miller, 1811.
Last Date of Publication: 1967

Date: 1758
Author: Richard Dodsley
Title: *The Miller of Mansfield* (a parody of *Henry V*)
Copy Text: Inchbald, *A Collection of Farces, and Other Afterpieces.* Vol. VII of VII. London: Longman, Hurst, Rees, Orme, and Brown, 1815. (Turned into another farce: *Harry La Roy*, Larpent 1775 Isaac Polack, 1813, and follow-up, *Sir John Cickle of Court*).

Date: 1756
Author: Arthur Murphy
Title: *The Apprentice. A Farce in Two Acts* (parodies *Hamlet* and *Macbeth)*
Copy Text: Inchbald, *A Collection of Farces, and Other Afterpieces.* Vol. III of VII. London: Longman, Hurst, Rees, Orme, and Brown, 1815, and *The British Drama* Vol. 1 of 2 Vols. London: Phil M. Polock, 1853.

Date: 1761
Author: Dr. John Hawkesworth
Title: *Edgar and Emmeline. A Comedy in Two Acts* (composite of *Macbeth* and *A Midsummer Night's Dream)*
Copy Text: Manuscript Larpent 185 compared to Inchbald, *A Collection of Farces, and Other Afterpieces.* Vol. VI of VII. London: Longman, Hurst, Rees, Orme, and Brown, 1815.

Date: 1763
Author: Unknown
Title: "The Humours of the Age" (a comic paraphrase on Shakespeare's "Seven Ages of Man")
Copy Text: Manuscript Larpent 222
Last Publication: Never published.

Date: 1777
Author: Isaac Jackson
Title: *All the World's A Stage, a Farce in Two Acts* (lines pastiche many Shakespeare plays, including *Othello*)
Copy Text: Manuscript Larpent 428 — includes additional scene not found in Inchbald, *A Collection of Farces, and Other Afterpieces.* Vol. IV of VII. London: Longman, Hurst, Rees, Orme, and Brown, 1815.

Date: 1796
Author: Samuel James Arnold.

Title: *The Shipwreck, a Comic Opera* (a *Tempest* Parody)
Copy Text: Manuscript Larpent 1146 compared to William-Henry Oxberry
(ed.), *New English Drama*. Vol. 11 of 22. London: W. Simpkin and R. Marshall, 1820.

Date: 1810
Author John Poole
Title: *Hamlet Travestie*
Copy Text: 1810 quarto

Date: 1823
Author: Anon.
Title: *Richard III: A Parody in Three Acts*
Copy Text: 1839 quarto

Date: 1848
Authors: Robert Barnabas Brough and William Brough
Title: *The Enchanted Isle* (a *Tempest* Farce)
Copy Text: *English Plays of the Nineteenth Century*, ed. Michael R. Booth.
Vol. 5 of 5 Vols. Oxford: Clarendon, 1976.

Forgeries (Four Plays):
Date: 1728
Author: Lewis Theobald
Title: *The Double Falsehood*
Copy Text: 1728 quarto

Date: 1795–6
Author: William-Henry Ireland
Title: *Vortigern, A Tragedy in Five Acts*
Copy Text: Manuscript Larpent 1110

Date: 1796
Author: William-Henry Ireland
Title: *Henry II*
Copy Text: 1832 quarto

About the Editor:
Jeffrey Kahan's Ph.D. was a study of Eighteenth-Century Shakespeare forgeries. His first academic book, *Reforging Shakespeare*, was published by Lehigh University, part of the Associated University Press consortium (1998). He has published articles and reviews in *Shakespeare Bulletin, EMLS, Upstart Crow, Renaissance Quarterly, Shakespeare Newsletter, Notes and Queries, The Ben Jonson Journal, ELN,* and *ANQ*.

Sample 5: Grant Proposal, Harry Ransom Humanities Research Center

Name: Jeffrey Kahan, Associate Professor
Institutional affiliation: University of La Verne

Length of residency requested: One month
Brief project title: Visual History of *King Lear*
Subject Code: PA Performing Arts

This is an application for funds to write a historical overview of *King Lear* in performance. Rather than simply restate the information found in other editions such as the Oxford and the Cambridge, I'm looking for underworked or overlooked materials, and the Ransom has them in ready supply.

The materials will be published as part of my 80-page introduction to a book of essays I am editing for Routledge. In my editor's introduction, I will comprehensively survey *Lear*'s claims to greatness among Shakespeare's plays, and how these claims are to some degree both substantiated and gainsaid by its complex source, print, and performance history. While this introduction will explore the play's critical and textual history, for the purposes of this application I will concentrate on the play's theatrical history and how it intersects with the Ransom's holdings.

Why the Ransom?

As I outline below, I believe that the Ransom offers a significant repository of untapped Shakespeare materials on the play, particularly concerning its visual history.

My Work Schedule and the Ransom's Materials.

Phase I would be occupied in the study of your visual materials, a necessary component in any attempt to bring the past alive to the present generation of readers. The Ransom Library contains strong collections of images, promptbooks, and playbills of American and British Shakespeare performance from ca. 1770 to the present, specifically the Theater Biography Collection and the Shakespeare Collection, as well as the Boydell Collection. Of special interest would be images of actors playing Lear, including Garrick, Kean, Macready, and Irving, as well as images of Ellen Terry and other actresses in the role of Cordelia. I think I might also learn quite a bit by studying your eighteenth- and nineteenth-century playbills, which detail what farces, fore- and afterpieces, and musical interludes accompanied a typical night's performance of *King Lear*.

In **Phase II**, I would be turning my attention to the Ransom's musical score for Irving's production of *King Lear*. The score may well serve as an invaluable resource in charting the dramatic emphases Irving and his cast placed upon specific parts of the play. These emphases, I suspect, will reveal the ways in which Irving continued to stress the play's melodramatic performance points.

In **Phase III**, I'd like to look at what I think are yet more hidden gems of the Ransom: lithographs and programs from the ca. 1905 production of the *Yiddish King Lear*, documents from a 1960s Marxist-friendly performance of the play in Russia, and a mimeograph of an early version of Stoppard's *Rosencrantz and Guildenstern Are Dead*, which was then called *Rosencrantz and Guildenstern Meet King Lear*. I am also interested in your more recent materials, including Donald Wolfit's promptbook from his production of *King Lear* (1944), as well as John Russell Brown's papers, which include his many essays on doubling in *Lear*.

Lastly, I'd be making notes on your many drawings and photos of *King Lear* costuming in the B.J Simmons Collection, as well as the collection's documents pertaining to David Hare's 1986 direction of the play for the National Theatre.

Ordering Images from the Ransom

For my last book, concerning the Shakespeare actor Edmund Kean (*The Cult of Kean* [Ashgate, forthcoming 2006]), I ordered about 15 images from the Ransom's Theater Collection. I would like to order all 20 images of actors, costumes, and staging for this book on *King Lear*.

A full vitae is attached for your perusal.

Yours respectfully,

Jeffrey Kahan.

Bibliography

Books

American Psychiatric Association. *Diagnostic and Statistical Manual of Mental Disorders: Primary Care Version.* 4th ed. Washington, D.C.: American Psychiatric Association, 1995.

Baker, Carlos. *Ernest Hemingway: A Life Story.* New York: Collier/Macmillan, 1969.

Bolman, L.G., and T.E. Deal. *Reframing Organizations: Artistry, Choice, and Leadership.* 3rd ed. San Francisco: Jossey-Bass/Wiley, 2003.

Brown, David G. *The Mobile Professors.* Washington, D.C.: American Council of Education, [ca. 1967].

Cameron, Kim. *Positive Leadership: Strategies for Extraordinary Performance.* San Francisco: Berrett-Koehler, 2008.

Canibe, Marcia I. "Economics of Library Binding." Master's thesis, School of Printing, Rochester Institute of Technology, 1988.

Carnell, Eileen, Jacqui MacDonald, Bet McCallum, and Mary Scott. *Passion and Politics: Academics Reflect on Writing for Publication.* London: Institute of Education, 2008.

Catasús, Bino, and Bengt Kristensson Uggla. "Reinventing the University as the Driving Force of Intellectual Capital." In *Intellectual Capital Revisited,* edited by Bino Catasús and Cristina Chaminade. Cheltenham, Gloucester; Northampton, MA: Edward Elgar, 2007.

Donoghue, Frank. *The Last Professors: The Corporate University and the Fate of the Humanities.* New York: Fordham University Press, 2008.

Downer, Roger G.H. "Innovation in Undergraduate Teaching: Student-centered and Research-led learning." In *Reinventing the Research University,* edited by Luc. E. Weber and James J. Duderstadt. London, Paris, Genève: Economica, 2004. 63–72.

Hanson, Victor Davis, and John Heath. *Who Killed Homer? The Demise of Classical Education and the Recovery of Greek Wisdom.* New York and London: Free Press/Simon & Schuster, 1998.

Hawes, Gene R. *To Advance Knowledge: A Handbook on American University Press Publishing.* New York: American University Press Services, 1967.

Hedges, Chris. *Empire of Illusion: The End of Literacy and the Triumph of Spectacle.* New York: Nation/Perseus, 2009.

Jenck, Christopher, and David Riesman. *The Academic Revolution.* New York: Anchor, 1969.

Kerr, Chester. *The American University as Publisher: A Digest of a Report on American University Presses.* Norman: University of Oklahoma Press, 1949.

___. *A Report on American University Presses.* 3rd ed. Ann Arbor, MI: Association of American University Presses, 1956.

Layzell, Daniel T. "Higher Education's Changing Environment: Faculty Productivity and the Reward Structure." In *Faculty Productivity: Facts, Fictions, and Issues,* edited by William G. Tierney. New York and London: Falmer Press/Taylor and Francis, 1999.

Luey, Beth. *Handbook for Academic Authors.* 4th ed. Cambridge: Cambridge University Press, 2002.

Menand, Louis. *The Marketplace of Ideas.* Issues of Our Time Series. Edited (general) by Henry Louis Gates, Jr. New York and London: W.W. Norton, 2010.

Munitz, Barry. "Managing Transformation in an Age of Social Triage." In *Reinventing the University,* edited by Sandra L. Johnson and Sean C. Rush, Coopers & Lybrand LLP. New York and Chichester: John Wiley and Sons, 1995.

Nelson, Cary. "Between Crisis and Opportunity: The Future of the Academic Workplace." In *Will Teach for Food: Academic Labor in Crisis,* edited by Cary Nelson. Minneapolis and London: University of Minnesota Press, 1997.

Olson, Tillie. *Silences.* Introduction by Shelley Fisher Fishkin. 1965. Reprint, New York: Feminist Press at the City University of New York, 2003.

Parsons, Paul. *Getting Published: The Acquisition Process at University Presses.* Knoxville: University of Tennessee Press, 1989.

Raeburn, John. *Fame Became of Him: Hemingway as Public Writer.* Bloomington: Indiana University Press, 1984.

Royle, Nicholas. *The Uncanny.* New York: Routledge/Taylor & Francis Group, 2003.

Sand, George, and Gustave Flaubert. *The George Sand-Gustave Flaubert Letters.* Translated by Aimee L. McKenzie. New York: Boni and Liveright, 1921.

Schmitt, Roland W. "A Symposium Summary." In *Reinventing the Research University: Proceedings of a Symposium Held at UCLA on June 22–23, 1994.* Los Angeles: University of California, 1995.

Shaw, B.N. *Academic Tenure in American Higher Education.* Foreword by John R. Fawcett, Jr. Chicago: Adams Press, 1971.

Shugg, Roger. *The Two Worlds of University Publishing.* University of Kansas Publications, Library Series, 31. [Lawrence?]: University of Kansas, 1967.

Sinnott, Jan, and Lynn Johnson. *Reinventing the University: A Radical Proposal for a Problem-Focused University.* Social and Policy Issues in Education, David C. Anchin Series. Edited (general) by Kathryn M. Borman. Norwood, NJ: Ablex, 1996.

Toth, Emily. *Ms. Mentor's Impeccable Advice for Women in Academia.* Philadelphia: University of Pennsylvania Press, 1997.

Websites, Institutional
(all Websites active as of September 17, 2010)

Bureau of Labor Statistics. http://www.bls.gov/news.release/union2.nr0.htm.

Federal Reserve Calculator. http://www.minneapolisfed.org/index.cfm.

"Joint statement of Norman Finkelstein and DePaul University on their tenure controversy and its resolution." DePaul University. September 5, 2007. http://news room.depaul.edu/.

Phobia Dictionary. http://www.blifaloo.com/info/phobias.php.

National Center for Education Statistics. http://nces.ed.gov/programs/digest/d08/tables/dt08_268.asp?referrer=report.

University of California Riverside Advance and Promotion Manual. http://academicper sonnel.ucr.edu/faculty/CNASAdvandPromoUCRiverside.pdf.

Websites, Individual
(all Websites active as of September 17, 2010)

Abumrad, Jad, and Robert Krulwich. "Agatha Christie and Nuns Tell a Tale of Alzheimer's." NPR online. http://www.wbur.org/npr/127211884.

Babauta, Leo. "Learn from the Greats: 7 Writing Habits of Amazing Writers." http://writetodone.com/2008/09/04/learn-from-the-greats-7-writing-habits-of-amazing-writers/.

Deresiewicz, William. "The Disadvantages of an Elite Education." http://www.theam ericanscholar.org/the-disadvantages-of-an-elite-education/.

Greenblatt, Stephen. "A Special Letter from Stephen Greenblatt." 2002 speech as the president of the Modern Language Association. http://www.mla.org/scholarly_pub.

Miller, Henry. On his writing. http://www.parisreview.com/media/4597_MILLER_H.pdf.

Olson, Gary A. "The Limits of Academic Freedom." http://chronicle.com/article/The-Limits-of-Academic-Freedom/49354/.

Simon, Stephanie, and Stephanie Banchero. "Putting a Price on Professors." *Wall Street Journal* online, October 22, 2010. http://online.wsj.com/article/SB100014240527 48703735804575536322093520994.html.

Wilson, Robin. "Tenure, RIP: What the Vanishing Status Means for the Future of Education." *Chronicle of Higher Education* online, July 4, 2010. http://chronicle.com/article/Tenure–RIP/66114/.

Film

Expelled: No Intelligence Allowed. Directed by Nathan Frankowski. Written by Kevin Miller, Ben Stein, and Walt Ruloff. Rocky Mountain Pictures, 2008.

Miscellaneous

Riley, Naomi Schaefer. "Cal State Mission Drift," *Los Angeles Times.* June 15, 2011.

Woo, Celeste, email, September 27, 2011.

_____. "Review of *Bettymania* "(currently under review at an academic journal).

Index